DERIVATIONS IN MINIMALISM

This pathbreaking study presents a new perspective on the role of derivation, the series of operations by which sentences are formed. Working within the Minimalist Program and focusing on English, the authors develop an original theory of generative syntax, providing illuminating new analyses of some central syntactic constructions. Two key questions are explored: first, can the Extended Projection Principle (EPP) be eliminated from Minimalist analysis without loss, and perhaps with a gain in empirical coverage; and second, is the construct 'A-chain' similarly eliminable? The authors argue that neither EPP nor the construct 'A-chain' is in fact a property of Universal Grammar, but rather their descriptive content can be deduced from independently motivated properties of lexical items, in accordance with overarching principles governing derivation. In investigating these questions, a range of new data is introduced, and existing data is re-analyzed, presenting a pioneering challenge to fundamental assumptions in syntactic theory.

Samuel David Epstein is a Professor in the Linguistics Department at the University of Michigan. He is co-author of *A Derivational Approach to Syntactic Relations* (with E. Groat, R. Kawashima and H. Kitahara), and co-editor (with N. Hornstein) of *Working Minimalism* (1999). He is co-founder (with S. Flynn) of the journal *Syntax*.

T. Daniel Seely is Professor of Linguistics and Chair of the Linguistics Program at Eastern Michigan University. His work in syntax has appeared in *Linguistic Inquiry* and *Syntax*. He is organizer and editor of 'Geometric and Thematic Structure in Binding' (1996), the first LINGUIST List online conference, and he is co-editor (with S. D. Epstein) of *Derivation and Explanation in the Minimalist Program* (2002).

In this series

66 ANTHONY R. WARNER: *English auxiliaries: structure and history*
67 P. H. MATTHEWS: *Grammatical theory in the United States from Bloomfield to Chomsky*
68 LJILJANA PROGOVAC: *Negative and positive polarity: a binding approach*
69 R. M. W. DIXON: *Ergativity*
70 YAN HUANG: *The syntax and pragmatics of anaphora*
71 KNUD LAMBRECHT: *Information structure and sentence form: topic, focus, and the mental representation of discourse referents*
72 LUIGI BURZIO: *Principles of English stress*
73 JOHN A. HAWKINS: *A performance theory of order and constituency*
74 ALICE C. HARRIS and LYLE CAMPBELL: *Historical syntax in cross-linguistic perspective*
75 LILIANE HAEGEMAN: *The syntax of negation*
76 PAUL GORREL: *Syntax and parsing*
77 GUGLIELMO CINQUE: *Italian syntax and universal grammar*
78 HENRY SMITH: *Restrictiveness in case theory*
79 D. ROBERT LADD: *Intonational morphology*
80 ANDREA MORO: *The raising of predicates: predicative noun phrases and the theory of clause structure*
81 ROGER LASS: *Historical linguistics and language change*
82 JOHN M. ANDERSON: *A notional theory of syntactic categories*
83 BERND HEINE: *Possession: cognitive sources, forces and grammaticalization*
84 NOMI ERTESCHIK-SHIR: *The dynamics of focus structure*
85 JOHN COLEMAN: *Phonological representations: their names, forms and powers*
86 CHRISTINA Y. BETHIN: *Slavic prosody: language change and phonological theory*
87 BARBARA DANCYGIER: *Conditionals and prediction*
88 CLAIRE LEFEBVRE: *Creole genesis and the acquisition of grammar: the case of Haitian creole*
89 HEINZ GIEGERICH: *Lexical strata in English*
90 KEREN RICE: *Morpheme order and semantic scope*
91 APRIL MCMAHON: *Lexical phonology and the history of English*
92 MATTHEW Y. CHEN: *Tone Sandhi: patterns across Chinese dialects*
93 GREGORY T. STUMP: *Inflectional morphology: a theory of paradigm structure*
94 JOAN BYBEE: *Phonology and language use*
95 LAURIE BAUER: *Morphological productivity*
96 THOMAS ERNST: *The syntax of adjuncts*
97 ELIZABETH CLOSS TRAUGOTT and RICHARD B. DASHER: *Regularity in semantic change*
98 MAYA HICKMANN: *Children's discourse: Person, space and time across languages*
99 DIANE BLAKEMORE: *Relevance and linguistic meaning: The semantics and pragmatics of discourse markers*

100 IAN ROBERTS and ANNA ROUSSOU: *Syntactic change: a minimalist approach to grammaticalization*
101 DONKA MINKOVA: *Alliteration and sound change in early English*
102 MARK C. BAKER: *Lexical categories: verbs, nouns and adjectives*
103 CARLOTA S. SMITH: *Modes of discourse: the local structure of texts*
104 ROCHELLE LIEBER: *Morphology and lexical semantics*
105 HOLGER DIESSEL: *The acquisition of complex sentences*
106 SHARON INKELAS and CHERYL ZOLL: *Reduplication: doubling in morphology*
107 SUSAN EDWARDS: *Fluent aphasia*
108 BARBARA DANCYGIER and EVE SWEETSER: *Mental spaces in grammar: conditional constructions*
109 MATTHEW BAERMAN, DUNSTAN BROWN and GREVILLE G. CORBETT: *The syntax–morphology interface: a study of syncretism*
110 MARCUS TOMALIN: *Linguistics and the Formal Sciences: The origins of generative grammar*
111 SAMUEL D. EPSTEIN and T. DANIEL SEELY: *Derivations in Minimalism*

Earlier issues not listed are also available

CAMBRIDGE STUDIES IN LINGUISTICS

General Editors: P. AUSTIN, J. BRESNAN, B. COMRIE,
S. CRAIN, W. DRESSLER, C. J. EWEN, R. LASS,
D. LIGHTFOOT, K. RICE, I. ROBERTS, S. ROMAINE,
N. V. SMITH

Derivations in Minimalism

DERIVATIONS IN MINIMALISM

SAMUEL D. EPSTEIN
University of Michigan

and

T. DANIEL SEELY
Eastern Michigan University

CAMBRIDGE
UNIVERSITY PRESS

CAMBRIDGE UNIVERSITY PRESS
Cambridge, New York, Melbourne, Madrid, Cape Town, Singapore, São Paulo

Cambridge University Press
The Edinburgh Building, Cambridge CB2 2RU, UK

Published in the United States of America by Cambridge University Press, New York

www.cambridge.org
Information on this title: www.cambridge.org/9780521811804

© Samuel D. Epstein and T. Daniel Seely 2006

This publication is in copyright. Subject to statutory exception
and to the provisions of relevant collective licensing agreements,
no reproduction of any part may take place without
the written permission of Cambridge University Press.

First published 2006

A catalogue record for this publication is available from the British Library

ISBN-13 978-0-521-81180-4 hardback
ISBN-10 0-521-81180-5 hardback

ISBN-13 978-0-521-01058-0 paperback
ISBN-10 0-521-01058-6 paperback

Transferred to digital printing 2006

Cambridge University Press has no responsibility for
the persistence or accuracy of URLs for external or
third-party internet websites referred to in this publication,
and does not guarantee that any content on such
websites is, or will remain, accurate or appropriate.

This book is dedicated to Elaine, Molly and Sylvie; and to Hannah, Piper and Charlie; and to our students: past, present and future.

Contents

	Acknowledgments	xiii
	Preface	xiv
1	**Orientation and goals**	1
1.1	Some methodological preliminaries	1
1.2	Outline and rationale	4
2	**On the elimination of A-chains**	14
2.1	Chains are not syntactic objects	14
2.2	A-chains are not specifiable under X' invisibility	20
2.3	A non-isomorphism between A-chains and successive cyclic A-movement	31
2.4	An alternative analysis without chains	42
3	**On the elimination of the EPP**	48
3.1	Introduction	48
3.2	The EPP	49
3.3	*There*-insertion and raising: more problems created by the EPP	56
3.4	The *conjecture* class of verbs	70
4	**More challenges to the elimination of the EPP: some movement cases**	113
4.1	Introduction	113
4.2	Evidence for successive cyclic A-movement as evidence for the EPP	114
4.3	The Bošković approach	116
4.4	Some alternative solutions	130
4.5	Lasnik's cases	164
5	**Exploring architecture**	174
5.1	Derivational architecture of C_{HL}	174
5.2	Some final notes on the derivational model; eliminating feature strength, and 'obligatory' transformational rule application	197

References	199
Index	209

Acknowledgments

We thank Andrew Winnard (Senior Commissioning Editor for Language and Linguistics), Helen Barton (Editor for Language and Linguistics), and Elizabeth Davey (Production Editor for Humanities and Social Sciences) of Cambridge University Press for their interest in our research, and for their patience, consideration and kindness during the production of this book.

We are also indebted to Catherine Fortin and Mary Beers for indispensable editorial and linguistic assistance. Steve Peter expertly prepared the entire manuscript and provided crucial input at all stages, which we gratefully acknowledge here.

We are very grateful to Scott Atran, Pam Beddor, Chris Collins, Diana Cresti, Josh Epstein, Justin Fitzpatrick, Jon Gajewski, Sam Gutmann, Mark Hale, Norbert Hornstein, Hisatsugu Kitahara, Rick Lewis, Peter Liem, Peter Ludlow, Fred Mailhot, Jim McCloskey, David Pesetsky, Esther Torrego, Christina Tortora, and C. Jan-Wouter Zwart for valuable discussion of many of the ideas presented here.

We also especially thank Jim McCloskey, Željko Bošković and Roger Martin, as well as Margaret Speas and Naoki Fukui, whose research challenging the EPP has significantly influenced the work reported here. We've also been influenced by Howard Lasnik's recent research supporting the EPP, which has helped to clarify the obstacles confronted in attempting to eliminate this principle.

We also owe a very special thanks to our colleague Acrisio Pires, who co-authored a manuscript with us, entitled "EPP in T?" (2004), which was written and submitted for publication during the writing of this book, and is discussed in Chapter 3. We also thank Acrisio for detailed and highly insightful comments on earlier drafts of many parts of this book, which have led to notable improvements in the final version.

We are extremely indebted to Noam Chomsky for his interest in our work, and for protracted discussion of many of the ideas presented here.

Needless to say, all errors are ours, and nobody acknowledged here necessarily agrees with any of the hypotheses presented.

Preface

> ...understanding always involves the notion of composition. This notion can enter in one of two ways. If the thing understood be composite, the understanding of it can be in reference to its factors, and to their ways of interweaving so as to form that total thing. This mode of comprehension makes evident why the thing is what it is. The second mode of understanding is to treat the thing as a unity, whether or not it is capable of analysis, and to obtain evidence as to its capacity for affecting its environment. The first mode may be called the internal understanding, and the second mode is the external understanding.... The two modes are reciprocal; either presupposes the other. The first mode conceives the thing as an outcome, the second mode conceives it as a causal factor.... It is true that nothing is finally understood until its reference to process has been made evident. (pp. 45–6)
>
> Process and individuality require each other. In separation all meaning evaporates. The form of process...derives its character from the individuals involved, and the characters of the individuals can only be understood in terms of the process in which they are implicated. (p. 97)
>
> The whole understanding of the world consists in the analysis of process in terms of the identities and diversities of the individuals involved. (p. 98)
>
> Excerpted from Alfred North Whitehead, *Modes of Thought*.[1]

Chapters 2 and 3 of this book are based in part on a manuscript written and circulated in 1999 and presented at the 1999 LSA Summer Institute Workshop on Grammatical Functions, 'SPEC-ifying the GF "Subject": Eliminating A-chains and the EPP within a Derivational Model'. Chapters 1, 4 and 5 are, to a good approximation, entirely new, as are many aspects of Chapters 2 and 3.

We thank Stanley Dubinsky and William Davies for inviting us to the workshop and we thank Howard Lasnik for his valuable commentary on this paper.

It should be noted that in the same year a Minimalist paper with certain similarities to our Chapters 2 and 3, concerning A-chains and the EPP, was independently written and distributed: Castillo, Juan Carlos, John Drury and Kleanthes K. Grohmann, 1999, 'Merge Over Move and the Extended Projection Principle', in *University of Maryland Working Papers in Linguistics* 8:63–103.

1. 1938. New York: The Free Press (a division of MacMillan Publishing Co. Inc.).

A revised version was then published as: Grohmann, Kleanthes K., John Drury and Juan Carlos Castillo, 2000, 'No More EPP', in *Proceedings of the 19th West Coast Conference on Formal Linguistics*, 153–166.

As further concerns the elimination of A-chains ('as we know them'), another recent analysis has appeared since the completion of Epstein and Seely (1999), that of Manzini and Roussou (2000), which regrettably we do not address here. Their analysis invokes quite different mechanisms than those proposed here. Earlier still (as recently pointed out to us by Norbert Hornstein, to whom we are indebted for doing so), Pauline Jacobson (1992) advanced an analysis of raising in a quite different framework in her 'Raising Without Movement'. More generally, there has existed for quite some time an unclarity, and we think interesting debate, both within and between frameworks, in both syntax and semantics (which we cannot comprehensively review here) concerning the proper treatment of the categorial status, internal structure and derivation of raising infinitives.

In this regard, it is important to note that at the very inception of GB theory (and the postulation of A-chains and the EPP), Chomsky (1981) explicitly addressed the broad issues at hand and explicated the nature of their importance in attempting to explain aspects of human knowledge of language, and its growth in the individual. As opposed to the GB-theoretic analyses he proposes, Chomsky (1981:92) considers an alternative:

> Consider...a different theory, call it "Theory II," which generates different s-Structures... lacking empty categories – traces or PRO. One might imagine other variants of Theory II in which some of the structures with gaps...have trace and others do not (perhaps movement-to-Comp might be distinguished from NP-movement in this way, for example). Theory II is rather different in its properties from Theory I. For example, Theory II does not observe the projection principle; furthermore, it assigns θ-roles to arguments that are not in θ-positions by devices quite different from those that are employed to relate operators such as wh-phrases to the variables they bind...Furthermore, it does not relate the properties of interpreted gaps to those of overt anaphors and pronouns with disjoint reference.... Theor[y] 1 and [Theory] II appear, at least, to be rather different in their conceptual and empirical properties; not so much in their coverage of data – presumably either can be developed in such a way as to deal in some manner with phenomena that are at all well-understood – but in their frameworks of unifying principles and assumptions about the nature of UG.

Portions of the following material were also presented at: the meeting of the Michigan Linguistics Society held at Eastern Michigan University (2001); Wayne State

University Department of Linguistics colloquium (2000); the LOT Summer school and the 1st Tools in Linguistic Theory Conference (TiLT), both held at the University of Utrecht (2001); and the LSA Summer Institute held at Michigan State University (2003). We thank the organizers and audiences there for their interest in and comments on our work.

We also each thank our graduate students for their many valuable contributions made during the presentation of this material in various classes (including some joint Eastern Michigan University – University of Michigan courses) and syntax workshops. In particular, we specifically acknowledge the following linguistics students from Eastern Michigan University: Scott Fults, Lydia Grebenyova, Neil Salmond, and Heather Taylor; and from the University of Michigan: Christopher Becker, Gerardo Fernandez-Salgueiro, Catherine Fortin, Rose Letsholo, Michael Marlo, Hamid Ouali, Andrea Stiasny, and Annemarie Toebosch; and (formerly at Eastern, and now at the University of Michigan) Dina Kapetangianni.

Abbreviations

CT   Chomsky, Noam. 1995. 'Categories and transformations', in *The Minimalist Program*, Cambridge, MA: MIT Press.
MI   Chomsky, Noam. 2000. 'Minimalist inquiries: the framework', in Roger Martin, David Michaels, and Juan Uriagereka (eds.), *Step by step: essays on minimalist syntax in honor of Howard Lasnik*, Cambridge, MA: MIT Press.
DBP   Chomsky, Noam. 2001a. 'Derivation by phase', in Michael Kenstowicz (ed.), *Ken Hale: a life in language*, Cambridge, MA: MIT Press.
BEA   Chomsky, Noam. 2001b. 'Beyond Explanatory Adequacy', ms., MIT. A revised version to appear in Adriana Belletti (ed.), *Structures and beyond: current issues in the theory of language*, Oxford: Oxford University Press.
DASR   Epstein, Samuel D., Erich Groat, Ruriko Kawashima, and Hisatsugu Kitahara. 1998. *A derivational approach to syntactic relations*, Oxford: Oxford University Press.

1   Orientation and goals

1.1   Some methodological preliminaries

1.1.1   A note on empirical coverage

Before outlining the book, we want to make aspects of our overall orientation clear, and we begin with two preliminaries.

Throughout, our primary goal (whether we attain it or not!) is explanation via deduction, not empirical coverage by (re-)description or stipulation (see e.g., Epstein and Seely 2002: Introduction, for further discussion). Of course, it is undeniable that empirical coverage is vitally important, but to adapt a point we believe was made by either Dirac or Thom,[1] consider the following scenario. First suppose we have some finite set of empirical findings, such as

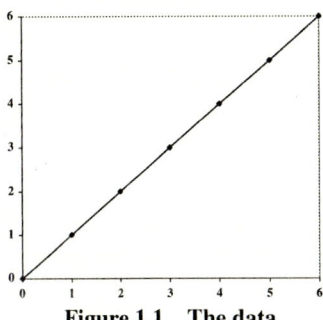

Figure 1.1   The data

From such findings we advance the non-finite hypothesis that x=y. Now consider

---

1. We are indebted to Josh Epstein for pointing this argument out to us. Despite his and our concerted efforts and numerous consultations, we have thus far been unable to determine the exact attribution, in particular, whether the argument is due to Dirac and/or to Thom, or someone else. We also thank Pam Beddor for very helpful discussion of and comments regarding the argument.

the following two competing theories. Theory 1 correctly predicts three of the data, namely (1,1), (3,3), and (5,5), e.g., as follows:

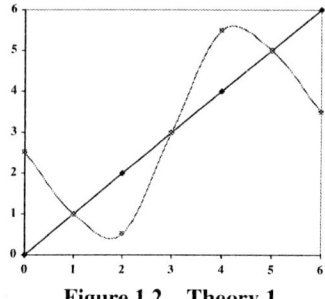

Figure 1.2 Theory 1

Now consider a different theory, Theory 2, which correctly predicts *none* of the data.

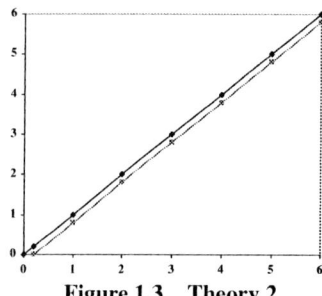

Figure 1.3 Theory 2

Clearly Theory 1 is 'empirically preferable' by a 'winning score' of 3–0. The point, as we understand it, is that Theory 2, despite getting none of the data correct, captures the data's overall (linear) pattern, and is 'closer to the truth' or 'more illuminating' than the empirically preferable Theory 1. Hence, we believe, Theory 2 is a better working or guiding hypothesis upon which to base future research. The 'balance' between coverage and insight is surely a delicate and vitally important matter, but our point here is only to re-emphasize the following: the empirical coverage of a theory (to the extent that it is ever precisely determined) is not the only issue at hand, if indeed our goal is explanation. (Needless to say, this study includes wide-ranging and detailed empirical analyses, and we do not explicitly seek a theory with zero empirical coverage as our goal!)

There are of course other scenarios, too, in which 'better empirical coverage' doesn't necessarily weigh in favor of one theory over another. Human scientific inquiry necessarily proceeds by decomposing the world into parts; for example, human knowledge of language is hypothesized to be an investigable aspect of the world, a part which has parts within it: syntax, phonology, semantics, morphology, pragmatics, etc., each with its own subparts. Thus, we *hypothesize* that a given fact is syntactic, and we try to cover the fact empirically. But it may well be that it is a mistake for a syntactic theory to cover a particular fact, since the fact may well be non-syntactic. Thus, covering more facts doesn't necessarily make a theory preferable. It can make it a worse theory than an empirically narrower competitor, if the extra 'winning facts', covered only by the 'winning syntactic theory', turn out to be, in fact, non-syntactic phenomena.

We include this discussion simply to identify our (undoubtedly unachieved but ultimate) goal, what Einstein (1954:282) called 'the grand aim of all science':[2]

> ...which is to cover the greatest possible number of empirical facts by logical deduction from the smallest possible number of hypotheses or axioms.

The centrality of 'minimalism' – operating in concert with the goal of empirical coverage – in all scientific explanation is evident from this perspective. (For an important, detailed discussion of the pervasive role of Minimalist method in scientific inquiry, see e.g., Freidin and Vergnaud 2001.)

The analyses that follow, we suspect, fall somewhere between Theories of Type 1 and 2. Of course, we certainly hope we got all of the data right, but needless to say, in any serious empirical inquiry, one never knows with certainty if they've truly discovered something or not. What is virtually certain is that we got at least some things wrong. Our hope is that where we are wrong, we are nonetheless 'close' like Theory 2, and thereby do not lead ourselves into a wildly wrong (Theory 1 type) hypothesis, that despite covering data is in fact 'way off track'.

1.1.2   Unclarity as a 'merely conceptual', hence non-empirical, issue

Another related issue concerning empirical inquiry is worth noting here. Certain

---

2. Einstein (1954:282) *Ideas and Opinions*, Bonanza Books, New York.

issues, e.g., examining the unclarity of a principle, it seems to us are sometimes viewed as a merely 'conceptual or philosophical issue, not really empirical, not real linguistics'. In many cases this seems to us an *empirically problematic* perspective to adopt. To the extent that a principle is unclear, its predictive content is unspecified, hence indeterminate. Thus unclarity is an empirical issue, and empirical issues are extremely (but not uniquely) important. The same holds true for contradictions within a theory or analysis. These are not conceptual, 'merely theoretical' non-empirical issues; rather, all the data is at risk of being unpredicted. (For an elegant unveiling of a contradiction embedded within Epstein *et al.* 1998, see Gajewski 2000.)

1.2 *Outline and rationale*

Our analyses are couched within and critically examine certain aspects of Chomsky's pioneering Minimalist framework (Chomsky 1991, 1995, 2000, 2001a). We develop and explore further a level-free architecture for UG, a so-called 'derivational approach' to syntactic relations, as initiated in Epstein (1994, 1999) and Epstein *et al.* (1998), and developed in Epstein and Seely (1999, 2002: Chapter 3). This eliminative derivational Minimalism seeks generative explanation (see below) through minimization, the latter, as noted, a highly characteristic, if not defining, goal of all scientific inquiry. (See Epstein and Seely 2002 for discussion, and the references cited there.)

1.2.1 *Eliminating A-chains*

One central 'observation' made here is that, under an independently motivated, contemporary and highly restrictive Minimalist hypothesis about what a syntactic object is (and is not), the postulate chain is in fact excluded by the theory. Thus, we seek to overcome the potential contradiction faced by adopting a chain-excluding restrictive definition of syntactic object, and concomitantly postulating chains, which fail to satisfy the restrictive conditions. We retain the restrictive definition, and seek to abandon the notion A-chain (see also Hornstein 1998). Chapter 2 explores only the elimination of A-chains, and focuses on the motivation for their postulation as a concept of UG, exploring some of the empirical motivation for A-chains in English, and the architectural aspects of UG that seem to have motivated this postulate. (We leave the role of head chains and A-bar chains within a derivational framework for future research.) We argue that the empirical support for A-chains in English raising constructions is negligible, and argue in addition that postulating A-chains engenders certain thus far unnoted empirical problems as well as fundamental (predictive) unclarities which are avoided by their elimination. We propose that there is no successive cyclic A-raising in such English constructions, but rather, by hypothesis, one fell swoop movement from theta to Case position.

We do not predict that successive cyclic A-movement is universally precluded, but rather, that English raising *to* checks no features whatsoever (although it may have semantic features, perhaps those of a modal operator). Consequently, under Chomsky's Minimalist explanation-seeking theory of transformational rule application, whereby all rule application is purposeful, there is no movement to or through Spec of raising *to*.[3] In other languages or English constructions there may well be abundant evidence for purposeful successive cyclic A-movement and intermediate feature checking. We thus do not propose that 'successive cyclic A-movement is universally excluded', or even that it is invariably excluded in English. 'Successive cyclic raising' has no real theoretical status; rather only local morpholexical feature checking does, and its overall distribution can be determined only by correctly characterizing the morphological features of all relevant lexical heads and the conditions regulating individual transformational rule application and derivations.

1.2.2   Derivations

If A-chains are eliminated and if certain information that A-chains encode is indeed important, namely the set of positions occupied by a mover and the order in which they were occupied over the course of a derivation, then such information must be expressed by other means. This, we suggest, can be achieved by adopting the derivational approach to syntactic relations. Under this level-free architecture, syntactic relations are, by hypothesis, deducible from the independently motivated iterative application of the two (perhaps unifiable; see Kitahara 1997) transformational rules, Move (Attract) and Merge. The idea is to *explain* the fundamental construct 'syntactic relation', e.g., c-command, as opposed to defining relations on already built tree structures, as is necessitated by a representational, 'rule-free' approach,

---

3. For a critical discussion of a possible problem confronting the particular Internalist-Functionalism inherent in contemporary Minimalist syntactic theory and analyses, see Epstein (2003).

such as GB theory. (In this regard see also Uriagereka's 1999 Multiple Spell Out proposal, eliminating the disjunction in Kayne's representationally applied 1994 LCA, by appeal to cyclic (derivational) structure building, and non-surface application of the LCA. See also Lasnik 2001 for an insightful overview of derivation and representation within the Minimalist framework.) Thus, in the rule-based Minimalist approach, iterative application of well-defined transformational rules is assumed (contra 'Move-α'). Thus, it would be odd indeed to pay no attention to the form of the rules, intermediate representations, and the mode of the iterative rule application. Similarly, Chomsky's (1995) abandonment of a virtually rule-free, hence 'all-at-once', theory of D-structure generation, invites, if not requires, investigation of the empirical content of the rules and their manner of application. If, contra Move-α, there is iterative well-defined (cyclic) rule application, then within such a theory, there are by definition intermediate representations, which are generated as output of one rule application, and input to the next. If their existence is postulated, arguably the central shift from GB to Minimalism, we should maximize explanation by trying to deduce as much as possible from these independently motivated, binary-concatenation rules, and their iterative application. In the derivational model, we seek to deduce grammatical relations from the formal properties of the rules and/or their partially ordered application. In this level-free model, each transformational output is 'evaluated' by both PF and LF, as opposed to the GB Y-model. As Chomsky notes (BEA:3), his phase-based approach is also level-eliminating in the following sense:

> In this conception there is no LF: rather, the computation maps LA to <PHON, SEM> piece-by-piece cyclically. There are, therefore, no LF properties and no interpretation of LF, strictly speaking, though Σ and φ interpret units that are part of something like LF in a non-cyclic conception.

In the derivational model developed here, not only do the rules themselves play a central explanatory role, but by virtue of feeding each transformational output to both PF and LF, each rule application is its own 'self-contained' Y-model (phasal) derivation. Again, the rule and the generative procedure play a central explanatory role. By contrast, in the 'rule-free' Principles and Parameters model, syntactic relations are necessarily *defined* on trees, and grammaticality is, by definition, *described* by filters that 'depict' illegitimate syntactic representations. Each mechanism is, by definition, non-explanatory, since definitions-on-trees, like definitions in general, do not explain. We believe that syntactic filters, describing illegitimate configurations, might be replaced with more deeply explanatory postulates; specifically, a generative procedure from which the described filtering effects can be deduced, consistent with Einstein's grand (minimizing) aim of all science, and consistent with Whitehead's (1938:98) view that '...nothing is understood until its reference to process has been made evident.'

Consonant with the Minimalist Program, we assume that lexical items (consisting of certain features) play a central and ineliminable role. Perhaps, if we can discover the properties of lexical items, including their individual properties (features) of attraction and repulsion, then the way they arrange themselves in groups, as trees (or 'sentences') will fall out and thus be explained.

As Epstein and Seely (2002) discuss, this seems very similar in spirit to J. Epstein's conception of the explanatory power of Agent-based Computational modeling in what he calls 'Generative Social Science' (J. Epstein 1999; see also Epstein and Axtell 1996). As J. Epstein (1999) notes:

> ...the central idea is this: to the generativist, explaining the emergence...of macroscopic societal regularities, such as norms or price equilibria, requires that one answer the following question: 'How could the decentralized local interactions of heterogeneous autonomous agents (i.e. individuals) generate the given regularity?'

J. Epstein (1999) assumes that one has explained the macroscopic societal regularity, to the extent that one can

> ...situate an initial population of autonomous heterogeneous agents in a relevant spatial environment; allow them to *interact according to simple local rules*, and thereby generate – or 'grow' – the macroscopic regularity *from the bottom up* [Our emphasis, SDE/TDS].[4]

In J. Epstein's terms, 'if you haven't grown it, then you haven't explained it.' For us, if you define relations on (or appeal in any other way directly to the macrostructure) tree representations, you have failed to explain their properties. For example, to perform an 'end-of-the-line' bottom-up compositional semantic interpretation,

---

4. See J. Epstein (1999) for interesting discussion of the historical roots of such forms of explanation, and for discussion of the usual scientific situation in which more than one initial microspecification generates the macrostructure in question (thereby requiring more tests to distinguish the competitors' comparative empirical adequacy).

exactly retracing the steps of the bottom-up local pairing of two categories (the syntactic derivation), seems highly suspect. Furthermore, this postponement of interpretation, until all transformations have applied and the macrostructure is complete, in turn seems to necessitate non-minimal mechanisms such as chain-based trace theory, a look-back device whereby the admittedly important aspects of the derivation are encoded in the 'enriched', arguably Inclusiveness-violating, derived macrostructure itself.

As argued in Epstein and Seely (2002), representational theories with enriched derivation-encoding representational mechanisms, e.g., trace theory, are thus really 'just' a kind of derivational theory (cf. Brody 1995, 2001), but, we would suggest, the wrong kind. An important similar argument, the spirit of which we follow here, appears in Chomsky's (1995) discussion of another kind of successive cyclic movement, namely head-movement, in which he advocates a return to rule-based, generative theories of human knowledge of syntax. (But note this account is still *not* entirely chain-free.)

> It is generally possible to formulate the desired result in terms of outputs. In the head movement case, for example [a case of raising from N-to-V followed by [$_V$ N+V], raising to Infl SDE/TDS], one can appeal to the (plausible) assumption that the trace is a copy, so the intermediate V-trace includes within it a record of the local N→V raising. But surely this is the wrong move. The relevant chains at LF are (N, t_N) and (V, t_V), and in these the locality relation satisfied by successive raising has been lost.... These seem to be fundamental properties of language, which should be captured, not obscured by coding tricks, which are always available. A fully derivational approach both captures them straightforwardly and suggests that they should be pervasive, as seems to be the case. (Chomsky 1995:224)

To summarize, we argue in Chapter 2 that, under independently motivated restrictions on the postulate 'syntactic object', there can be no 'enriched representational objects' such as chains, as one would expect if the derivational approach is on track. (Nonetheless, many Minimalist analyses continue to assume chains.)

1.2.3   The EPP

If there is no movement to or through the specifier of raising-*to*, this in turn necessitates the abandonment of standard formulations of the EPP. We explore the elimination of the EPP in Chapter 3. We suggest that it is the EPP, an unclear and (to the extent that it is clear) questionable principle, which motivates movement to Spec, *to*, and such movement is argued to be empirically problematic in Chapter 2.

Thus, in Chapter 3, we seek to eliminate the EPP as a universal principle, following those that have already challenged its efficacy in other domains, including McCloskey (1986, 1996, 1997) and within recent Minimalist assumptions, Martin (1999), and Bošković (2002).

One of the leading ideas of our exploration is that the EPP is redundant with numerous other independently motivated mechanisms of the grammar. While Epstein (1990) has argued that *certain* redundancies are empirically supported by evidence concerning varying types and degrees of grammaticality (see also Chomsky 1965), we argue here that the EPP is not independently motivated. Given its widespread redundancy with other principles, we argue for its elimination as a universal principle of grammar. Thus, in this respect we follow Chomsky's methodological lead regarding (empirically unsubstantiated) redundancy, as reflected in e.g., the following:

> Repeatedly, it has been found that these [redundant principles with overlapping empirical coverage SDE/TDS] are wrongly formulated and must be replaced by non-redundant ones. The discovery has been so regular that the need to eliminate redundancy has become a working principle in inquiry. (Chomsky 1995:5)

But suppose one adopts this strategy, seeking to eliminate such redundancy.[5] How do we determine which of the overlapping principles should be targeted for modification or elimination so as to remove the redundancy? It takes at least two to be redundant. One issue is of course the nature of the empirical overlap. Here the idea we follow is that there are multiple independently motivated principles, each overlapping with, i.e. intersecting, the empirical domain of the EPP; hence, it's the EPP that should be targeted for modification or elimination. In addition to the redundancy, the EPP remains unclear – 'a pervasive mystery' according to Lasnik (2002). Furthermore, on some formulations, the EPP (as a 'macro phrase-structural' principle) seems to exhibit precisely the formal properties prohibited by the very

---

5. For extremely illuminating discussion of Minimalist method, including the elimination of redundancy, see Kitahara (2003). For other important discussion of Minimalist method, see e.g., McGilvray (1999) and Smith (1999). For a highly critical perspective, see Lappin, Levine and Johnson (2000a). For important discussion of Lappin, Levine and Johnson's perspective, see Holmberg (2000), Reuland (2000), Roberts (2000), Piattelli-Palmarini (2000), Uriagereka (2000), and Epstein and Seely (2002: introduction). See also Lappin, Levine and Johnson (2000b) for a response to some of these responses. See also Edelman and Christianson (2003) for criticism of Minimalist method, along with Phillips and Lasnik's illuminating (2003) response.

heart of the derivational Minimalist attempt to *explain* macrostructure properties by deducing them from lexical properties, a minimal theory of transformations, and by hypothesis, language-independent principles of efficient computation.

The redundancy concerning the EPP (much of which has already been noted by previous researchers, as we'll discuss in some detail) can be informally illustrated as shown in Figure 1.4.

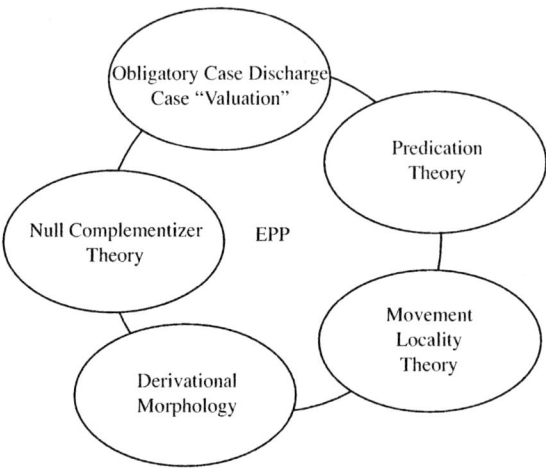

Figure 1.4   The EPP

Of course, we do not claim to have 'demonstrably eliminated the EPP'.[6] What we hope to have done instead is to suggest that analytical reliance on the EPP is reliance on something quite unclear, hence empirically problematic in its unclarity. Moreover, where it is clear, the EPP: (i) is highly redundant in its welcome empirical effects with numerous other independently motivated mechanisms; (ii) is empirically problematic to the extent that the predictions are clear (see Chapter 2); and (iii) (as noted above, on at least some formulations) violates both the spirit and letter of 'Minimalist law', threatening to mislead us into believing we have a genuine explanation of human knowledge of (un)grammaticality when we say, 'This data can be readily accounted for by the EPP.'

---

6. The five postulates intersecting the EPP might (contra this diagram) also display certain intersections with each other. This issue is not investigated here, nor do we *demonstrate* that the combined intersections with the EPP entirely subsumes this principle.

The remainder of Chapter 3, as well as Chapter 4, discusses just some of the challenges to trying to eliminate appeal to the EPP. In what remains of Chapter 3, we explore two non-movement challenges. The first is '*there*-insertion', and the general question of what forces the presence of expletives in the absence of the EPP. Here we rely on Minimalist extensions of Fukui and Speas's (1986) observation that 'obligatory Case discharge' creates a redundancy with the EPP. Currently, if Case (or unvalued φ-) features appear on a 'Case-assigning' head, they are uninterpretable, hence must be discharged. We adopt the view that expletives facilitate Case discharge (following Groat 1995 and Lasnik 1995). The second challenge investigated in Chapter 3 is the purported motivation for the EPP that stems from so-called BELIEVE-type verbs (i.e., those that can select an infinitival complement, but do not assign accusative Case). These motivate the EPP, since if indeed these verbs are Caseless, we cannot rely on Case discharge to force expletives into the derivation. Thus we seem (unwillingly) compelled to appeal to the EPP to state the fact in need of explanation, namely, the required presence of the expletive. In this discussion, we conduct an in-depth analysis of the verb *conjecture*, since it has been argued to be the archetypal BELIEVE-class verb. We suggest that the evidence that *conjecture* fails to check Case is weak, and there is evidence that we provide indicating *conjecture* is in fact an accusative Case-assigner, but displays curious semantic constraints on the conditions under which accusative is assigned. We follow Martin (1999) in hypothesizing that perhaps there may not exist any BELIEVE-class verbs, in which case 'they' provide no motivation for the EPP, since obligatory Case discharge is by hypothesis adequate to cover those phenomena thought to require appeal to EPP. We also discuss limitations of the Case discharge account in light of a further challenge, namely nominal forms of *conjecture* (altogether lacking accusative Case) taking an infinitival complement. Here we explore alternative independently motivated hypotheses regarding: (i) the structure of infinite complements to nouns, namely, that some are CP projections (see Ormazabal 1995); and (ii) the properties of null complementizers (as pioneered in Stowell 1981 and in Pesetsky 1991) heading such CPs. Here we adopt the leading idea of Martin (1999), namely that there is a redundancy between Null Complementizer Theory and the EPP. We nonetheless reject Martin's specific analysis of null C^0s. We adopt instead the null C^0 analysis proposed independently of the EPP in Bošković and Lasnik (2003). Following Epstein, Pires and Seely (2004), we show how this analysis of null C^0s can be exploited to cover certain EPP effects, revealing yet another potential redundancy – this one between the EPP and morpholexical properties.

Chapter 4 explores some movement-based challenges to the elimination of the EPP. The phenomena explored here all involve evidence that a DP has moved *through* the specifier of an infinitival on its way to its PF position. Since we've argued that the specifier of non-control (e.g., raising) *to* is not a checking position, the EPP, then, is apparently needed to describe such cases. These are what Bošković (2002) refers to as 'intermediate EPP effects'. In this chapter we examine relevant phenomena concerning Binding Theory, Reconstruction, and Quantifier Float (*all*-stranding). We examine an EPP-eliminating approach to these phenomena advanced in Bošković (2002). Bošković's basic idea is to exploit yet another redundancy, one between the EPP and movement locality, both forcing intermediate landing sites. Although this exploitation of the redundancy is a potentially very important part of eliminating the EPP, we nonetheless note some potential problems confronting Bošković's account. We then explore some alternative solutions, in particular adapting the independently motivated analysis in Torrego (2002), in order to capture certain 'intermediate EPP-effects' without reliance on the EPP. This approach presumes not that there is a redundancy between EPP and movement theory, with each forcing movement through the same position, but instead incorporates the hypothesis that the movement is not actually taking place through the EPP position; hence, there is no argument for retaining the EPP based on such data. We also briefly review analyses proposed by Williams (1982, 1989, 1994) and Bobaljik (2001), which call into question the general viability of a Sportiche (1988) type analysis of Quantifier Float, instead suggesting that such quantifiers are in fact adverbs, indicating nothing regarding the EPP. Finally, important arguments for the EPP as advanced by Lasnik are examined.

The final chapter, Chapter 5, returns to and explores the central point from which we began: namely, the abandonment of the (phaseless) four-level or two-level Y-model and the postulation instead of a level-free architecture of UG. Within this derivational approach, we advance the null hypothesis assuming phases, namely that each rule application is a self-contained Y-model derivation (phase) of its own. (For one aspect of comparison with Chomsky's 'bigger phase' approach, see Epstein and Seely 2002.) We suggest that each representation generated is interpreted by PF and LF. Many representations crash, but since crashing subderivations can be embedded within larger derivations, convergence can be obtained. That is, there is so-called non-fatal crashing, which can be overcome by subsequent operations yielding convergence in a derivation containing a crashing subderivation (see also Epstein 2003 for discussion of a related issue concerning Chomsky's DBP and BEA models). We explore a deep question that arises concerning how 'grammatical' vs. 'ungrammatical' can possibly be characterized in derivational approaches – what we call 'The (Sam) Gutmann Problem'. Among issues explored here are matters concerning what it means to have the endpoint of one derivation constitute the initiation point for another, as is assumed in any derivational approach. We call this 'derivational recursion', as distinct from recursive rule application, and suggest that the two are intimately related; in fact, within our model, they are one and the same. Specifically, we are led to assume that, following Chomsky, agreement checking is done through Probe-Goal matching, but we argue that Case cannot be checked in situ, but requires a more local relation, what was described as 'spec-head', an 'M-command' notion barred under the derivational account of c-command. We propose, following DASR, a way to characterize (certain) spec-head relations, but without appeal to representationally defined notions like m-command or government. In addition, we show that the derivational model provides no way to characterize the traditional notion of 'covert movement', since within our model, each representation generated is interpreted by PF and LF. Similarly, re-cycling, i.e. reapplying cyclic rules at different levels or within different components, is simply inexpressible. We also argue that the derivational model allows us to eliminate feature strength (see Lasnik 1999). Each representation generated in the unfolding derivation is directly inspected by PF (and LF), and features detected are either PF-illegitimate, inducing (sometimes only temporary) crashing, or legitimate; therefore, no appeal to strength, over and above interface legitimacy, is necessary.

To sum up, following Epstein and Seely (2002:86),

> Our proposals constitute what we believe to be the specification of the null hypothesis regarding the organization of a 'multiple splits' derivation-based model of UG lacking levels altogether. Our analyses are far from conclusive, but, we hope, contribute to the ongoing and (we think) exciting attempts to explicitly identify and seek explanatory maximization in formulating the theory of the biologically determined aspects of human knowledge of language, as begun and continued in Chomsky's routinely pioneering work.

2 On the elimination of A-chains

2.1 Chains are not syntactic objects

To begin, we need to clarify precisely what an A-chain is, and whether it 'qualifies' as a legitimate syntactic object. Arguably the clearest recent definition of 'syntactic object' is in Chomsky's (1995) Categories and Transformations (henceforth CT); and the definition provided there is, to the best of our knowledge, maintained in Chomsky's subsequent work (Minimalist Inquiries (MI), Derivation by Phase (DBP), and Beyond Explanatory Adequacy (BEA)). This definition in many respects parallels that of 'syntactic constituent' or 'syntactic category' in previous frameworks and plays a similarly fundamental role, as we'll see. After examining the Minimalist definition of 'syntactic object' we will then investigate the formal properties of the copy theory of movement, and the implications of copy theory for chains. Once this is done, the unnoticed entailment that chains are not syntactic objects emerges.

2.1.1 Syntactic objects

What counts as a syntactic object is tightly constrained: such objects are limited to lexical items and objects recursively built from them. The definition plays a direct role in the central goal of 'minimizing' the technicalia invoked in much Government Binding analysis. In fact the definition of 'syntactic object' constitutes the formal embodiment of the Inclusiveness condition, and perhaps more generally characterizes the minimalist approach. The formal definition is as follows (for further discussion see MI, p. 42):

(1) Syntactic Objects:
    a. Lexical items (CT, p. 243)
    b. $K = \{g, \{a, b\}\}$, where a, b are objects and g is the label of K (CT, p. 243).

c. K = {g, {a, b}}, where a, b are features of syntactic objects already formed (CT, p. 262).

Syntactic objects are of fundamental significance since only they are visible to, and hence manipulable by, the computational system of human language (C_{HL}).[1]

---

1. CT is arguably inconsistent regarding the criteria for syntactic accessibility. We believe the most natural interpretation of CT is that given in our text above, namely, that only syntactic objects (SO) as formally defined in (1) are accessible to syntactic operations. Thus, if X is a SO, then X is accessible to operations; and if X is not a SO, then it is inaccessible. This view has strong conceptual support; for one thing, it is not clear why a formal definition of SO is given unless it is assumed that only SOs are accessible. Moreover, the claim that only SOs are accessible is clearly appealed to in CT. Thus, CT states: 'And WHOSE cannot raise because it is not a syntactic object at all, hence not subject to movement.' p. 263. See also our later discussion.

    On the other hand, it is to be noted that a somewhat different criterion of syntactic accessibility is also arguably given in CT. CT includes the following passage (and a number of others similar in content to it): 'We assume further that the principles of UG involve only elements that function at the interface levels; nothing else can be "seen" in the course of computation, a general idea that will be sharpened as we proceed.' (p. 225)

    From this quote it seems to follow that X is syntactically accessible only if X is interpretable at the interface. (This interpretation of what is accessible to the syntax is adopted by recent research; thus Hornstein (1998) builds his argument against chains on the assumption that '...the objects interpreted at the interface determine the units of syntactic manipulation.')

    Note that both of these criteria for syntactic accessibility are problematic within CT.

    If we assume that only those elements that meet the definition of SO given in (1) are syntactically accessible, then it follows that lexical features are NOT accessible. Although lexical items are SOs, individual features of lexical items apparently are not. Features are not lexical items (although lexical items consist of sets of features), and hence (1a) does not entail that features are SOs. That features are SOs does not follow from (1b). [We assume that the word 'object' in (1b) refers to syntactic objects; for note that if the word 'object' in (1b) ranged over things like features, then (1c) would be entirely unnecessary.] And (1c) only implies that an object constructed out of features is a SO, but not that the features themselves are SOs. [Note that the actual SO given by (1c) is K, and K itself is the object {g, {a, b}}, and this object K is not a feature but rather it is a complex object composed of features (and the label 'g').] So it follows from (1) that features are not SOs. If only SOs are syntactically accessible, and if features are not SOs, then it follows that features are inaccessible to the syntax. However, the entailment that features are inaccessible to the syntax is directly contrary to the thrust of CT, as a large part of CT in fact explores the consequences of the idea that features are accessible to syntax. Indeed, in CT, features are argued to participate in the most fundamental syntactic operations; specifically, Move/Attract, Deletion, Agreement.

    On the other hand, if only interface interpretable elements are accessible to the syntax, then another problem emerges. It follows that if X is not interpretable, then X is not visible/accessible for computation. But it follows from this, in turn, that [−interpretable] features are not visible to the syntax since they are not interpreted at the interface. And if that is the case we seem to disallow feature checking, which is 'a core property of C_{HL} (i.e. the computational system of human

2.1.2 Copy theory and chains

Under copy theory, a mover and its 'trace' are identical. Thus in (2), there is exactly one DP, *Mary*, which is said to have two occurrences, *Mary*^{1} in subject position, and *Mary*^{2} in direct object position (superscripts are used only for ease of exposition).

(2)   Mary^1 was arrested Mary^2

Importantly, there is only one *Mary* in the numeration, and there is only one *Mary* in (2), with the result that Inclusiveness (no new features are added in the course of the derivation) is satisfied under the copy theory. In fact, one can regard copy theory, or at least the abandonment of trace theory, as necessitated by Inclusiveness.[2] If the copy trace were not a subset of the features of the mover, then features would thereby be added in the course of the derivation, and this would violate Inclusiveness. However, if the mover and its copy-traces are identical (satisfying Inclusiveness), but the chain is to be multi-membered, then a chain cannot consist of just the mover and its trace(s), for 'they' are actually ONE AND ONLY ONE thing. Thus, under copy theory the chain is not {*Mary*, t} as in standard non-copy theory. Nor can the chain be {*Mary*^{1}, *Mary*^{2}}, for this is not the intended chain: Recall *Mary*^{1} and *Mary*^{2} are IDENTICAL (superscripts used here for exposition only), and

---

language)...' (p. 228). CT clearly assumes that [−interpretable] features are accessible to the syntax; the work is in large part devoted to exploring exactly this assumption.

   A solution to the problems outlined above is to assume that only SOs are accessible, but add to the definition of SO syntactic features; thus, features, lexical items, and elements formed from them are SOs, and only they are syntactically accessible. The addition of features to the definition of SO, which is in fact done in DBP, does not affect the argumentation regarding chains presented in the text above.

2. We are indebted to Noam Chomsky (personal communication) for extensive discussion of the copy theory, and its historical development. In classical theory, a mover and its trace are distinct; they are featurally distinct and therefore are subject to different grammatical constraints. For example, with A-movement of an R-expression, as in passive, the mover is an R-expression subject to BT-C while its trace is an anaphor subject to BT-A. Note further that because they are distinct, some mechanism for referentially associating a mover and its trace is required. (For contemporary discussion of copy theory and its entailments regarding the phonetic unrealizability of 'traces' see Nunes 1999, 2001 and 2004.)

   These characteristics of the traditional view of movement are incompatible with Minimalism and the main reason involves the overarching constraint of Inclusiveness. Inclusiveness disallows mechanisms like indexing. It also disallows traces, as entities featurally distinct from their antecedents, since such a trace does not occur in the numeration, and, by Inclusiveness, it can't be 'created' in the course of a derivation. Copy theory as identity, however, is consistent with Minimalist tenets. If a mover and its trace are identical, then indexing is not required and Inclusiveness is not violated.

therefore the set {*Mary*¹, *Mary*²} is equivalent to the unit set {*Mary*}. This is not the intended characterization of the chain since, whatever else the chain is hypothesized to be in (2), it is certainly an object different from (the unit set containing) just the DP *Mary*. Thus, under copy theory, chains are characterized in terms of the POSITIONS occupied by the different occurrences of the mover since although the occurrences are identical, the positions of those occurrences are not. The fact that identity, in turn, requires appealing to positions in the definition of chains is perhaps most clearly stated as follows:

(3)   Suppose, then, that *a* raises to target M in S, so that the result of the operation is S', formed by replacing M in S by {N, {*a*, M}}, N the label. The element *a* now appears twice in S', in its initial position and in the raised position. We can identify the initial position of *a* as the pair <*a*, *b*> (*b* the co-constituent of *a* in S), and the raised position as the pair <*a*, K> (K the co-constituent of the raised term *a* in S').... *though* a *and its trace are identical, the two positions are distinct* [our emphasis, SDE, TDS]. We can take the chain CH that is the object interpreted at LF to be the pair of positions. (CT, p. 252)

What then is the chain associated with (2)? The chain will consist of the (one and only) DP *Mary* and the positions of its two occurrences. The position of a category C is defined, or identified, by the (representational) sister of C; i.e. if we know the sister of C, we know the position of C. (Interestingly, notice, that representational sisters are invariably *created* by the minimal, binary rules Move and Merge. This fact plays a central role in the DASR attempt to deduce/explain syntactic relations and will play a central role in what follows.) Assuming the characterization of chains in (3), what this means is that the chain in (2) consists of two members, each a pair where the first element of the pair is an occurrence *a* of the mover, and the second element of the pair is the 'co-constituent,' i.e. the sister, of *a*. Thus the two-membered chain in (2) is:

(4)   (<Mary¹, Infl'>, <Mary², V>)

Notice that this notation is somewhat misleading. If the position of *Mary*¹ is to be characterized in terms of the sister of the occurrence of *Mary*¹, then the sister of *Mary*¹ is the entire I' constituent [*was arrested Mary*²], not just the label 'I'' (the label itself is not a sister to anything nor is it a syntactic object[3]). Consequently, if

---

3. See Collins (1999, 2002) and Seely (2000) for further discussion of the syntactic 'inertness' of labels.

18 *Derivations in Minimalism*

chains must be defined in terms of the 'position of the occurrences' of a single category, and positions are defined in terms of the sister of an occurrence, the correct (Bare Phrase Structure) characterization of the chain of (2) is as in (5), containing two members: (i) *Mary*^{1} and its Infl$'$ sister; and (ii) *Mary*^{2} and its verb-sister:[4]

(5)   (<Mary^1, {was {was, {arrested, {arrested Mary^2}}}}>, <arrested Mary^2>)

That is, the sister of the occurrence of *Mary*^{1} is the entire I$'$ (or T$'$) *was arrested Mary*^{2}. And the sister of the occurrence of *Mary*^{2} is the verb *arrested*. Importantly this specification of a chain includes complex phrases (i.e. terms) and ENTIRE derived tree representations (e.g. the I$'$ *was arrested Mary* in (5)).

So far, we have reviewed the restricted definition of 'syntactic object', and we have established how chains must be defined under the copy theory of movement – in terms of multiple occurrences of the positions of the mover. We will next argue that chains are not syntactic objects.

2.1.3 Why chains are not syntactic objects

The chain in (5) does not meet the restrictive definition of 'syntactic object' given in (1). (5) is not a lexical item (or a feature of a lexical item) and it satisfies neither condition (1b) nor (1c). Merge and Move each take two objects, join them together (as a set), and then project one or the other thereby creating a label for the object that results. But chains do not have a label at all and there is no projection of the required sort. A chain is a set of 'discontinuous' positions each expressed as a relation between an occurrence of a mover and the entire derived syntactic representation which is its sister. A chain thus seems to be defined in terms of grammatical functions or relations, as in (5), in which *Mary*^{1} is Spec, IP (= subject) and *Mary*^{2} is direct object of V.

Since chains are not syntactic objects, and since the C_{HL} has access only to syntactic objects, it follows that chains are invisible to C_{HL}. For all intents and

---

4. Notice that the Spec, IP, i.e. *Mary* in this case, could itself be a complex term (=subtree) as in *The tall woman was arrested* rendering a chain-representation even more 'complex', or structurally detailed. Here and throughout, we will use the terminology *tense/Tense phrase*, vs. *Infl/Infl-phrase* interchangeably, unless otherwise indicated.
   Notice also that both <Mary^1, {was {was, {arrested, {arrested Mary^2}}}}> and <arrested Mary^2> appear in the A-chain representation (5). Thus, among other things, the chain representation is itself *internally* redundant.

purposes, then, chains do not exist in the syntax. This predicts that no computational operation of any sort can refer to them.[5]

2.1.4 A potential problem: substantive reference to A-chains

We have revealed that, on formal and independently motivated grounds, chains are invisible to C_{HL}. In fact, if we are right, this follows from the most fundamental definition that the theory incorporates, that of 'syntactic object'. Nonetheless, elsewhere in CT, and subsequent work, 'chains' (CH) are treated as if they are syntactic objects, visible[6] to C_{HL}. For example,

(6) a. '...CH violates the uniformity condition...' (CT, p. 258)
    b. 'Only the head of an A-chain (equivalently, the whole chain) blocks Matching under the Minimal Link Condition.' (DBP, p. 16)
    c. '...domain and minimal domain ...are defined "once and for all" for each CH...' (CT, p. 299)
    d. 'In the present framework, the natural proposal is to eliminate the chains CH_1 and CH_2, leaving only the well-formed chain CH_3.' (CT, p. 300)
    e. 'Only the head of a chain CH enters into the operation of Attract/Move.' (CT, p. 304)
    f. 'The operation Move forms the Chain CH=(a, t(a)), t(a) the trace of a. Assume further that CH meets several other conditions (c-command, Last Resort, and others)...' (CT, p. 250)

A theory-internal inconsistency has now emerged: the above passages presuppose that chains are visible to the C_{HL}, and yet they cannot be visible to the C_{HL} since they are by definition not syntactic objects. As a final note, let us consider an apparently more serious problem: CT (p. 281) seeks to deduce that 'terms cannot be erased' (see also footnote 1). CT notes that given the syntactic object $\{A, \{a, b\}\}$, erasure of b would yield $\{A, \{a\}\}$. CT then notes that this is by definition not a syntactic object according to the formal definition of syntactic object in (1) above. CT asserts that 'erasure of a full category cancels the derivation.' The logic is clear: if a non-syntactic object ever appears, the derivation is cancelled. Thus, it would

---

5. See Hornstein (1998) for a similar conclusion based on different argumentation.
6. If chains are 'invisible' as we have argued above, then it precludes both operations manipulating chains and operations referring to chains (e.g. a chain can't be part of the structural description of an operation).

seem that chains, not being syntactic objects, wouldn't just be invisible, but would cancel the derivation. Since all convergent derivations involve chain formation in the CT framework, it would seem that all derivations are cancelled. In what follows, we will disregard this important property of CT and will assume, less problematically, that chains are (just) invisible to C_{HL}, i.e. they do not induce derivational cancellation. (We will later return to the prohibition against term erasure, entailed by the definition of syntactic object, since it is this aspect of the theory that forces the presence of a 'trace' – an enduring trace present throughout the derivation – in every departure site. Following DASR, we seek to eliminate trace theory, at least in A-movement.) We turn now to further arguments against A-chains.

2.2 A-chains are not specifiable under X' invisibility

This section has two goals. The first is to strengthen the argument that chains do not exist. It is suggested that chains are not only invisible to the syntax but in fact are invisible in LF representations as well; thus, they do not exist in the mapping to LF, nor in LF representations, and hence they do not exist at all.[7] Implications of this conclusion are then explored.

2.2.1 Could chains be visible, but only at LF?

One approach to the problem raised above maintains both the restrictive definition of 'syntactic object' and the prediction that chains are not syntactic objects and therefore are not visible to C_{HL}. This would seem to imply, correctly we think, that chains are not objects manipulated by C_{HL}. This may be right since a chain, as exemplified by (5), as opposed to certain parts of it, never appears to undergo syntactic operations, such as Merge or Move. (We return to this issue below.) Notice that the non-manipulability of chains, if correct, does not logically preclude the visibility of chains at the LF interface. C_{HL} might operate only on syntactic objects but there is nothing in the theory which forces it to CREATE only syntactic objects, i.e. only objects that are visible to itself. In a modular system it is perfectly feasible for the products produced by component A to be inaccessible to A but these products nonetheless constitute visible input to component B. Imagine a robot, for example,

---

7. We are assuming, following Chomsky's recent work, that chains cannot exist at PF since chains, as we've detailed above, contain syntactic structure (e.g. the I' in (5)) and such structure is arguably PF-uninterpretable.

that was designed to paint cars on the assembly line but that was not designed to detect the colors in any way – it's 'blind'. Obviously this robot cannot 'see' what it produces. But imagine that there is another 'seeing' robot that was designed to detect colors and takes as its input the painted cars produced as output by the blind painter robot. This seeing robot could perfectly well perform operations based on color, like putting a certain kind of bumper on the blue cars or a certain kind of tinted window on the green ones. In theory, then, it is possible for the C_{HL} to create but not see chains and then to pass those chains over to the interface, perhaps as a 'set of instructions,' which are interpretable/interpreted at the interface.

However, we now argue that at least within the CT analysis this logical possibility is precluded. The form of the argument is this: chains are defined in a certain way given copy theory (see section 1.2); however, (we'll show that) on the required definition, one element of a chain is invisible at LF, and therefore the entire chain is uninterpretable at LF. Recall the Passive (2) and the chain of movement (5) associated with it, both repeated (superscripts are used only for exposition):

(2)   Mary[1] was arrested Mary[2]

(5)   (<Mary[1], {was {was, {arrested, {arrested Mary[2]}}}}>, <arrested Mary[2]>)

The first member of the chain is composed of the occurrence *Mary*[1] and its sister, the I' {was {was, {arrested, {arrested Mary[2]}}}}. But note that at LF, this I' is invisible since under bare relational phrase structure theory it is neither minimal nor maximal, under the following hypothesis (see also Muysken 1982, Speas 1986, Freidin 1992):

(7)   X' Invisibility Hypothesis (Chomsky 1995, p. 242):
        A category that does not project any further is a maximal projection XP, and one that is not a projection at all is a minimal projection X^{min}; any other is an X', invisible at the interface and for computation.

This is well motivated to the extent that single-bar projections seem not to participate in operations in C_{HL}, as CT notes. Thus single-bar projections do not assign or receive Case; they do not participate in agreement relations; they do not bind or control and are not bound or controlled; they do not move, delete, or insert, nor do they undergo Merge.[8] Representationally, then, it is claimed that the (entire category) I' is 'invisible at the interface.' But this has an important consequence: if I' is invisible, then the (representational) chain specification that includes it is unspecifiable at the interface; i.e. part of the chain is invisible hence uninterpretable at the interface. As a concrete illustration, recall that the position of $Mary^1$ in (2) is defined in terms of its sister, the simplest assumption. But the sister to $Mary^1$ in the LF representation is a single-bar projection, assumed to be invisible to C_{HL} and invisible at the interface.

To consider the matter in more detail, note that at the point in the derivation before attraction (movement) of *Mary*, the structure is {*was* {*was*, {*arrested*, {*arrested* $Mary^2$}}}}, or more conspicuously:

(8)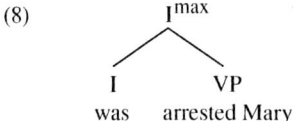

I^{max}

I VP
was arrested Mary

This I projection (within a derivational, relational, bare theory of phrase structure) is maximal, at this point in the derivation, since it does not project further. However, once *Mary* is attracted to Spec, I, I^{max} in (8) will project and hence will no longer be maximal. Nor will it be minimal since it dominates the I^0 *was*. Thus once the application of Attract is completed, (this derivational operation (rule) yielding a representation) the intermediate projection I' (which is neither a maximal nor minimal projection) is created and once the I' is created, it is invisible 'at the interface and for computation.' Thus chains, as defined, are not specifiable even as representational objects within an LF representation.

---

8. Notice, however, that single-bar categories do presumably undergo compositional semantic interpretation (thanks to Diana Cresti p.c. for helpful discussion of this issue). Thus if single-bar categories are indeed invisible, there would seem to be no way to perform compositional semantic interpretation at LF. A solution to this daunting problem is readily available in the Epstein *et al.* (1998) framework, within which the single-bar category is interpreted when it is still a maximal projection, before being demoted to a single-bar by virtue of concatenation with an element that will become its specifier. This derivational approach to interpretation would also 'explain' why single-bar categories are present in LF, but invisible. How can X be present in representation R but not visible in representation R? This too could come about derivationally, X'-projections are fossils of what were once X^{max}.

2.2.2 Avoiding reference to X': motherhood instead of sisterhood?

Thus, if in fact X' is invisible, and reference to it in definitions is precluded, then, indeed the X' sister cannot be used to specify the positional occurrence of a category in Spec. Lasnik (2002:7) and Chomsky (2001a:39) seem to provisionally accept our argument, and so proceed to suggest that an alternative approach to chain-specification can be maintained while also maintaining X' invisibility. They suggest that the X' invisibility problem we note can be circumvented by exploiting the 'motherhood' relation, instead of the 'sisterhood' relation, to specify positions of occurrences. The basic idea is as follows; consider

(9)   [$_{IP}$ Mary^1 [$_{I'}$ was arrested Mary^2]]

Instead of referring to the X' sister (I') to specify the positional occurrence of *Mary*^{1}, we can instead refer to the mother, IP, that is, the head of the chain is the occurrence of *Mary* immediately dominated by IP. Thus no reference to the (by hypothesis) invisible X'/I' is made, yet the occurrences are nonetheless positionally specified. There are at least three potential problems confronting this approach as we understand it.

First, what exactly does the A-chain look like, what is an A-chain, under the positional specification of occurrences employing motherhood? The head of the chain (*Mary*^{1}) is Spec, IP, i.e. it is immediately dominated by the *category* IP = 'the entire tree', not just the label 'IP' which is not a term. So, in order to specify the positional occurrence of *Mary*^{1}, we need to specify what the category IP is. (This parallels the fact that we similarly needed to specify the (invisible) *category* I' under the sisterhood approach.) Thus the first member of the chain, *Mary*^{1}, might be specified as follows:

(10)   {<Mary^1, IP>}

But this is insufficient since the 'IP' must be specified, and the bare phrase structure specification of IP is as follows, yet crucially it includes reference to/specification of I'. Thus, under the motherhood approach, the head of the chain is the occurrence of *Mary* immediately dominated by the category IP:

(11)   {<Mary¹, {was { Mary¹ {was {was {arrested {arrested Mary²}}}}}}>
         ───
                        underlined= the category IP

The problem is that the motherhood approach ('*Mary*¹ is immediately dominated by IP') requires specifying the entire IP (not just the label), but specifying IP in bare phrase structure requires in turn specifying I′, which is by hypothesis invisible, hence unspecifiable. If we are on track then, the appeal to motherhood does not in fact circumvent the problem of referring to (invisible) X′ projections.[9]

One might argue that the motherhood approach could be made to work by specifying the first member of the A-chain as in (11), and ignoring the invisible I′ set – attending only to the 'leftmost' *was* as the 'immediate dominator'. This amounts to a label- (or node-label) based approach.[10] Within this label-based approach the specification of the positional occurrence of the A-chain head (*Mary*¹) would seem to be tantamount to the following, which importantly is not a syntactic object under the restrictive definition in (1) above.

(12)   { <Mary¹, {was {Mary¹}}

Informally, this specifies that there is an occurrence of *Mary*, namely, *Mary*¹, which is immediately dominated by the IP label, namely *was*. Another potential problem with this label-based motherhood approach is that under Collins' (1999, 2002) label-free system, reference to 'the immediately dominating node-*label*' is precluded, since there are no labels. In fact, Seely (2000) attempts to deduce labellessness from a derivational theory of relations within which syntactic relations are just and only the relations created by the generative procedure. As Seely notes, since the label was never operated upon by transformation, it is in no (derivational) relations, and being in no relations, it is tantamount to being absent from a syntactic representation, thereby explaining Collinsian labellessness. Following Seely, a derivational

---

9. Our only claim here is that if X′ is invisible, then there remains potential unclarity regarding the implementation of the motherhood alternative.
10. As assumed in DBP (fn. 68): 'Other apparent distinctions between X′ and XP dissolve – largely or completely – with more systematic reinterpretation of relations and operations in terms of labels rather than phrasal categories, as in MI and here.' Yet DBP (fn. 2) earlier says: 'In what follows there is no use of labels except for the new object gamma, which has the label of either alpha or beta, determined (in the best case) by algorithm. This item is similar to the locus that determines the next operation in the system developed by Collins (1999, 2002), who proposes that labels be eliminated more generally.' Thus the status of labels within DBP is unclear to us.

approach seems to prohibit the 'mother-label' (in fact any label-based) approach to specifying occurrences, driving us back to mother-*category* specification, which in turn confronts the X' invisibility problem, just like the sisterhood approach does.

A second potential problem with the motherhood approach to X' invisibility is that the positional specification of the chain tail in Passives might, under certain proposals, require direct reference to X'=V', the immediate dominator/mother of the direct object occurrence. That is *Mary*^{2}, the direct object occurrence of *Mary*, would be positionally specified as 'the occurrence of *Mary* immediately dominated by V'' if indeed there is, or can be, a Spec, VP in Passives. If there can't ever be Spec, VP in Passives, then there is no problem specifying the chain tail occurrence since as Chomsky notes (see Chomsky 2001a:40) within the motherhood approach, the immediate dominator of a direct object occurrence in a Passive is the maximal projection 'VP'.

The third and final potential problem is that under the motherhood-based representational specification of A-chain, we confront exactly the same kind of redundancy that confronts sisterhood. As Epstein *et al.* (1998), Epstein (1999) note, binary Merge and Re-Merge are operations that create sisterhood and motherhood relations (two-membered sets). There is a serious redundancy (the type of which has been addressed regarding earlier theories, by e.g. Rizzi 1986, Brody 1995) within any analysis whose RULES create such relations, and yet the very same relations are again stated in representational specifications of the objects (like A-chains) created. We think it's worth exploring the elimination of such redundancies, especially if they are empirically problematic (see below), not just redundant, under the hypothesis that representational constructs like A-chains are difficult if not impossible to specify under the restricted definitions proposed. If impossible to specify, as we suggest here, then the theory has the attractive property that its restrictive definitions *disallow* redundant (and problematic) specification, i.e. there is no way to formally specify an A-chain, under the theoretical apparatus proposed. Disallowing the specification of that which we (provisionally) think should not be stateable is an attractive property of a (Minimalist) theory. Of course the 'larger' issue is to determine how much of the theory is formulated derivationally, and to what extent is such derivational specification in fact inconsistent with the concomitant postulation of representational postulates.

The preceding discussion concerns the Chomsky-Lasnik motherhood approach which seeks to provide a solution to the problem we have raised regarding the sisterhood approach, *under the assumption that X′ is invisible*. We have argued that, contra Lasnik and Chomsky, under X′ invisibility, the motherhood approach might not provide an adequate solution.

Of course all the problems created by X′ invisibility as proposed in e.g. CT (following Muysken and Freidin) concerning chain-specification disappear if the X′ Invisibility Hypothesis is abandoned. Of course, the matter is entirely empirical, so what is the syntactic and interpretive status of such projections? Are they targetable? Are they specifiable in definitions? The matter seems far from clear. For example, recently, Lasnik (2002) in discussing Epstein and Seely (1999), and proposing the motherhood approach, says the following regarding targeting of X′:

> There is actually very little evidence in the literature that intermediate projections cannot be targeted by operations (mildly surprising for something so widely believed), but I have no particular reason to doubt the claim, so I will assume it is correct. (Lasnik 2002:7)

As another example, DBP seems less 'supportive' than CT of X′ invisibility's empirical content and its conceptual underpinnings. Thus in discussing Epstein-Seely (1999), DBP writes:

> Take the notion of occurrence as X′ sister. The empirical and conceptual arguments for X′ invisibility are slight. The conceptual argument relies on the assumption that X′ is not interpreted at LF, which is questionable and in fact rejected in standard approaches.

To clarify, we have never intended that e.g.

(13)   John [$_{I'}$ will sleep]

appears at LF as, and is thus interpreted at LF as:

(14)   John

an interpretation which would be necessitated if 'X′ were not visible at LF.' We assume X′'s must be interpreted at LF. But how can they be if X′'s are 'invisible for computation and interpretation' (CT). The hypothesis is that, (in contrast to the GB Y model), it must not be the case that LF is reached only after all transformations have been applied, and hence after X′ has been projected and rendered invisible!

That is, it must be that LF is reached 'derivationally' (Epstein *et al.* 1998, Uriagereka 1999, Chomsky MI, DBP). But if that is the case, then, X′ can in principle be interpreted at the derivational point at which it has no immediate dominator – i.e. at the point of creation, when it is still a full-fledged maximal projection, not yet demoted to an invisible X′ by subsequent projection induced by Merge/Move (see Chomsky BPS: fn. 10 and McGilvray 1999). This then is the 'X′ as representational fossil' approach to the question: 'If X′s are invisible, what are they doing in mental representations?' Answer: 'they were, at an earlier point of the derivation, X^{max}, at which point they were visible, but in output representations they have been rendered invisible.' X′s (i.e. sets like {kick him}) ARE interpreted at LF, precisely because LF is reached multiply and at a time when the set is still a visible, hence interpretable, maximal projection. This requires online, immediate compositional interpretation (as suggested in Epstein *et al.* 1998). This is then our take on the view that conceptually X′s cannot be invisible.

As concerns the empirical issue, Chomsky (DBP, p. 40) continues:

> The empirical argument is that it allows incorporation of (much of) Kayne's (1994) Linear Correspondence Axiom, within an impoverished (bare) phrase structure system [fn. 68]. But that result, if desired, could just as well be achieved by defining 'asymmetric c-command' to exclude (X′, YP) (a stipulation, but not more so than X′ invisibility).

Two points regarding this: first, '*the* empirical argument' suggests there is but one. We are not sure about this (although in theory development one often suffices). Second, within the derivational approach we develop here, c-command and asymmetric c-command (more generally, syntactic relations) cannot be DEFINED on representations in order to achieve a specific result. Relations instead are hypothesized to be derivational, derivative constructs, so we are not sure that this result could 'just as well be achieved by re-defining asymmetric c-command to exclude the X′ YP relation.' We do agree with DBP that X′ Invisibility is a stipulation, but as we'll note in a moment, it may be possible to derive it. Thus, one can view Kayne's LCA as providing yet another argument for X′ invisibility.[11] Of course, as with any theo-

---

11. Informally, the LCA states that a category X precedes a category Y, iff: (i) X asymmetrically c-commands Y, or (ii) Z precedes Y, and Z dominates X. If single-bar projections were visible to such linearization, then, the wrong result would obtain, as follows. The single bar projection asymmetrically c-commands all members of the specifier. This predicts that the members of the single bar projection precede the members of the Spec. However, the Spec asymmetrically c-commands all members of the single bar projection, thus the members of the Spec should precede the members

retical construct, we are not asserting that X′ invisibility is true, but provisionally assuming that it might be, as hitherto motivated, and are trying to determine the properties and predictions of one theory incorporating the construct in question.

Note furthermore that we can attempt to derive X′ invisibility from properties of the derivational model that we develop (see the Appendix of Epstein and Seely 1999 for extensive discussion). The basic idea is that an X′ is invisible since it was not merged with anything at any point in the derivation. Rather, an X′ projection is created by the rule of Merge itself; an X′ is the by-product of Merge. Thus if X and Y are merged, X or Y projects. If X re-merges (moves) to the Spec of Y, then Y projects to produce Y^{max}, thereby demoting Y to an X′, i.e. an intermediate projection. But this X-bar itself was never merged with any category and hence cannot participate in any relations with respect to any category; it is rendered syntactically inert, i.e. invisible.[12]

2.2.3   Chains are redundant with Merge and Move

We now hypothesize that the non-existence of chains (here we focus on A-chains) is just the right result. Consider again the chain

(15)   (<Mary^1, [was arrested Mary^2]>, <Mary^2, arrested>)

As noted, the first member of the chain, namely (<*Mary^1*, [*was arrested Mary^2*]>, where *Mary^1* is the Spec of IP and [*was arrested Mary^2*] is an I′) specifies the entire tree (if I′ were visible, which it is not, given X′ invisibility). What information does the chain contain? Crucially, the sister relations or, under Chomsky and Lasnik's alternative proposal, mother relations. But notice that *sister and mother relations entirely restate precisely the relations established by the application of the rules Merge and Move*, which create sisters and mothers, and only these relations, while nothing else in C_{HL} does. Thus the chain, a representational construct,

---

of the single bar projection. Thus, if single bar projections were visible, linearization by the LCA would be impossible, since the LCA would produce instructions to PF like 'X precedes Y and Y precedes X' – for each and every [Spec + X′] structure. Such symmetrical instructions (due to the symmetrical, mutual c-command, (sisterhood) relation between single bar and Spec) are presumably unimplementable by the PF component. Thus, the LCA is yet another mechanism requiring the invisibility of single bar projections, and this, in turn, strengthens our argument against chains based on such invisibility.

12. See Kayne 1994: sec. 3.5 for a different approach. See also the Appendix to Uriagereka (1998:506), authored by J. Nunes and E. Thompson, for a clear, succinct explication of the LCA.

restates formal properties of the rule applications. Thus 'the chain' is in fact already (successfully) specified internal to the rule of Move; specifically, chains are defined within the structural description of Move. Chains are thus, in a clear formal sense, 'inside', or part of, the rule of Move. This is consistent with the general 'derivational program': to show that representational approaches are inadequate (not internally consistent) and are redundant since the theory already incorporates derivational mechanisms (which are in our view mistakenly ignored), which themselves are not only non-problematic but empirically adequate and arguably explanatory; i.e. the independently motivated simple rule X+Y → [$_Z$ X+Y] is sufficient to specify the chain which is not even specifiable within the representational analysis (cf. Brody 2001).

In summary, we have thus far presented three arguments against chains:

(i) Chains are not Syntactic Objects and are therefore inaccessible to syntactic operations; they are invisible to the syntax.

(ii) Chains 'contain' an invisible X', which renders them unspecifiable to the syntax and to LF. (Thus, even if chains were Syntactic Objects, they would nonetheless not 'exist' for the syntax.)

(iii) The information encoded in chains is in fact already contained in the syntactic operations Merge and Move. (Thus, even if chains did not contain invisible X's, they can and should nonetheless be eliminated since they are redundant with independently motivated, irreducible syntactic operations.)

The question that emerges is this: If there are no chains, then how is the important information which the 'representationalist' sought to provide in chains to be captured? Our answer is that the information is, even in the 'representational approach', already present in the derivation itself.

This derivational analysis, to be considered in detail below, is entirely consistent with certain perspectives expressed in CT; in particular

(16) A chain CH=(a, t(a)) formed by Move meets several conditions, WHICH WE TAKE TO BE PART OF THE DEFINITION OF THE OPERATION ITSELF [our emphasis]. One of these is the c-command condition...(Chomsky 1995:253).

Thus chain conditions are 'part of the rule' including the c-command condition on chains, with c-command arguably also a derivational relation expressed by the operation Move/Attract itself, as argued in Epstein *et al.* (1998), and Epstein (1999).

Before turning to further details of chain formation, one more note concerning X' invisibility and derivationality is worth stating. If X' projections are indeed invisible to C_{HL}, predicting, apparently correctly, that they play no role in Case, Agreement, Binding, Control, and Movement, there remains still the question of theta-assignment. Consider, for example, the assignment of an external theta-role to *John* in

(17) $[_{VP}$ John + [v + [V_{likes} + $DP_{the\ cake}$]]]

In the Structural Description of Merge

(18) Merge the DP *John* and the [v + [V_{likes} + $DP_{the\ cake}$]]

the underlined v-projection is still maximal. In the output representation, this v-projection vP is a 'demoted' invisible single bar projection of v. Thus, at least in the case of theta-role assignment to Spec, if it is indeed theta-assignment by the sister of Spec, consonant with a Montagovian compositional bottom-up semantics (see Higginbotham 1985, Berwick and Epstein 1995, Epstein *et al.* 1998), it seems the relation can't be defined representationally but can be expressed (or is already expressed) within the Structural Description of the rule. Once the rule applies, it is too late; the theta-assigner (sister of Spec) is now an invisible little v'. This argument extends to 'inner Specs' in a Larsonian shell structure, too, as well as to *wh*-movement to Spec, CP. In fact, it pertains to all movement to Spec, the canonical checking position.[13] Notice that the independently motivated mechanics nicely preclude appeal to anything like the projection principle – applying to all levels, within a derivation. This principle type is excluded on minimalist assumptions (CT p. 220) and within many current analyses. As we see, given X' invisibility, the Projection Principle is not simply superfluous or overly determined. Rather, this representational principle is incompatible with core assumptions since theta-marking *relations* are not represented in tree structures given X' invisibility.

After Merge of an argument into Spec, vP, a representationally visible theta-marking relation between sisters no longer exists. This is consonant with Bošković

---

13. On the interpretation of Agr-less Larsonian shell structures, and their creation in the LF component, see Epstein (1998).

and Takahashi's (1999) hypothesis – motivated on different grounds – that theta roles are assigned features and accords with the rule by rule derivation envisioned in DASR. Crucially, in LF representation, the sister of Spec, an X′ projection, is invisible. Again, this would seem to 'force' a derivational implementation of compositional semantics. To the extent that 'Spec-of' X′ is a Grammatical Function, these would be invisible, under X′ invisibility, once Spec is created. Thus (some) GFs are also 'inside' the independently motivated rules, wherein the Grammatical Functions already 'reside', given Merge and Move. This seems to us very much a return to Chomsky (1965); e.g.

> Suppose we have a sequence of rewriting [i.e. PS] rules *associated with [such] rules is each grammatical function*... [our emphasis, SDE, TDS] (p. 70).

As *Aspects* (p. 71) similarly says, grammatical functions are 'directly derivable' from the PS *rules* and representing such information in trees is thus unnecessary.

We hope to have provided, thus far, compelling arguments that 'representational chains' are, on a number of different, independently motivated grounds, unrepresentable. In fact, as noted, since chains are by definition not syntactic objects, CT (p. 281) predicts that their presence invariably cancels the derivation. We have also suggested that the information specified or represented in a chain is in fact already expressed in the Structural Description of the sister- and mother-creating transformational rules Merge and Move. This conceptually desirable reduction of chains to properties of transformational rules would seem to work only if chain formation is isomorphic to movement. The *complete* reduction of chains to rules is potentially threatened if there is some other chain formation algorithm since then chains or their members might not correspond exactly to the positions (departure site and landing site) of any given single movement operation. Exactly this non-correspondence appears to be the case in CT's analysis of successive cyclic A-movement. Let us turn then to a consideration of that analysis, within which chains are not isomorphic to Move.

2.3 *A non-isomorphism between A-chains and successive cyclic A-movement*

CT proposes arguably one of the most detailed analyses of standard English

32   *Derivations in Minimalism*

Successive Cyclic A-movement phenomena. This analysis is particularly important to our present concerns as it seeks to construct an account of A-movement and chain formation consistent with minimalist explanatory goals. We first review the analysis, which postulates A-chains non-isomorphic to Move/Attract.[14] A number of potential problems are revealed, ultimately leading us to our hypothesis that there is no successive cyclic A-movement, at least in the cases under consideration here, nor a universal 'Extended Projection Principle' (see Chapters 3 and 4).

The central case examined is:

(19)   we are likely [t^3 to be asked[t^2 to t^1 build airplanes]]]] (= Chomsky 1995:ex. 88)

Certain aspects of the analysis of (19) were dealt with above. Recall, for example, that the traces, unlike the traces of pre-minimalist frameworks, are identical to *we*; in short *we*, t^3, t^2, and t^1 are the same category, namely *we*.[15] Furthermore, the chains associated with (19) are characterized in terms of positions (sisters of the departure and landing site(s)) and problems with this have already been discussed. Of central concern for present purposes, however, is how the chains are formed, whether automatically via movement (or some other derivational method) or through a representational chain formation algorithm. We note here that CT does seem to suggest that chains are formed through, and are isomorphic to, movement. On a number of occasions, a 'strictly derivational' approach to computation is assumed; for example, '. . . the two elements of the chain CH *formed* by this [i.e. the movement] operation. . .' (CT, p. 250) and, as noted in section 2.1.4: 'The operation Move forms the chain CH. . .' (CT, p. 250). However, the matter is not clear. As we'll see in a moment a non-isomorphic analysis is in fact proposed. Again, we are particularly interested in this non-isomorphism since it potentially challenges the argument that chains are fully redundant with Merge/Move.

2.3.1   +/− interpretability of features

Under Inclusiveness, the features that make up lexical items play a central defining

---

14. Unless otherwise specified, the arguments presented in this subsection concern the CT analysis of successive cyclic A-movement, but our arguments, as we will note in later discussion, extend to subsequent analyses of this phenomenon.
15. We hope the reader is not confused by our notation in which the identical copies of *we* are indicated by 't'. A more conspicuous representation would thus be:

    (i)   we are likely we to be asked we to we build airplanes role in the form and function of the operations of the computational system. For example, operations like Move/Attract F scan lexical items and apply depending on the features that are detected. Features are of various types. Cut one way, there are semantic, phonological, and formal features (Chomsky 1995:230). But features are also intrinsic or optional (p. 231); weak or strong (p. 232); and plus or minus interpretable (p. 276).

This explicit appeal to features (already implicit in GB analyses of Case, Theta-assignment, Agreement, etc.) requires revision of various components of the computational system. For instance, Move-α is replaced by Move-F since the latter is claimed to better accord with minimalist tenets.[16] Furthermore, Move is subject to Last Resort, which is (initially in CT) stated as follows:

(20)   Move F raises F to target K only if F enters into a checking relation with a sublabel of K (p. 280).

It is then revised in terms of *attraction* (attributed to Frampton in Chomsky 1995: 297, fn. 14):

(21)   K *attracts* F only if F is the closest feature that can enter into a checking relation with a sublabel of K.

Thus, F can raise only if a checking RELATION is thereby created. We take a checking *relation* to be a structural relation between F and a *sublabel* of the target K (and, of course, between F and K).

Next, the 'operations of checking and deleting' become:

(22)   a. A checked feature is deleted when possible (i.e. rendered invisible at LF but still accessible to computation).
        b. A deleted feature is erased when possible (thus it is inaccessible to computation) (p. 280).

The central idea is to show that by appealing to the independently motivated notion of [+/−interpretable] lexical features, stipulations within earlier formulations

---

16. Chomsky points out that: 'The underlying intuitive idea is that the operation Move is driven by morphological considerations: the requirement that some feature F must be checked. The minimal operation, then, should raise just the feature F: we should restrict alpha in the operation Move Alpha to lexical features' (p. 262). (Cf. Chomsky 2000 and Epstein *et al.* 1998 which reject feature-movement.)

34   *Derivations in Minimalism*

of checking theory can be eliminated.[17] Naturally enough, a [−interpretable] feature is not a legitimate object at LF and hence must be eliminated before LF (since if it appears, the derivation crashes at LF). Features that are [+interpretable], on the other hand, may be present at LF given Full Interpretation, and they are accessible to computation (cf. footnote 1). Chomsky's use of [+/−interpretable], and the changes in the computational operations that it requires, is conceptually and empirically motivated. Since filters on representations (like principles) are, by definition, non-explanatory (simply specifying an ill-formed representation) the elimination of filters and their reduction to arguably ineliminable lexical features, seems to us a compelling, explanatory development of Chomsky's theory.

2.3.2   How are chains formed?

With the above preliminaries regarding features in place, we can now consider chain formation with successive cyclic A-movement. Recall our motivation: we argued above that not all the information encoded in a chain is representable, and even if it were, the information is redundant with, hence derivable from, the computational operations Move and Merge. The argument is strongest where chain formation is isomorphic to Move, in which case the two elements involved in each Move/Merge become sisters, which are then used (unnecessarily and impossibly given X′ invisibility) to specify the positional members of the resulting chain. Our reduction of chains to the Move/Merge operations is (potentially) threatened if chain formation is not isomorphic to Move, which as we'll now see, is the case for at least some chains of successive cyclic A-movement.

Chomsky assumes an implicit undefined chain formation algorithm that is not clear with respect to (23) (see CT pp. 300–301):

(23)   we are likely [t^3 to be asked[t^2 to t^1 build airplanes]]]]

The following three movements/attractions (the standard ones, in the standard successive cyclic order) are clearly assumed to apply in the derivation:

---

17. In particular, the analyses of trace-deletion in Lasnik and Saito (1984, 1992), along with cases of verb-trace deletion associated with verb raising over negation violating the Head Movement Constraint. Perhaps central is the attempt to explain the Case Filter under appeal to the notion of Interpretability. Below we suggest that, contra the CT analysis, Case may in fact be a PF uninterpretable feature, i.e. not an LF uninterpretable feature (see Epstein 1990).

(24)   1st: move *we* from t^1 to t^2 position
         2nd: move *we* from t^2 to t^3 position
         3rd: move *we* from t^3 to matrix Spec, IP

Three distinct chains are claimed to be formed:

(25)   a. $CH_1 = (t^2, t^1)$
         b. $CH_2 = (t^3, t^1)$
         c. $CH_3 = (we, t^1)$

Notice that each of these three chains terminates with t^1, the theta position. Keeping in mind that the chains above consist of positions occupied by a single lexical item (i.e. the four occurrences of the one and only *we* in (23)), the question is: How do these chains arise?

It can't be that chain formation is isomorphic to Move. In the derivation of (23) there was EPP-checking movement from the t^2 to the t^3 position, and from t^3 to *we*; but, under the analysis presented in CT no chain, nor chain link, corresponding to these movements is formed (even though 'move forms the chain CH,' CT p. 250). Moreover, there are chains where the two positions were not related by any single-application of Move/Attract, e.g. both CH_2 and CH_3.[18] Each contains two positions not directly related by movement. Thus, it is proposed that there is both movement without chain formation and chain formation without movement.

Notice that CH_1 does indeed consist of two positions that were related by movement. That is, there was movement from the t^1 position to the t^2 position (presumably for EPP checking), and such movement forms the chain CH_1. By contrast, CH_2 consists of two positions not related by movement: there was no single movement from t^1 to t^3 position. Finally a slightly different relation to movement is expressed in CH_3. The two members of this chain are indeed such that the head *we* was a landing site of movement, and the tail (t^1) was a departure site of movement, but, notice that there was no single movement (Attraction operation) moving *we* from

---

18. Furthermore, while it might be possible under copy theory (i.e. under identity) to move *we* from t^1 to t^2; and then to move *we* again from t^1 but this time to t^3 (recall that t^1 is identical to *we*); and then to move it a final time from t^1 to *we* (which would yield (25), but now with chains isomorphic to Move); this is not what is proposed (see CT p. 283). The latter two movements would presumably violate the Minimal Link Condition. They also run afoul of a CT constraint (proposed a bit later in the discussion) that a trace is inaccessible to movement (thus the first movement from t^1 to t^2 would render the occurrence t^1 invisible, preventing any move from this position).

36 *Derivations in Minimalism*

the t^1 position directly to the matrix subject position. (Note that we are leaving aside here the problems noted above, including the fact that chains are not syntactic objects; that they can't even be formed by Move; and that they cannot appear in LF representations.)

It must be that there is an implicit chain formation algorithm not isomorphic to the move operation. This is problematic since it entails that some chains are, while others are not, isomorphic to Move, yet the chain formation algorithm is not defined, nor addressed. But this is potentially problematic since chain formation in (23) must be representational (non-isomorphic to Move) whereas a 'strictly derivational' view of computation is assumed, stating that the chain structure in which chains and movement are (sometimes) 'divorced', as in successive cyclic raising, is motivated as follows:

(26)   It is 'natural, particularly if successive cyclic raising is necessary in order to remove all [−interpretable] features...' (CT p. 300).

But a question, to be addressed below, is whether we need a theory with well-defined transformational rules; e.g. Move/Attract as well as the representational construct A-chain, leaving aside how to define 'A-chain' and how to define chain formation so that the derivation of (23) yields (25).

In a theory with chain formation isomorphic to movement, we would seem to have a case of redundancy in which one or more of the postulates Move vs. Form Chain might be reduced to the other.[19] Below, we will argue that the system with both Move and Form Chain overgenerates: the problems we raise are thus not ones of mere superfluousness or redundancy, which is not to deny the often noted and important redundancy between Move and Form Chain (Rizzi 1986, Brody 1995). We will argue that where chain formation sometimes is and sometimes is not isomorphic to movement, there is so much apparatus that the generative procedure is 'overburdened' and hence 'operationally' inadequate to the task of correctly characterizing certain aspects of human knowledge of syntax.

2.3.3   Chains and the chain condition

CH_3 in (25) is assumed to be the only legitimate LF chain; CH_1 and CH_2 are each illegitimate since they violate the Chain Condition. How the Chain Condition

---

19. But see Poole (1996) who notes that Chomsky (1993) has both Move and Form Chain. Poole embraces the two in his attempt to allow OPTIONAL MOVEMENT, which he argues forms no chain, but is allowed under the assumption that derivational economy 'counts' only Form Chain.

(henceforth CC) is violated, however, is not clear. Earlier versions of CC, a representational description (which Chomsky seeks to deduce, see below), state that

(27)   An A-chain is headed by a unique Case position and must terminate in a unique theta-position (Chomsky 1986).

Both CH_1 and CH_2 terminate in a theta-position (t^1) in (23), here repeated:

(23)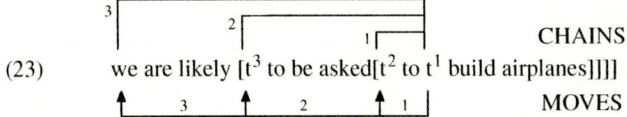
we are likely [t^3 to be asked[t^2 to t^1 build airplanes]]]]

Thus we assume that this means that CH_1 and CH_2 in (25) are each illegitimate by virtue of being headed by a Case-bearer, i.e. a category whose [−interpretable] Case feature has not been erased. But herein is a potential problem. We assume that in the numeration *we* bears the [−interpretable] Nominative Case feature. It is Merged into the position of t^1 and then moves successive cyclically to and through the positions of t^2 and t^3 and finally lands in Spec, matrix TP. Each movement leaves behind an identical copy. Therefore all occurrences of *we* bear the Nominative Case feature, under identity. Now, the [−interpretable] Case feature of *we* in the matrix Spec, TP position is deleted and erased by virtue of its being in a proper checking relation with the matrix T. And here, we believe, lies an important part of the CT analysis, not fully discussed in CT. Notice that *we* and its traces t^3 and t^2 are implicitly assumed to be NON-identical (see Hornstein 1998, and the references cited therein); i.e. if we are interpreting the analysis correctly, *we* gets its Case checked and deleted, and therefore its sole chain-mate in the representation, namely the identical copy trace t^1, also gets its Case automatically deleted – rendering the pair a legitimate LF object, namely CH_3. But notice that the copy traces t^3 and t^2 – identical to *we* – do NOT get their Case checked automatically when the Case of *we* is checked. They thus retain their uninterpretable Case feature and so CH_1 and CH_2 are each claimed to be illegitimate. Why, and how, is the Case retained on t^2 and on t^3 but eliminated on t^1, even though they are each supposed to be identical to *we* which DOES have its Case checked in the matrix subject position? We think it is assumed that 'automatic' feature deletion, for a trace which is identical to the mover, somehow, occurs only when that trace is in a chain the head of which is checked. Indeed, it is stated that '...features of a chain are considered a unit: if one is affected by an operation, all are' (Chomsky 1995:381, fn. 12). We think this must mean that feature deletion occurs ONLY in a chain. And what this means is that even though t^2 and t^3 are identical to the Case-checked *we*, they act independently with respect to feature deletion by virtue of being in no chains containing the Case-checked *we*. This seems a questionable result, in that 'two identical elements' (really, there is but one) undergo differential treatment, one has its Case checked and deleted, while the identical 'other' does not.

To summarize, Chomsky's chain formation algorithm is not defined. We infer that it is not isomorphic to movement. Furthermore, the mechanism by which CH_1 and CH_2 somehow retain Case is potentially problematic under copy (=identity) theory. Finally, if these chains are illegitimate, then the derivation of (23), which represents a grammatical sentence, would seem to be ruled out within the analysis, crashing at LF since it contains the two illegitimate chains. We take up this latter issue in the next subsection.

2.3.4 Derivation-internal deletion of derivation-internally created copies and chains

Assuming that CH_1 and CH_2 in (23) are illegitimate, how is a well-formed (convergent) LF representation of this grammatical sentence generated? A seemingly 'natural move' is to eliminate the offending chains. We suggest in this subsection that this is in fact problematic on a number of grounds.

CT states that the offending chains (CH_1 and CH_2 in (23)) can be removed by

(28) ...STIPULATING [our emphasis, SDE, TDS] that the raising of α heading the chain CH=(α, t) deletes the trace formed by this operation – that is, marks it invisible at LF.... At LF, then, all that is "seen" is the chain CH_3, which satisfies the Chain Condition. (p. 301)

Besides being a stipulation, this deletion procedure raises a number of questions. First, it would seem to delete something that needs to be retained, namely the trace t^1. Under (28), however, this trace would be deleted as a result of the first movement, from the t^1 to t^2 position. But that is not the intended result since if t^1 is deleted the chain CH_3 (= (*we*, t^1)) assumed to be the one legitimate LF chain, can't exist at LF. Thus it is stipulated that this deletion applies to the moving head of a chain but only if the chain has more than one member, i.e. by stipulation, the initial move is exempted from the trace deletion stipulation in (28). Second, the deletion of the trace is tied to movement ('...the raising of α [heading the chain CH=(α, t)] deletes the trace formed by this operation...'). But for this to work, notice that we must form chains derivationally AS MOVEMENT OCCURS; i.e. the chains CH_1,

CH_2, and CH_3, even though some of them do not directly correspond to movement, must be formed derivationally so that t^2 and t^3 are created by moving the head of a non-singleton chain and are thus rendered invisible. To illustrate, under this analysis moving from the t^2 to t^3 position does not form an isomorphic chain containing these two positions (see (25)). In addition, the analysis must ensure that immediately after this move from t^2 to t^3 position, the chain CH_2, namely (t^3, t^1) is (somehow) formed. With this chain formed, the stipulation (28) can now apply as desired (i.e. t^3 is indeed, at this point, before the final move, a chain-head) so that move from t^3 to *we* constitutes movement of the head of a non-singleton chain, and as such, leaves an 'invisible' trace in the t^3 position. But forming these chains, which are not isomorphic to movement, simultaneously with movement is curious as some of the chains (specifically, CH_2 and CH_3) do not correspond to movement. Thus, the undefined chain formation algorithm, sometimes forming chains non-isomorphic to Move, must apply derivationally, i.e. after movement from t^2 to t^3 but before movement from t^3 to *we*.

There are still further questions confronting the purported deletion process. We can't just delete chains nor whole copies since to do so is to delete terms and this is expressly disallowed (to delete a term is to destroy a syntactic object and that cancels a derivation, CT, p. 281). Moreover, deletion (and erasure) is presumed to be constrained by the checking operation:

(29)   a.   A checked feature is deleted when possible.
            b.   Deleted α is erased when possible (CT, p. 280). (Deleted means invisible at LF but accessible to C_{HL}; erased means invisible and inaccessible.)

So what is proposed is that the chains presumed to be illegitimate, CH_1 and CH_2, can be 'eliminated' in the desired sense if certain features of 'traces' are deleted, namely formal features. The whole trace can't delete since it is a term. Its phonological features have already been stripped away by Spell-out and thus are not available for deletion. Its semantic features by their very nature don't enter into checking relations and hence are not subject to (29). And '...therefore, a formal feature F of an intermediate trace of an argument may erase, and indeed must erase if possible' (CT, p. 301).

But problems emerge. First, deletion of an element 'marks it invisible at LF.' Presumably some notation/marking would be needed for this (unlike erasure), but such notation is disallowed by inclusiveness.

Second, an apparent contradiction arises. It is stated that '...the intermediate deleted traces do not enter into interpretation' (CT, p. 301). But recall that it's not the whole trace that deletes, just its formal features. Deletion of these formal features does not affect the semantic features; indeed, '...semantic features remain' (CT, p. 301) (not being subject to (29)). How semantic features can be present but not interpreted is unexplained.

Moreover, the chains resulting from the deletion of the formal features of the intermediate traces can be informally thought of as 'a single "linked chain"... with "defective" intermediate traces...' (CT, p. 301); but earlier, it is stated that linked chains do not fit the current framework. Indeed, any chain linking would be a process distinct from Merge/Move, and distinct from the partially redundant, and partially unspecified derivational operation, Form Chain.

Yet another question is: which formal features delete? The only candidate is the [−interpretable] Case feature since all other formal features are [+interpretable]. But it is odd that this should render the trace 'defective' when in all other contexts it is exactly what is required for convergence. And there is something else of concern about this: the formal feature deletion operation deletes the very formal feature that would be deleted anyway on the simplest assumption that if an operation affects X then it equally affects all (identical) occurrences of X. But now the formal case feature on the intermediate traces is NOT eliminated by virtue of CHECKING deletion and erasure, since neither t^3 nor t^2 is in the checking domain of a Case-checker. Thus there must be different means, in addition to checking, whereby Case is eliminated, a conceptually questionable state of affairs. In addition, eliminating an illegitimate object (one containing a [−interpretable] feature) is generally not allowed; on the contrary, such features are retained and constitute the basis of all LF crashing.

It can be noted that however the details of the deletion process might be worked out, the 'bigger picture' seems counterintuitive. The chains are created (by an undefined chain formation algorithm) – some do correspond to movement, some don't – only to be eliminated since they are uninterpretable/illegitimate at LF (even though *we* in the matrix Spec, TP did get Case-checked and is identical with the members of the offending chains). Are there, or should there be, syntactic entities (i.e. chains) that require a less restrictive definition of syntactic object than (1), which are never in the numeration, nor in the LF representation nor in the PF representation, but are nonetheless CREATED by C_{HL} in the course of computation and then ELIMINATED by C_{HL}, in subsequent computation, before the interfaces are reached? CH_1 and CH_2 are precisely such objects. We propose that the answer is negative.

Note, finally, the trace-deletion or trace-invisibility analysis is extended to A movement of expletives. This should then yield the welcome result that, in the following, the 'intervening' trace of *there*, being invisible, does not prevent attraction by the matrix INFL of 'the Case and phi features of "books"'.

(30)   there seem [t to be some books on the table]

Note however that 'marking the intervening trace invisible *at* LF [our emphasis: SDE, TDS]' (CT, pp. 300–1) is too late, i.e. if the trace is a problem, marking it invisible AT LF means that whenever *books* tries to raise, the *t* is still there; i.e. we can't mark *t* invisible AT LF and then subsequently raise features of *books*, since that would be to apply a transformation AFTER the LF representation is derived. (But see DASR and below for a theory in which precisely such ordering is possible.)

To summarize, we saw in section 2.1 that chains are by definition not syntactic objects, nor are they visible in the LF representation. Moreover, we have shown that chains may not even be creatable, given the X' Invisibility Hypothesis (section 2). In addition, chains would seem to restate independently motivated properties of simple, virtually conceptually necessary transformational rules (Merge and Move/Attract). In this section, we argued that even if chains were somehow created and were somehow visible syntactic objects, certain other serious problems concerning chains arise. The chain formation algorithm in CT is undefined, for example. But clearly some chains are isomorphic to Move and other chains are not – this is illustrated in the central example of successive cyclic A-movement that we examined. Under the analysis of (23) with the chain structure in (25), CH_1 (isomorphic to Move) and CH_2 (non-isomorphic) must somehow be formed intra-derivationally, to feed the *stipulation* that movement of the head of a chain with greater than one member leaves an 'invisible' trace. Moreover, (elements of) the chains CH_1 and CH_2, regardless of what algorithm forms them, are deleted before LF. Thus they are created by the derivation and then are deleted, having no effect on output, and allowing the possibility of somehow simply deleting illegitimate objects before LF, raising serious questions about possible over-generation of what should crash at LF by virtue of the (undeleted) presence of illegitimate objects.

In the next section we will propose an alternative analysis within which the relevant chains (and even the traces) are never generated, and therefore the problems associated with eliminating them are avoided, yet the LF output of successive cyclic

A-movement envisioned in the standard analysis *is* generated, in that there simply are no intermediate traces, as opposed to there being invisible ones.

We have presented a variety of difficulties with the analysis of successive cyclic A-movement. Let us turn our attention to possible solutions.

2.4 An alternative analysis without chains

2.4.1 A-movement in one step

Consider again (23), repeated below:

(23)   we are likely [t^3 to be asked[t^2 to t^1 build airplanes]]]]

Suppose, for the sake of argument, that the only Chain appearing in the LF representation of (23) is CH_3 (i.e (*we*, t^1)), a two-membered chain with *we* the sole Case-checked chain head in a non-theta position, and the other occurrence of *we* (= t^1) the sole member in theta-marked 'Caseless' position, the archetypal A-chain. Assuming that this is the chain structure appearing in the LF representation, the question is: 'How is this chain generated?' This question might be answered with another: 'What's the simplest assumption about the derivation that produces this chain?' We think the simplest analysis avoids all the complex problems noted above that were associated with the creation and deletion of CH_1 and CH_2, including, more specifically the creation and deletion of the intermediate traces t^3 and t^2. In the simplest world, these traces and the chains CH_1 and CH_2 would not even be created. The simplest way to obtain this result is to assume that Movement through the infinitival subject positions does not in fact occur. Thus the question of whether traces – invisible, deleted, or erased – are left in these positions does not arise, nor does the question of how to formulate the implicit chain formation algorithm assumed to construct CH_1 and CH_2. In addition, notice that if there is no movement through these intermediate infinitival subject positions, movement and chain formation would be isomorphic even in this derivation too; i.e. there would be a single movement from the theta position directly to the Case-checking position, namely the matrix finite Spec, TP position. Thus, if a chain is formed, it is isomorphic to Movement. As noted above, in fact a chain cannot be created since, by definition, chains are not syntactic objects and can't be positionally defined in terms of sisters or mothers given the X′ Invisibility Hypothesis. This raises the distinct possibility that UG has only the elementary operation Move, and not also an isomorphic elementary operation Form Chain.

If all these welcome results can be obtained by assuming that there is no successive cyclic A-movement in such cases, why is it assumed that movement is successive cyclic? There are two answers. One lies primarily with the Extended Projection Principle. Specifically, movement through these intermediate Spec (TP) positions is assumed to be required so as to check and delete a postulated uninterpretable ('EPP') feature in Tense/*to*, or to satisfy the EPP viewed as a non-checking structural requirement. Another answer is movement locality; for example, at least as early as Chomsky (1975) and most recently in Bošković (2002), it is assumed that successively cyclic A-movement is necessitated by 'locality restrictions' on A-movement.

In the following chapter we examine the EPP as the catalyst of successive cyclic A-movement, suggesting that the EPP has been a suspect 'principle' from its inception and remains undesirable even in its most recent incarnations. We argue that there is no EPP and hence problematic successive cyclic A-movement, as examined in this chapter, can't be driven by the EPP. We take up the locality-based approach in Chapter 4, suggesting that it too may be problematic, leading us ultimately to the hypothesis that no principle motivates successive cyclic A-movement, at least not in English raising and ECM constructions, and hence that there is no such movement in these cases.

2.4.2   The elimination of A-traces: derivation vs. representation

It has been suggested in the literature that perhaps there are no A-traces. Given the hypothesized non-existence of the chains CH_1 and CH_2 (see (25)) in such cases as (23), along with our observation that chains are in fact uncreatable, unrepresentable non-objects, a closely related question arises: If there is indeed one fell swoop movement from the Caseless theta position to the Case-checked theta-less position, is the trace in the theta position necessary? We think the answer is negative, as proposed in DASR, which suggests a wholesale elimination of traces. Let us pause for a moment and consider what we believe is an important issue regarding the possible elimination of A-chain traces, more specifically an issue regarding 'representationality' and 'derivationality'.

44 *Derivations in Minimalism*

Chain-based analyses are often called 'representational' as opposed to 'derivational'. In fact however this is a serious misnomer leading to much confusion, we think. A-chains, including the trace(s), represent the derivational history of A-movement and thus the A-chain is (at best) not necessary since it merely encodes aspects of the now reified derivation itself given Chomsky's rule-based minimalist approach. The idea that A-chains, including traces, notationally encode derivational histories is not new. Consider the following case:

(31) $[_{S_1}$ John INFL $[_{VP_1}$ be [believe $[_{S_2}$ t′ INFL have been $[_{VP_2}$ kill t]]]]
'John is believed to have been killed'

with respect to which Chomsky (1981:45) writes:

> ...*John* bears the GF [NP,S_1] by virtue of its actual position in [(31)], and bears the relations [NP, S_2] and [NP, VP_2] by virtue of the positions of its traces t′, t respectively. Suppose we associate with each NP in S-structure a sequence $(p_1,...,p_n)$ which, *in an obvious sense, represents the derivational history of this NP by successive applications of Move-α* [our emphasis, SDE, TDS].

And later in the same passage, 'function chains' are proposed:

> Correspondingly, let us associate with each NP in S-structure the sequence of GFs $(GF_1,..., GF_n)$, where GF_i is the GF of the element filling position p_i in the S-structure configuration: the NP itself for i=1, a trace in each other case. If NP was base generated, then GF_n is its GF at D-structure, a GF-. If NP is a non-argument inserted in the course of a syntactic derivation, then GF_n is the GF associated with the position in which it was inserted, a GF-non-theta. Let us call (GF1,..., GFn) the 'function chain' of the NP filling GF1...*the function chain [is defined] in terms of successive applications of Move-α*... [our emphasis SDE, TDS].

Similarly, Chomsky (1986:95) regards 'a chain [as] the S-structure reflection of a "history of movement".'

Thus, in the principle-based, 'rule-free' GB theory adopting the standard Y-model, structure building RULES are virtually 'propertyless' ('Move anything anywhere optionally') while principles, and their (defining) application to output representations constitute the substance of the theory. Note however that such systems by definition retain a rule, namely Move-α, and hence are unavoidably mixed, containing one rule, and principles. 'Rule-free' is thus a misnomer of the Principles and Parameters approach. Within that framework, nothing 'should', nor could, be deduced directly from (the accidental) properties of the amorphous rule 'Move anything anywhere optionally' as it blindly applies in any one of an infinite number of ways that it logically could. As a result of this approach, the idiosyncratic properties of successive rule application must be *encoded* so that the output representation (to which necessarily descriptive, representational constructs such as traces and principles/filters apply) 'in an obvious sense represents the derivational history.' Herein lies the motivation for trace theory and for representational chains. The derivation (successive rule application) is in fact recognized as vitally important, but direct appeal to the derivation is 'forbidden' in a 'rule-free' system so that the output representations must invoke technicalia to encode derivational history – since it is clearly relevant. Chain theory and trace theory are annotational look back devices encoding derivational history, tracking where categories were derivationally, and marking those locations in the output representation. With the Minimalist elimination of S-structure, perhaps even more encoding of the derivation is necessary, since, ignoring the split-off to PF, LF representation is the sole level of syntactic representation.

Importantly, notice that such trace theoretic, chain theoretic, principle-based so-called 'representational' theories, are crucially a kind of derivational theory to the extent that traces and chains are precisely 'look back' notations whereby the (empirically important) derivation that produced the output representation is encoded. *Thus 'representational' theories are in fact, just one kind of derivational theory* (for related discussion see Epstein and Seely 2002). The question then is not: 'which is preferable, derivational or representational theory?', but rather 'Which type of derivational theory is preferable, one which refers to the existing rules and derivation itself, or one that instead has incorporated rules and derivations, but does not appeal to them and instead encodes derivational history in output representations containing traces and chains?'[20]

---

20. One notable exception is the work of Brody (1995), who proposes a representational theory with (purportedly) no derivation at all. As Brody (personal communication) rightly points out, Brody's (1995) representational approach and Epstein *et al.*'s (1998) derivational approach are not diametrically opposed. Rather both seek to eliminate 'mixed theory' incorporating constrained rules and also filters.

46 *Derivations in Minimalism*

The conviction that trace theory is indeed a representational 'coding trick' necessitated by the failure (or within principle-based theory, the inability) to recognize the importance of the constrained application of explicitly defined rules themselves (the derivation) is in fact expressed in Chomsky (1995). With respect to another kind of movement, namely successive cyclic head movement, discussed as an illustration of general properties of movement, CT writes:

> It is generally possible to formulate the desired results in terms of outputs. In the head movement case, for example [a case of raising from N to V followed by [$_V$ N+V] raising to Infl] one can appeal to the plausible assumption that the trace is a copy, so the intermediate Verb-trace includes within it a record of the local N–V raising. But surely this is the wrong move. The relevant chains at LF are (N, t_N) and (V, t_V), and in these, the locality relation satisfied by successive raising has been lost...
>
> These seem to be fundamental properties of language, which should be captured, not obscured by coding tricks, which are always available. A fully derivational approach both captures them straightforwardly and suggests that they should be pervasive, as seems to be the case. (CT, p. 224)

We (largely) agree, except that we would push the derivational approach more fully, and assume that even in the LF representation the trace-tail of the chains (namely the tails t_N, and t_V) are absent as well, as are the chains, since each 'in an obvious sense represents (an aspect of) derivational history.' The matter at hand is ultimately architectural concerning the very structure of the language faculty. If interpretation is postponed, as in GB theory, until all transformations have applied, then the information must be encoded representationally via mechanisms like trace theory. If, however, unlike GB, the rules and operations are well-defined, i.e. 'real', then the possibility arises that the rules themselves may be sufficient to express syntactic relations. See Epstein *et al.* (1998) and below.

Similarly, in the case of A-movement, we would assume (with Epstein *et al.* 1998) that there are no traces, not even the chain-tail trace. The information represented by the trace tail of the chain is already part of the derivation, e.g. for direct objects the relation is expressed by 'Concatenate/Merge theta marker V and DP'. Traces of the DP are only 'coding tricks' needed in order to represent the derivation later in the sole interpreted representation, namely the LF representation generated at 'the end of the line', only after all transformations have applied, as in the Y-model. Recall from section 1 that A-chains are not syntactic objects (see

(1)) and are in fact unrepresentable during computation derivationally and at LF, as argued above. But crucially, in the Minimalist framework, unlike GB there is no prohibition barring appeal to properties of the explicit existing rules (namely, Merge, Move/Attract) and there is in fact an explanatory incentive to deduce from the application of these independently motivated reified rules, as much as can be deduced.[21]

21. Lasnik (1999) provides a different argument that there are no A-traces. Following Chomsky (1995), he assumes that there is no Reconstruction in A-chains. He then notes that if there are no A-traces, Reconstruction in A-chains will be blocked, given the trace-dependence of Reconstruction.

3 On the elimination of the EPP

3.1 Introduction

Suppose, as proposed above, there is no successive cyclic A-movement through spec of TP in constructions such as (1), but movement is rather one fell swoop:

(1)   we are likely [to be asked [to __ build airplanes]]]]

If correct, then standard formulations of the EPP, which force successive cyclic movement (perhaps redundantly with movement locality, as we'll see below), must be abandoned. We thus reject the EPP as a structural requirement and as a feature-checking requirement of raising *to*. In fact, we propose that *to* in such cases checks no features at all and hence, given that operations are purposeful, there is no movement to the intermediate spec TPs.[1] Under our analysis, Move is one fell swoop, from theta to case-checked position. The creation of intermediate traces, the deletion of these traces, the formation of chains (and whether they are linked), chain deletion, and the question of semantic features, or lack thereof, borne by intermediate traces, simply do not arise; nor do pervasive problems associated with trying to determine what in fact the EPP is. Stated in terms of Attraction, the matrix T (*be/are*) does in fact attract the closest potential feature checker, which in this instance is *we*. Neither instance of *to* attracts. Movement of *we* in one step does

---

1. As Esther Torrego (personal communication) points out, raising *to* could fail to be a checker, yet still have interpretable features, including perhaps Tense features. In this regard, note that Stowell (1991:568) claims that '. . . infinitival complements in Raising Structures [are] not. . . INTERNALLY specified for Tense' [our emphasis SDE, TDS]. This leaves open the possibility that Stowell's observations are correctly formalized by postulating that *to* is a Tense, which inherits its particular Tense specification (e.g. PAST, PRESENT) from a locally c-commanding Tense, something like 'controlled tense'. (Interestingly, Chomsky 1957 suggests that control *to* is 'semantically vacuous.') For present purposes we leave open whether *to* is a tense specifier and if so, how tense is specified on it. Our main point is that it does not check syntactic features.

not 'skip' any potential intermediate checking position, there being no feature to force movement (=re-merge) to create the position. Thus, all relevant locality requirements (and specifically the feature-relativized MLC) are satisfied.[2] In precisely such instances, then, what looks like 'long distance' A-movement is possible (in fact forced) and this in turn allows the simplest analysis of successive cyclic A-movement: there is simply no such thing in such cases. If this is on the right track, it suggests that there is no EPP at all, a welcome result. In this chapter, we investigate some of the history, formal properties, and current perspectives regarding the EPP. We then turn to some of the consequences of eliminating the EPP as concerns non-A-movement cases, i.e. existential structures, ECM and *believe*-class verbs, and infinitival complements of nominals. In Chapter 4, we focus on the proposed elimination of the EPP as concerns movement cases beyond the 'successive cyclic' structures already examined.

3.2 The EPP

3.2.1 The mysteriousness of the EPP

It has recently been claimed that 'The EPP has been ...a pervasive mystery since it was first formulated by Chomsky (1981)' (Lasnik 2002:1). We agree. Simply put, the EPP is ill-understood. There are a number of reasonable strategies one could adopt: assume the principle for now with an eye toward its future clarification. Another, which we propose here, is to try to clarify the principle now so as to clarify the predictive content and explanatory depth of the theory. (The methodological issue of *when* to address which unclarity is always open to debate.) One form of clarification is elimination. The EPP can be clarified to the extent that it is eliminated. Attempting to eliminate the EPP will, at best, allow us to deduce the 'EPP's' properties and effects from independently motivated principles. At worst, the attempt will have the 'therapeutic value' (Chomsky 1995) of determining which of the EPP's properties and effects can (and perhaps can't) be deduced. It's not that we are on an 'Anti-EPP campaign'. Rather we seek to better understand the

---

2. Note that in standard theory subjacency would be violated, and it is this principle that forces successive cyclic movement (see Chomsky 1975, and for a recent appeal to movement locality seeking to eliminate the EPP see Bošković 2002 and Chapter 4 below). Under Attract and the MLC there is no violation. See Ferguson and Groat (1993) for the reformulation of Rizzi's (1990) Relativized Minimality, in terms of 'Feature-Relativized Minimality'.

organization, hence empirical content of UG through the elimination of any appeal to the 'pervasive mystery' referred to as 'the EPP'.

3.2.2 The unclarity of the formulation of the EPP

Originally, the EPP was the configurational requirement that clauses have a subject (see Chomsky 1981) as expressed by a Standard Theory PS-rule, namely

(2)   S → NP Infl VP

But a problem with this statement of the EPP is that it represents a form of construction specificity of just the sort that, for principled reasons, is avoided within the Principles and Parameters (and Minimalist) approach. Note further that for us there can be no syntactic macro-structure representational requirements since we seek to explain such requirements by appeal to features of heads, as locally manipulated by the generative procedure. This is consistent with Derivational Minimalist explanation.

Neither problem, construction specificity nor representational stipulation, arises within the Minimalist approach of Chomsky (1995) and much subsequent work, within which the EPP shifts from a requirement on clausal structure to a morphosyntactic requirement of feature checking. The basic idea is that there is some feature, an 'EPP feature', which attracts a DP to Spec position. This seeks to subsume the EPP under the more general feature-checking mechanisms of Case and Agreement. The reduction of the EPP to morpholexical feature checking by a functional head is conceptually desirable. It eliminates the pure and perhaps ill-defined stipulation that 'clauses' must have a 'subject'. Moreover, feature checking is a general phenomenon. Rather than being a formally unique and descriptive 'principle', the EPP is reduced to the (empirically and conceptually) motivated process of lexically driven checking.

But there are problems: it is unclear just what this EPP feature is. CT, for example, argues that it's a D feature,[3] whereas it is suggested in other work (Chomsky

---

3. Note that there is a potential contradiction within the CT analysis of the EPP-as-D feature. On the one hand, CT argues that it is only [−interpretable] features that trigger Attract or Move, consonant with the idea that syntactic operations are driven by the need to attain interface interpretability. To trigger Move, then, the D feature of T must be [−interpretable]. But, D is a categorical feature and categorical features are claimed to be [+interpretable] (see CT, p. 277). So, either we must loosen the fundamental generalization that movement is invariably driven by [−interpretable] features (arguing

2001a) that it is the person feature (or an 'occurrence' feature or an 'edge feature' Chomsky 2004). Moreover, even if the EPP-feature were specified, we have the still unanswered question of whether it is a 'strong feature' (as in CT p. 232) or not; and thus the question of the level of application of the EPP (is it derivationally satisfiable (Lasnik 2002); is it an Everywhere principle Chomsky (1995:123);[4] or is it (at least) a PF principle (see Bošković and Lasnik 2003)?

Additional unclarity in the formulation of the EPP has recently developed with the re-emergence of the EPP as 'some kind of' a structural requirement (see Lasnik 2001 and Chomsky 2001a, 2001b). Yet a further issue is that the EPP has been argued to be neither featural nor configurational but instead a 'semantic' requirement on theme-rheme or information structure (see Rothstein 1983 and Williams 1980). This leaves unclear what even the basic formulation of the EPP is. Moreover the crosslinguistic status is in question. For example, Alexiadou and Anagnostopoulou (1998) argue that it is a parameterized principle, whereas others assume it is universal. In addition, Lasnik (2001) argues that the EPP has the added property of being optionally assigned, and thus is apparently not an inherent lexical feature. Needless to say, there are also empirical problems created by the EPP (as noted in the last chapter and discussed further below). One can rightly argue that some level of unclarity confronts every principle, but it seems to us that the EPP has distinguished itself in this regard.

3.2.3 Redundancy with other principles

The EPP has in its many varying and unclear forms been deemed not only mysterious, but to the extent that it is clear, 'highly' redundant with other principles of Universal Grammar.[5] The redundancies include Case/Agreement, Theta theory, Locality conditions on Movement, and the theory of null complementizers. For example, Fukui and Speas (1986) and more recently Martin (1999) argue that in a finite clause like

(3)   __ has [Mary left]

Mary raises to Spec, TP not only to satisfy EPP but also to check Case and

---

that D as the EPP feature is [−interpretable]) or we may need to abandon D as the EPP feature; alternatively we could argue that D is uninterpretable *in T*.

4. Thanks to Hamid Ouali (personal communication) for pointing this out to us.
5. But see Bošković (1995) who argues, following the form of argument presented in Epstein (1990) that the redundancy, in the case of the EPP, might well be empirically motivated.

Agreement features. In fact, it's been argued that in all finite clauses the EPP overlaps with Case/Agreement checking in a spec-head configuration.

There is also claimed to be redundancy with aspects of semantic structure; thus, Rothstein (1983) (see also Williams 1980) argues that EPP effects follow from predication, while Chomsky (as reported in Bošković 2002) 'suggests that EPP effects are a result of a universal thematization requirement.'

Moreover, redundancies have been identified concerning the EPP and the theory of movement locality: for instance, most recently Bošković (2002) argues that successive cyclic A-movement is induced not only by the EPP but also locality conditions on movement (see also Chomsky 1975).

Finally, Epstein, Pires, and Seely (2004) claim that the EPP is also redundant over a thus far recalcitrant domain, assumed to require the EPP, namely infinitival complements of nominals. This domain by hypothesis is in fact covered without appeal to the EPP, as we will review below.

3.2.4   Non-redundant EPP satisfaction

There are, we think, few cases (at least in English) where there is no redundancy, i.e. where there is alleged to be pure EPP checking. One case has already been examined, successive cyclic A-movement, and we argued that such cases of 'pure' EPP checking are highly problematic. Other cases include ECM and raising infinitival complements to nouns, both of which will be considered later. Another case of pure EPP satisfaction occurs in the following central, and problematic case, to be examined momentarily:

(4)   *there seems a man to be outside

In fact, under the analysis in DBP this problematic case is derived via two non-redundant operations satisfying the EPP: *a man* moves to satisfy *to* and *there* is inserted as a pure EPP checker.

What we would like to suggest, given the problems noted thus far, is that even these 'residues' of the EPP should be analyzed not by looking for an independently motivated EPP feature – thus far undiscovered – but by eliminating the EPP. Thus, the general research strategy we adopt is:

(5)   a.   In the many cases where the EPP applies redundantly, appeal to it is unnecessary.

We also adopt the following empirical hypothesis:

> b. In the few cases (in English) where the EPP applies non-redundantly, it is making the wrong predictions.

If both (5a) and (5b) are maintainable, the EPP is eliminable; i.e. it's superfluous or false.

Before turning to detailed examinations of these pure EPP checking cases, there is one other issue to consider regarding the EPP over and above its mystery, unclarity, redundancy, and 'purity', namely, its empirical inadequacy as argued by McCloskey (1996). As we will argue the Irish salient unaccusatives, which McCloskey claims violate the EPP, exhibit interesting parallels with English raising infinitivals.

3.2.5   Inadequacy: McCloskey's elimination of the EPP

We are by no means the first to suggest that the EPP might not be a principle of UG. The important work of Martin (1999) was considered above, for example. In addition, Jacobson (1992) and Manzini and Roussou (2000), propose analyses inconsistent with the EPP; Castillo, Drury and Grohmann (1999) as well as Bošković (2002) reject the EPP, while Chomsky (2001a) entertains the possibility of its elimination. We will not review all of these works here, instead we would like to very briefly consider the important work of McCloskey.

To begin with, McCloskey (1996) notes an unclarity regarding the EPP:

> With the advent of the Internal Subject Hypothesis, it becomes crucially unclear what position this principle referred to. Is it properly construed so as to require that the internal subject position always be structurally realized? Or is the requirement that there be a structural subject to be construed rather as a property of functional projections, as suggested in Chomsky (1993)? If there are many inflectional projections between C and V, which one of them, if any, is privileged by the Extended Projection Principle? (p. 242)

Like McCloskey's (1996) treatment of Modern Irish, we have attempted to eliminate the EPP as an overarching principle governing English, by appeal to presumably ineliminable (independently motivated) morphosyntactic features of (certain) lexical items. Specifically we've argued that raising *to* checks no features and hence that there is no infinitival Spec, TP in raising constructions. Interestingly, the constructions ('salient unaccusatives', in McCloskey's terminology) which McCloskey claims violate the EPP (having no VP-external 'subject') seem quite closely related to the subjectless projections we claim occur in English. McCloskey's 'salient unaccusatives' are exemplified by

(6)   Mheadaigh   ar a   neart
        increased   on his   strength
        'His strength increased' (p. 243)

We have claimed that the infinitival *to* selected by a Raising predicate never has a Spec position at any point in the derivation (and this of course is inconsistent with the EPP). Thus, there is no movement through Spec-*to* in the following

(7)   John seems (to you) [__ to be [t happy]

McCloskey characterizes the Irish salient unaccusative verbs, the ones inconsistent with the EPP, as follows:

> these are verbs which s-select a single argument, which mark that argument with what is traditionally taken to be a preposition and which seem to entirely lack a structural subject. The verb itself appears in the so-called 'analytic form' (McCloskey and Hale 1984), the finite form of which encodes no information about person, number and gender. (p. 243)

It seems unlikely to be accidental that the verb types assumed to 'escape the effects of the EPP' in Irish and in English are so closely related morphologically, taking only internal arguments, and lacking person, number and gender, by hypothesis. In fact, with *seem* it even parallels Irish in taking an internal PP argument, e.g. the dative experiencer. What about cases without an experiencer, e.g.

(8)   John is likely [__to be happy]

(Here again we claim that the *to* selected by *likely* (a raising predicate) checks nothing in its Spec.) Here, *likely* seems to be selecting an internal 'clausal' argument which is *not* a PP, whereas the Irish salient unaccusatives always select an internal PP argument. Notice, however, that what is selected by *likely* is *to*, which 'looks' just like a preposition. Perhaps these *to*-projections, Merged with the Raising predicates are in fact PPs, making such constituents internal PP arguments, just like in Irish salient unaccusative constructions. Here, we follow Chomsky (1980, fn. 7) who notes that *to* appears in infinitivals, and *to* is also a preposition, writing 'A deeper understanding of language may show that the properties of contemporary English, in this regard, are more than fortuitous.' Whether the *to* selected by a raising predicate is a preposition is an issue we leave for further research.[6]

As a final comparison between the Irish salient unaccusatives, and the *to*-projection Merged with a raising predicate, it should be noted that the Irish and English examples may not be identical in their Tense features. McCloskey (p. 272) claims that the Irish salient unaccusative verbs are specified for Tense (and perhaps Mood as well). Stowell (1982), however, claims that 'the infinitival complements in Raising structures [are] not internally specified for Tense.' We are not altogether clear about Stowell's claims, (in particular, is the complement *externally* specified for Tense?) but regardless, we note that he is talking about 'Clauses having Tense' whereas we are concerned with the featural properties of *to*, so the 'translation' between the GB framework within which Stowell was working and the morpholexical approach of more contemporary theory is unclear. In addition, notice that Stowell seems *not* to be saying that the infinitival complement to the Raising predicate is tenseless, but rather that it has no inherently specified tense 'of its own'. The general question remains, what exactly are the features of *to* selected by a raising predicate?

We leave this issue open here. But it is interesting to note the apparent similarities between Irish salient unaccusative constructions and English infinitivals selected by a Raising predicate: two constructions in two languages, seeming to have few if any common properties at first glance, which, if McCloskey and we are on the right track, are very closely related indeed, sharing numerous features, and in turn, mitigating against the existence of an overarching principle like the EPP. This kind of analysis goes some distance toward achieving the central goal of linguistic theory: make UG restrictive enough to account for the acquisition of any given single grammar (this grammar being the only one the child can hypothesize) but make UG permissive enough to allow for the fact that the child can acquire *any* human grammar. If the kind of argument just provided is on track, then acquiring construction-specific aspects of English and acquiring construction-specific

---

6. We've said earlier, following Torrego (personal communication), that *to* maybe bears tense features. Prepositions are not usually associated with tense. However, they may be as in e.g. *I went for an hour*, *I went on Saturday*. And, if Emonds (1986) is right that subordinating conjunctions and prepositions and complementizers are conflated, then to the extent that complementizers bear tense, then 'prepositions' (or whatever the ultimate label is) also bear tense.

56 *Derivations in Minimalism*

aspects of Irish might be achieved by the *same* apparatus, since the two constructions, are, at a certain level of analysis (ours and the acquirer's by hypothesis) identical. The theory therefore need not incorporate any construction-specific apparatus, or language-specific apparatus; there is just one grammar, human, the central Chomskyan hypothesis from the start.

3.3   There-*insertion and raising: more problems created by the EPP*

3.3.1   *The central problem*

A central claim of this section is that the EPP is in fact engendering a number of serious problems which in turn motivate a series of problematic solutions, all of which, we argue, can be avoided with the elimination of the EPP. Consider then the central data in (9), which has been particularly important and troublesome to current theorizing, motivating a number of unattractive, and we suggest unnecessary, postulates.

(9)   *there is likely [a man to be [[a man] outside]

In a moment, we will consider the details of recent analyses. Before doing so, however, notice that under our proposal that raising *to* checks no features (hence, there is no EPP in the standard sense), (9) is straightforwardly excluded: if there is no successive cyclic A-movement, then there can be no 'partial A-movement' as in (9). Specifically, *a man* can't raise to spec of *to* since no features would be checked as a result.

Notice that analyses embracing the EPP license precisely such movement, thereby creating the central problem of the overgeneration of (9). In the framework of Chomsky (1981) these examples were excluded by the Case Filter applying at S-structure. The S-structure representation is filtered, since *a man* is caseless. In the Minimalist framework of assumptions, there cannot be appeal to the Case Filter, nor to an S-structure level of representation. More broadly, it is proposed that there are no filters internal to C_{HL}. This is proposed presumably because it is thought to be true that filters never explain why it is that certain elements are prohibited, rather, filters by definition state the prohibition. In the Minimalist framework, all constraints on representation must be stated as 'bare output conditions' – conditions imposed from outside C_{HL}, by the systems that take C_{HL}-generated interface LF (and PF) representations as their input.

In GB the Case Filter and S-structure are axiomatic; hence the question 'Why is it that certain NPs/DPs are Case marked at S-structure?' is not addressed. In the Minimalist framework, not only is the question posed but a compelling answer is provided. Case is by hypothesis uninterpretable, so it must be checked and erased before LF, under the entirely natural assumption that LF representations must contain only interpretable features. Thus the Case Filter is eliminated, and in a certain sense, explained.

However, under the deeper minimalist mode of explanation, (9) raises an interesting problem, which is this: nothing prohibits the Movement of *a man* from its initial position to the position it occupies in (9) above, i.e. subject of the infinitival; in fact, it is the EPP that licenses such movement. Moreover, the movement is sufficiently local, and is, it seems, attested in grammatical ECM constructions, which seem to exhibit the same 'pure EPP' movement:

(10)   I expect [a man to be [[a man] outside]

In addition to being sufficiently local, the move satisfies Enlightened Self-Interest (Lasnik 1995) adopted in CT, (p. 346) and Suicidal Greed (MI, p. 127). That is, under the assumption (which we reject) that *to* does check some 'EPP' feature in its spec, the movement does result in feature checking in the grammatical ECM cases and thus seemingly identical 'pure EPP' movement is licensed in the ungrammatical (9).[7] In effect, the EPP unifies ECM and raising, exactly the wrong result. Consequently, supplementary mechanisms must be postulated so as to allow (force) the pure overt EPP movement in (10) but disallow the pure EPP movement in (9); and it is these supplementary mechanisms, we argue, that are potentially unnecessary.

Returning to (9), in the covert component, *a man*, or some features of *a man* can raise into the matrix clause for the purpose of agreement and Case checking (assuming for present purposes, with DBP, that *there* is a pure EPP checker). This covert movement/attraction too is hard to prohibit, since precisely such movement is allowed overtly, assuming (as we do not) successive cyclic A-movement as in:

(11)   a man is likely [a man to be [a man outside]]

---

7. Notice that the adoption of Greed, whereby the Mover must have features checked, would exclude (9) the problematic case, but also the grammatical ECM case (apparently). See Bošković (1997) for arguments favoring Greed over Enlightened Self-Interest.

58 *Derivations in Minimalism*

That is movement from the subject of the infinitival to matrix subject position must be allowed. Assuming such movement takes place covertly in (9), the derivation would seem to violate nothing, clearly the wrong prediction. In addition, even if covert movement of features and categories is prohibited, as in the probe-goal analysis of Chomsky (2001a), the problem still persists. That is, the copula *is* can probe the goal *a man*, which has moved to spec of *to* to check the EPP feature, thereby checking Case and agreement features. The satisfaction of the matrix EPP is achieved through the insertion of *there*, which is assumed to be a pure EPP checker. So again, (9) is overgenerated.

This problem has been noted and solutions proposed. We now review those solutions and argue that they, like the EPP which initiates the problem, yield yet further problems.

3.3.2   Problematic solutions: a domino effect?

In the Minimalist Inquiries (MI) framework of Chomsky (2001a), and subsequent work (particularly Chomsky 2001, DBP) the problematic example (9) is excluded by a derivational economy constraint, Merge-over-Move, which is a traffic rule, favoring application of one type of operation over another at a particular derivation-internal point at which either operation 'could' in principle apply. The analysis of (9) is as follows. At the following stage of the derivation,

(12)   __ [to be [a man outside]]

there are two ways in which the EPP-feature of *to* could be checked.[8] *A man* could move to Spec of *to*/T (just as occurs in successive cyclic A-movement) or *there* could be inserted into Spec *to*/T. Thus it appears we have a case of local derivational optionality. A number of problems now arise. The first has already been noted: what prevents raising *a man* to Spec of *to*, an important case of pure EPP checking, and inserting *there* in the matrix Spec TP, as a pure EPP checker (Chomsky DBP) thereby overgenerating (9)? In order to prevent this, it would seem that some form of look-ahead is necessary e.g. 'at the derivational point (12), raise *a man* to Spec of *to* but only if you subsequently raise *a man* to the matrix spec – yielding

---

8. Although it's not critical for our overall argument, we assume the feature-strength cycle, which states that a strong feature must be checked by the operation immediately following its introduction, i.e. we are assuming here that the EPP is satisfied as soon as possible.

a man seems to be outside' (and not (9)).⁹ But, how can we avoid such 'computationally costly' look-ahead (see Collins 2001) and non-Markovian optionality? The MI answer is twofold; the postulation of (i) the numeration, and (ii) the economy principle of Merge over Move.

By appeal to economy conditions, insertion (Merge) of *there* is a simpler operation than Move (=Remerge). Thus, the principle

(13)   When both Move and Merge are 'possible', choose the formally simpler operation MERGE (MI, p. 17).

Thus by feature-cyclicity and 'Merge over Move', the next operation from (12) Merges *there*, yielding EPP feature checking in the structure:

(14)   [there to be [a man outside]

Further merging applies yielding

(15)   [is likely [there to be [a man outside]]

Next the EPP of *is*/T must be checked. The EPP feature of *is* can now 'see' only *there* in (15), the closest EPP checker. *A man* is too far away to be attracted by *is*. Thus *there* raises yielding

(16)   There is likely to be a man outside.

Importantly, examples like (9) are not generable: raising of *a man* in the embedded infinitive is blocked, since merger of *there* is preferred over Move *a man*.¹⁰ However, a new problem now emerges: the analysis thus far proposed forces *there* insertion in (12). How, then, do proponents of successive cyclic A-raising generate

---

9. Interestingly, this is a modern form of the age old problem: once successive cyclic movement is licensed, what prevents 'partial movement' as in the case above?
10. It seems to us, following Epstein (1990), that examples like (9) might be correctly excluded by phonetic requirements, not by a problem with semantic interpretation, i.e. the LF illegitimacy (uninterpretability) of structural Case. That is, the example 'sounds wrong', but seems to 'mean right', as was predicted/stated by the Case Filter. In the analysis just reviewed, the example is ungenerable given Merge over Move. It is unclear whether or not this predicts that (9) is known to be anomalous by someone who 'knows English' due to their knowledge of phonetic (phonosyntactic) requirements, or not. We return to this important issue below.

cases such as (11) – where Move applies over Merge? This phenomenon, in part, motivates the numeration. As a preliminary formulation, to be modified below, assume the following. Each derivation begins with an initial selection of lexical items, which in effect constitute all the lexical items that will be used in that derivation. Thus, the derivation of (12) remains as traced above. But, the problem of undergenerating (11), successive cyclic A-movement, is solved by appeal to the numeration: in fact, there is no *there* in the numeration of (11); and thus at the derivational point (12) Merge over Move allows Move of *a man* because Merge of *there* is not a logical possibility, i.e. (13) is inapplicable. (Note further that *a man* has its Case and agreement features checked in situ, the details of which do not directly effect present argumentation. Thus, *a man* can't raise to *to* since *a man* is inactive, in effect it cannot raise since there is no reason to.)

It should be noted now, however, that this Merge-over-Move analysis encounters at least two potential new problems, as is pointed out in MI. First, unlike the case just discussed, there are derivations in which: (i) *There* is in the numeration, yet (ii) Move nonetheless applies, contra Merge-over-Move. These grammatical cases have been noted in the literature but are not generable. An illustrative example is

(17)   there is a possibility that [proofs will be discovered ~~proofs~~]

At the derivation-internal point shown in (18)

(18)   __ [will be discovered proofs]

there are two ways to satisfy EPP, Move *proofs* or Merge *there*, which is indeed in the Numeration. Paradoxically, in this case we need to do Move over Merge. Notice the right result could be obtained if *there* was not, at this point, visible in the numeration (since there would then be nothing to Merge, movement of *proofs* would be allowed). This is precisely the tack initiated in MI and pursued in subsequent work (DBP and BEA). It is proposed that CPs and vP (where v is the 'light' verb head of transitive constructions, MI, p. 15), but not TP, are *phases*. A derivation is generated phase-by-phase, each phase having its own separate Numeration, called a 'lexical array'. Thus, since the embedded CP is a phase in (17), we can begin the derivation with just and only the lexical elements required to generate this CP. Thus, when we get to stage (18) of the derivation, *there* is *not* in the (embedded CP's) lexical array. Thus Merge over Move applies, yet Move is allowed, since we have, at this point, no *there* 'in hand' to Merge. Thus passive is allowed in the embedded CP. Raising of *a man* in (9), on the other hand, is *not* allowed, since TP is not a phase, and no other phase category exists that has a lexical array which excludes *there*. In short, *there* is visible throughout the derivation of (9), and must be merged in the embedded infinitival, as desired. (For arguments against appeal to the numeration cf., among others, Collins 1997:4 and Frampton and Gutmann 2002.)

This phase-based, numeration-dependent, Merge over Move analysis, in turn, encounters at least one potential conceptual and one potential empirical problem (see also Epstein and Seely 2002 and Epstein 2003). One potential empirical problem concerns the actual statement of the phase analysis. First, only CPs and vPs can be phases. The empirical motivation is clear enough, but is the naming of CP and vP as phases purely descriptive and ad hoc, allowing us to Move, as if *there* were not in the numeration? MI says that CP and vP are a natural class since the lexical arrays associated with these two category types

> determine a natural syntactic object SO, an object that is relatively independent in terms of interface properties. On the 'meaning side' perhaps the simplest and most principled choice is to take SO to be the closest syntactic counterpart to a *proposition: either a verb phrase in which all theta roles are assigned or a full clause including Tense and force*. [our emphasis SDE TDS] (MI, p. 20)

The difficulty here is that, returning to the problematic case (9), within the matrix VP as well as the matrix TP, all theta roles *are* assigned and hence this VP would therefore seem to be 'propositional'. If it is propositional, then it is a phase (all propositions are phases). Thus the following VP is predicted to be a phase:

(19)   [$_{VP}$ seem [a man to be [a man outside]]

Since this is a category with all theta roles assigned, it is a proposition, hence a phase, and as such has its own lexical array [*seem, a, man, to, be, outside*] crucially excluding *there*. Since it is a phase excluding *there*, raising of *a man* is allowed, since Merge of *there* is impossible (since *there* is not in the lexical array associated with this phase). Finally *there* can be inserted after this (VP) phase is complete, and (9) is overgenerated.[11] To prevent this result, MI assumes that the VP-phases are 'limited to transitive v with phi-features and external argument' (MI, p. 22).

---

11. One might argue that the matrix VP is not propositional hence not a phase, because it lacks tense. Notice, however, that vP is assumed to be a phase/propositional yet it lacks tense. If one wanted to

This would prevent the overgeneration. Since the VP (19) does not have an external argument, it can't be a phase, so *there* is visible in the NUM throughout, and must be merged in the Spec of the embedded TP. But the naturalness of phases including 'a verb phrase in which all theta roles are assigned' is lost (since all theta roles are assigned in (9)). Also lost is the idea that phases are 'propositional' (if propositional, then a phase). This is lost since the VP (19) seems propositional. But it is by the MI hypothesis not a phase. In addition, limiting phases to transitive v with an external argument seems descriptive.

The naturalness of the idea that phases are propositional is also potentially called into question by vP phases that do not seem propositional in any clear sense. Consider

(20) [$_{vP}$ who bought what]

This is a phase, but seems un-propositional. Note, it might be non-propositional since it's a double-question, or it might be non-propositional since it exhibits vacuous quantification, due to the fact that neither *wh*-operator binds a variable.

Finally there is another potential problem similar to the one noted in Epstein *et al.* (1998). Recall, in characterizing the lexical arrays associated with phases, MI states that a 'Lexical Array should determine a natural syntactic object SO, an object that is relatively independent in terms of interface properties.' The potential problem is that, in 'the act of' selecting an array, how can one determine that it can yield – by as yet unapplied derivational operations – a natural syntactic object, and moreover one that is 'relatively independent in terms of interface properties'? This suggests that lexical array selection might require look-ahead which 'envisions' the entire derivation and can 'see' whether the LF and PF representations, each a set generated by the derivation, are, or are not 'relatively independent in terms of interface properties.' Stated another way, we can't know whether a vP is a legitimate phase, with its own lexical array, until the derivation is over, and we are at the interface with respect to which a phase is characterized.[12]

In addition, the notion 'relatively independent in terms of interface properties', in contrast to 'convergent' (the latter entertained but rejected in MI as the character-

---

argue that propositions (hence phases) require tense, then vP would be excluded and (9) would still be overgenerated since the matrix TP (namely T + (9)) would be propositional, hence a phase.

12. One possible way to avoid such look-ahead is to freely generate, and (thus sometimes) crash. See Frampton and Gutmann (2001) and Epstein (2003) for possible problems confronting crash generation within a derivational framework.

ization of 'phases'), is not well-defined. To the extent that this definition is lacking, and the notion 'propositional' is unclear, the hypothesis that vP and CP are phases remains ad hoc – explicitly designed to render *there* as if invisible at derivation-internal points at which Move is required, and Merge must be postponed.

Finally, another potential problem confronting Merge-over-Move is sentences involving 'short Passive' such as

(21)   there was a proof discovered [a proof]

Recall that TP is not a phase. Moreover, crucially, a vP lacking an external theta role is also not a phase. This stipulation was incorporated so that no sub-phase (lexical array) lacking *there* would allow Movement of *a man* over Merge in the embedded clause.

(22)   there seems [there to be a man outside]

Crucially [*seems to be a man outside*] MUST NOT be a phase. If it were, then the Lexical Array for this vP-phase would lack *there*. This in turn would incorrectly allow *a man* to move to the Spec of the infinitival to satisfy the EPP: Merge-over-Move would allow this, since *there* is not in the sub-array, so Merge is not a possibility, thus licensing Move. To prevent this, it is stipulated that vP lacking an external theta role is *not* a phase.

But if this is so, it is arguably 'construction-specific' and short Passives (noted in MI), as in (21) are ungenerable. Consider the derivational point

(23)   [discovered a proof]

To generate (21) Move of *a proof* is required. But since TP is never a phase, and vP lacking en external theta role is not a phase, there are no phases in (23). Thus *there* remains visible in the lexical array throughout. Merge-over-Move then prohibits *a proof* from moving, and instead requires *there*-merger in this position. *There* then raises, yielding

(24)   there was [there discovered a proof]

64   *Derivations in Minimalism*

Although (24) is grammatical, the analysis incorrectly renders *there was a proof discovered* ungenerable.

3.3.3   Further issues concerning there-*insertion and raising*

The Merge-over-Move analysis not only requires supplementation to account for cases like (17) where *there* is in the numeration yet Move applies instead of Merge, but also needs to account for cases, where again, Move preempts Merge as noted in MI:

(25)   a.   JOHN expected [a proof to be discovered a proof]
                = MOVE applies downstairs
     b.   *JOHN expected [JOHN to be discovered a proof]
                = MERGE *John* downstairs, then Move *John* upstairs, by shortest Move

The problem here is that at the following stage, Merge, in particular Merge-*John* into Spec, TP, to satisfy the EPP is possible, yet Move is in fact preferred, in seeming violation of Merge-over-Move.

(26)   [T to be discovered a proof]

In order to prevent such Merge (recall TP is never a phase, hence the Merge-able category *John* is present in the lexical array) and thereby force Move, MI proposes the following:

(27)   Pure merge in theta position is required of (and restricted to) arguments

Let us examine the status of (27). First of all, (27) is really two principles, stating both a requirement and a restriction, which together amount to one half of the traditional theta criterion:

(28)   a.   If X is an argument, then X must be first-merged into a theta position.
     b.   If X is a non-argument, then X must not be first-Merged into a theta position.

(This too might be regarded as a vestige of (aspects of) D-structure.) What does not follow from (27) (= (28a) and (b)) is the second half of the theta criterion, namely that all theta roles must be assigned, a matter we put aside for present purposes.

(27) is called a 'principle' in MI but we are not sure of its status, hence its mode of application. It seems to us that, given 'Merge-over-Move', we must block, at the derivation-internal stage represented by (26), the merger of *John*, which Merge-over-Move demands at this very stage of derivation. Thus, it seems that (27) is not a principle (i.e. not a filter on representation; in fact it can't be, if the assumption is that there are no filters internal to C_{HL}), nor can it be a BOC, since we are trying to prevent a particular operation (Merge-*John*) from applying at a derivational-internal point, yet the operation seems required by Merge-over-Move. What is done then is to adopt (27), making Merge of *John* into Spec, TP an impossibility in (26), hence allowing Move. Thus (27) must constitute a constraint on the operation of the rule Merge. With this constraint in part *defining* Merge, the merger of *John* in (26) is, in fact, impossible – this simply is not Merge, as defined in (27). Since Merge, so defined, is not an option, Merge can't apply and Move is therefore allowed by Merge-over-Move, the right result.[13]

One possible problem with this theta constraint on Merge is that it excludes, but perhaps shouldn't, cases like

(29)   *John seems that Bill sleeps.

(30)   *I was in England last year [the man]

Intuitively, at least, this type of example should not be excluded by the incorporation of a constraint on rule application such as (27). Rather, this would seem to represent a class of examples each of which constitutes a good candidate for being correctly excluded by the Bare Output Conditions of the C-I system, external to C_{HL}. Informally, there is nothing wrong with the sound, and there is nothing wrong with the linear order of the categories – replace the verb *seems* with the verb *thinks*, and it is grammatical. So, it seems to us that what is wrong with this example is the meaning, in particular this kind of co-occurrence of a non-theta marking verb,

---

13. Note that (27) does raise some difficulties for the Pronominal Argument Hypothesis (PAH) of Jelinek (1984) (see also Baker 1993). For the PAH certain nominals (in, for example, Mohawk) are claimed to be base-generated in an A'-position and to bind a pronominal in an A-position. Similarly Left Dislocation in English seems not to be an instance of Move: *John, I wonder if Mary likes him*. If *John* is simply merged in, (27) would require that this is a theta-position. Why the pronoun must be bound would then be a question. Moreover, Bošković and Takahashi (1999) argue that optional scrambling violates Greed. They postulate that the scrambled element is 'base generated' in the A' phonetic scrambled position, and then is driven by theta-checking into the theta position – at LF.

and an argument *John*. If so, the difficult question we face is: Should the interpretive anomaly of such co-occurrence be explained by a constraint on the operation of Merge, or by appeal to independently 'necessary' lexical semantic (theta) properties and bare output conditions (the theta criterion as a BOC) which define the interpretability/legibility of an LF representation? The answer isn't clear to us. But our intuition accords with that of Chomsky (1986:98–9), who writes, with respect to examples like these:

> We might express many of these ideas by saying that there is a principle of Full Interpretation (FI) that requires that every element of PF and LF, taken to be the interface of syntax (in the broad sense) with systems of language use, must receive an appropriate interpretation – must be licensed in the sense indicated. None can simply be disregarded. We cannot have sentences of the form (88) 'I was in England last year the man', interpreted as 'I was in England last year', disregarding 'the man'.

Later:

> It is, then, a mistake to construct a *rule system* [our emphasis SDE, TDS] that bars [such examples]. Such rules would simply restate some complex facts that follow from quite general syntactic properties of human languages. There is, then, no justification on the basis of these constructions for enriching the class of available descriptive devices to permit these facts to be stated directly in a rule system – an undesirable move in any event.

We should note that it is not entirely clear to us whether these comments from Chomsky (1986) pertain to a 'Universalized' Rule system such as the one currently under consideration within which Merge and Move (or certain aspects of them) are universal. Regardless, such a constraint on Pure Merge, is a stipulation. Thus, the following question is not answered:

(31) Why is it that an argument cannot be Pure merged into a non-theta position, nor a non-argument Pure merged into a theta position?

An alternative analysis, appealing to Bare Output Conditions expressing the Theta Criterion at LF, in effect following Chomsky (1986), addresses and maybe even answers the question, predicting seemingly correctly that such examples are in a very circumscribed way, in part, uninterpretable. It isn't clear that the Merge-constraint captures this.

Another potential problem with constraining the operation of 'Pure Merge' in this way is that the notion 'Pure Merge' must be distinguished from 'impure' Merge, where impure Merge is Move/Re-Merge. It is perhaps a mistake to differentiate Pure from Impure Merge in this way, since recall, Merge-over-Move is assumed to be naturally economical since Merge is a sub-operation of Move. But given the above theta-constraint on 'PURE' Merge, which does not apply to the landing site of Impure Merge (=Move =Remerge), it is not clear which operation, Merge or Move, is (intuitively) simpler, hence more economical, since 'Pure Merge' has certain theta-constraints on its operation that do not constrain Impure-Merge =Move =Remerge, e.g. an argument *can* be (re-merged (moved)) to a non-theta position, whereas, pure merger of an argument into a non-theta position is barred by the proposed theta constraint (27) on Pure Merge. Thus, the first assumption of the Merge-over-Move analysis ('Merge, being a subcase of Move, is simpler hence preferred') is now perhaps itself unmaintainable.

In sum, the EPP seems to be creating a domino effect: since Spec of *to* must be filled, a case of pure EPP satisfaction, the analysis incorporates a number of arguably problematic mechanisms, including: (i) postulation of the numeration, (ii) the traffic rule Merge-over-Move, (iii) phases, and (iv) the theta based constraint on Merge, i.e. (28), incorporating half of the Theta Criterion.

3.3.4   Some advantages of a derivational analysis

Let us now consider under our own analysis those cases that engendered the problematic Merge-over-Move constraint, the postulation of phases and the theta-theoretic constraint on Merge which amounts to part of the traditional Theta Criterion.

Under our approach, the spec of *to* in examples like (9), repeated below, checks no feature. Thus Greed, ESI, or Suicidal Attract (the latter proposed in MI) prohibit movement to this position. That is a welcome result since all the difficulties presented above arise because *to* is claimed to have some EPP feature, and hence must be checked by something:

(9′)   there seems [a man to be [a man here]]

Cases like (9′) are perhaps the central loopholes created by the 'translation' of the GB Case Filter at SS, to the much preferable, but 'delayed-enforcement' Minimalist analysis of Case as uninterpretable at LF. For us, Merge-over-Move is simply not needed for these, or related, cases. The derivation does not have to be blocked since the derivation simply does not arise. For us, the element *to* has no features to check and therefore *a man* cannot move to Spec of *to* since no features could be checked there. Two derivations, then, are possible: *there* is merged into the matrix position, yielding *There seems to be a man here*; or, *a man seems to be here* is derived in one fell swoop movement (how Case and agreement are checked in such instances will be taken up a bit later).[14]

Since we don't need Merge over Move to block (9'), we do not need to incorporate postulates like numerations and phases designed to handle the cases where Merge-over-Move does not happen, but rather Move happens, even though Merge was in principle applicable, e.g.

(32) there is a possibility that [a man will be arrested ~~a man~~]

Recall, finally, that the constraint Merge-over-Move, left in this simple form, runs afoul of theta theory. As is noted in MI, in (33)

(33) John expects [~~John~~ [$_{TP}$ to be arrested a man]]

after the spec-less infinitival TP is built, Merge-over-Move forces merger of *John*, perhaps overgenerating such examples, but certainly undergenerating, leaving us no way to derive:

(34) John expects [a man [to be arrested ~~a man~~]]

Since TP is never a phase, and the embedded VP is not a phase, since it has no external argument, *John* is visible in the lexical array throughout. In order to block *John*-insertion in the embedded clause, the proposal that arguments must and can merge only into a theta position is made (see (27)). We have argued,[15] by constrast, that such derivations are excluded since movement to or through spec of *to* is impossible under our analysis.

---

14. Consider the derivational stage:

    (i) seems there to be a man here

    derived by Merge-over-Move. If *there* is a pure EPP satisfier and the EPP is a purely structural principle; i.e. not feature checking, then, it is unclear how *there* should induce an intervention effect blocking superraising under the probe-goal analysis.

15. The idea that the elimination of the EPP (and thus not moving to spec of raising *to* successive cyclically through Spec-T) can solve various problems within the Merge-over-Move account in MI is independently proposed in Castillo, Drury and Grohmann (1999). We leave to future research a comparison of their approach with those aspects of our analysis directly concerning the EPP, Merge-over-Move, and successive cyclic A-movement.

3.3.5 On ECM

If the ECM *to* checks no features, as seems to be true even under GB exceptional case assignment analyses, then Movement to the Spec of this *to* should be prohibited, just like it is prohibited in (9′). However, as shown in (34), movement to this Spec-of-*to* position in ECM apparently does occur, a central concern in Minimalist accounts. Why is there overt movement to this position? The standard is that movement to this spec applies since T's EPP feature must be checked. But we would like to suggest a different approach, one that parallels our claim that raising *to* has no features. Thus we seek to unify ECM and Raising *not* by assuming that both involve movement to Spec *to*, but rather by postulating that neither involves movement to Spec *to*. That is to say, in fact, the ECM subject is not moving to such a position.

We would like to suggest, following in large part independently motivated analyses of Johnson (1991), Koizumi (1995), and Lasnik and Saito (1991) that ECM is an 'optical illusion'. In fact, the ECM subject does not occupy the Spec of *to* at Spell-out, consistent with our assumptions that this *to* is not a feature checker. Suppose that the ECM DP has overtly 'object raised/shifted upstairs'. If this overt-shift analysis is correct, nothing occupies Spec of *to* overtly. We, unlike others, would claim in addition that nothing even moves through Spec of *to*. Thus, the ECM DP is shifted (object shift for Case from the ECM verb in a spec-head relation) to the left of the ECM verb, but the ECM verb also raises to the left of the shifted object DP (for reasons unclear to us) yielding the correct word order. Nothing is ever in Spec TP. This is represented in (35).

(35)   I believe a man ~~believe~~ [$_{\text{Specless-TP}}$ to be [~~a man~~] outside
(Note that 'copies' are shown here only for purposes of derivational exposition; no actual copies or traces are present under the derivational approach that we adopt.)

Just like 'long distance A-raising', for us this is not successive cyclic A-movement. Rather it is one fell swoop to upstairs spec of *believe*, thereby answering the vexing question: if there is no 'exceptional case marking', but only spec-head, why does the DP move to spec of *to* overtly in ECM? While it can't in Raising? Our answer is that it doesn't move to Spec *to* in ECM, just as it fails to in Raising. Thus we reject two central cases of non-redundant so-called 'pure' EPP-checking.

3.4 The conjecture class of verbs

3.4.1 The Problem

Another challenge to attempting to eliminate the EPP concerns the *conjecture* class of verbs, as discussed in Bošković (1997:135, ex. 117); see also Brody (1993). There are certain ungrammatical data that appear to be excluded only by analyses which appeal to the EPP; i.e. these data, like successive cyclic A-raising and ECM, appear to display pure EPP effects. To begin, Bošković (1997:80) argues that members of the *conjecture* class of verbs each have the following properties:

(36) *Conjecture* class verbs:
  a. Assign subject theta role
  b. S-select proposition (thus disallows a Control-PRO complement)
  c. Assign no ACC Case
  d. Take an infinitival complement

The relevant data presented by Bošković (1997:79) are as follows (* and ? from Bošković):

(37) *John has conjectured [PRO to like Mary]   (illustrates (36b))

(38) *John has conjectured Mary to like Peter   (illustrates (36c))

(39) ?Mary has been conjectured to like Peter   (illustrates (36d))

Under Bošković's analysis, example (37) is excluded because *conjecture* s-selects propositions and Control infinitives cannot be interpreted as propositional. In (38) s-selection is satisfied since the complement is propositional, but since, Bošković argues, *conjecture* fails to assign ACC Case, *Mary* is not Case checked and the example is correctly excluded. The marginal example (39) is argued to provide crucial evidence that *conjecture* does indeed take an infinitival. *Mary* moves to get Case, unavailable from *conjecture*. Bošković notes that the example (39) is 'slightly marginal', and attributes this to the passivization of a [−ACC] Case-assigning verb, but not to a selectional violation. We are not sure of the formal status of the ban against passivizing [−ACC], proposition-selecting verbs. As evidence for this ban, Bošković (p. 80) offers the following example, characterizing its status with a question mark:

(40)   ?It has been conjectured that Peter likes Mary

So, Bošković is arguing that (39) and (40) have roughly the same status, due to the passive ban, while selectional violations seem far worse.

(41)   *Mary wants very much that Peter will graduate

Bošković conjectures that (39) is not a selectional violation; i.e. *conjecture* has the lexical property of allowing infinitival complements – or has no lexical property barring them.

Given these properties of *conjecture*, the following (arguably ungrammatical case)[16] can be excluded under the standard assumption that expletive *it* requires Case.

(42)   *John has conjectured [it to seem that Peter is ill]

However, Lasnik (2002) notes that without the EPP, the following example, which simply omits the expletive, is overgenerated.

(43)   *John has conjectured [__ to seem Peter is ill]

Without the EPP, nothing forces Spec, TP to appear, and if nothing is forced into Spec, TP, it isn't clear why (43) is ungrammatical. It certainly isn't excluded by a Case requirement on expletives since there is no expletive. Nor can we appeal to Case-discharge requirements on a Case assigning head, if, as we have argued, *to* in such cases has no feature checking properties, and as Bošković argues *conjecture* lacks Case. Nor can we appeal to selection, if, as discussed above, *conjecture* does allow infinitival complementation, as suggested by the 'mere marginality' of the passive infinitival example (39) above, which recall, Bošković argues only violates the passive ban, not selection. How then can (43) be excluded without the EPP?

---

16. We suggest later that (42) (or analogs thereof) are, in fact, relatively well formed.

3.4.2 On the properties of conjecture verbs and the documented unclarity of the data

3.4.2.1 Does conjecture *take an infinitival complement?*

Before proceeding with some possible answers, we would like to point out what we believe to be possibly serious unclarities surrounding the data used to determine properties of the *conjecture* class of verbs, verbs argued to motivate an independent EPP.

One straightforward approach to excluding (43) above is to assume that members of the *conjecture* class of verbs simply do not select an infinitival complement. But, as just noted, Bošković does not pursue this approach based on the status of (39) and his analysis of it as fully consistent with *conjecture* selecting an infinitive. The status and analysis of (39) are thus crucial to the argument that (43) motivates the EPP. However, as documented in the literature, the status of passive infinitivals like (39) is not altogether clear. For example, Martin (1999, fn. 16) differs from Bošković in his judgments regarding Passive infinitivals with *conjecture*. Contra Bošković, Martin judges the following as having the same status, which he calls 'at best marginal':

(44)   a. Mary was conjectured to like Peter
           b. Mary was remarked to like Peter

By contrast, Bošković presumes they are different, as indicated by the fact that Bošković (1997:78) reports that Bošković (1994) had suggested that *remark* belongs to the BELIEVE class of verbs (i.e. those that assign subject theta role, do not check ACC Case and take an infinitival complement), writing:

> In Bošković 1994 I suggested that *remark* belongs to this class of verbs. However it seems to me now that *conjecture* is a better candidate *for most speakers* [our emphasis SDE, TDS]. (pp. 78–9)

(Bošković 1997:199, fn. 7 however reports that one of his informants accepts *Mary has been remarked to like Peter*, noting 'for this speaker *remark* does belong to the BELIEVE class.')

This indicates unclarity about the status of *conjecture* and its relation to *remark*. Moreover, as Martin (1999, fn. 16) also notes, Bošković's analysis requires some kind of independent selection, distinct from s-selection, dictating whether or not infinitival complements are allowed. This is because Bošković claims a distinction in the status of (44a) and (44b), claiming (44b) is worse, yet the two verbs are assumed to have identical s-selectional properties. Bošković calls this 'other selection' l(=lexical)-selection, under which an X^0 selects particular lexical items and not others. As for our own judgments, we are quite unsure about these data, perhaps indicating further unclarity.

In the remainder of this chapter, we examine *conjecture* in great detail precisely because Bošković (1997), and later researchers following him, e.g. Lasnik (2002), consider it *the* most likely candidate for membership in the class of so-called BELIEVE verbs.

As Martin (1999) further notes, the hypothesis that *conjecture* assigns an external theta role, but assigns no 'internal' Case, runs counter to part of Burzio's Generalization. Of course Burzio could be wrong, but the inconsistency may also indicate that *conjecture* is misclassified (perhaps on the basis of what may be unclear data). We will return momentarily to Martin's re-analysis of *conjecture* under which it is a verb consistent with Burzio's Generalization. Before doing so, we consider what seems to us to be a factual unclarity regarding the Case-assigning properties of *conjecture*, to which we now turn.

3.4.2.2 Does conjecture *assign Case?*

Recall that Bošković proposes that *conjecture* assigns no Case. He provides the following supporting data (p. 79):

(45)   *John has conjectured something/it
       (indicated grammaticality judgement from Bošković, p. 79)

First of all, it is not clear to us that the quantificational *something* and deictic referential *it* yield identical ungrammaticality; i.e. we are not sure whether such data should be collapsed with slash notation. But, let's assume with Bošković that the examples with *something* and *it* are ungrammatical, and equally so. Bošković compares such purportedly ungrammatical cases with the following grammatical cases with *wager/admit*.

(46)   a.   John wagered all his money on the Bulls.
       b.   Mary admitted her mistake.

wager/admit are argued to have ACC Case to assign, while *conjecture* does not. But notice that no two members of the last three examples constitute a minimal pair. That is, the indefinite complements (*something/it*) used to support *conjecture*'s purported *lack* of ACC-assigning powers differ from the definite complements used to support the hypothesis that *wager/admit* by contrast *do* have ACC Case to assign. Moreover, the perfective form of *conjecture* is used while *wager/admit* appear in the simple past tense. With *something/it* as complement, forming a true minimal pair with (47), *wager* too seems significantly degraded:

(47)   John (has) wagered something/it

Once again, though, the data isn't clear; we can't determine the comparative grammaticality of (45) vs. (47). We henceforth indicate such indeterminacy with the symbol '±'. Our unclarity is further compounded by the following 'discourse' effects. If the reference of *something/it* is fixed, as it could be by e.g. 'right dislocation', the examples improve:

(48)   John wagered something, namely five-hundred dollars.
       John wagered it, the $500 he owes you (here, a bare amount '500' is less acceptable than a definite description, presumably due to the specificity of it).[17]

Notice also that temporal adverbials might improve the examples still further:

(49)   John can't place another bet, he has *already* wagered something, namely $500.

With all of this in mind, reconsider Bošković's example supporting the claim that conjecture lacks ACC Case:

(45)   *John has conjectured something/it.

What if we fix the reference here? Can a DP appear, and arguably be Case checked by *conjecture*?

(50)   a.   John has conjectured something, the first law.
       b.   John has conjectured something, that the first law is true.

---

17. Further complicating the experiments, there may in fact be two *wagers*: *I wager* (= reckon) *that she likes him* vs. *I wager* (placed a bet of) *x* (e.g. a monetary amount) *on y* (an outcome).

(51)   a.   John has conjectured it, the first law.
       b.   John has conjectured it, that the first law is true.

Again, our judgments are unclear, but it seems that the (b) examples, in which the interpretation of *something/it* is propositional, are better than the (a) examples, which lack this propositional interpretation. Thus we tentatively propose, contra Bošković, that

(52)   *Conjecture* class verbs:
       Do assign ACC Case, but only if the ACC Case recipient can receive propositional interpretation.

       With Bošković, we assume that conjecture
       a.   Assigns subject theta role
       b.   S-selects proposition (thus disallows a Control-PRO complement)
       c.   Takes an infinitival complement

With these properties of *conjecture* postulated, in particular that it s-selects a proposition and (contra Bošković) can ACC assign to propositional-NP/DPs only,[18] consider the following cases where *conjecture* takes a direct object NP/DP but the context supplies the direct object with propositional interpretation:

(53)   ASSERTION: John conjectured that the Bulls would win.
       a.   That's interesting, I conjectured that too.
       b.   That's interesting, I conjectured something too, namely that $2 + 2 = 4$.
       c.   That's interesting, since he conjectured it AFTER they played the game!
       d.   That's interesting, I conjectured the same outcome.

18. Returning to (46b), it is interesting to note here that Bošković's example, arguing that *admit* can assign ACC, has a DP object that apparently has a propositional interpretation.

   (i)   Mary admitted her mistake = Mary admitted [THAT she was mistaken]

   It does not mean: Mary admitted $[2 + 2 = 5]$, where $2 + 2 = 5$ *is* the mistake. Recall Bošković's other example demonstrating ACC assigning powers,

   (46b)   John wagered all his money on the Bulls.

   Here too there is a propositional interpretation involved; namely, John wagered all his money [THAT THE BULLS WOULD WIN]. We leave the properties of *admit* and *wager*, focusing instead on the properties of *conjecture* (claimed to be an archetypal example of a BELIEVE-type verb).

e. Then John conjectured something foolish (=reduced relative, not small clause).
f. No he didn't. In fact John conjectured nothing.

These seem better than Bošković's example *John has conjectured something/it. With our hypothesis that *conjecture* can assign ACC (at least under certain circumstances) in mind, let's return to another case argued to indicate that *conjecture* lacks ACC:

(54)   *?John has conjectured Mary to like Peter.
       (cf. *John has conjectured that Mary likes Peter.*)

Why is this out if, as we have suggested, *conjecture* can assign ACC Case? Under our hypothesis *Mary* cannot receive Case since *Mary* is not propositionally interpretable. This makes at least three predictions. First, that the passive infinitival should be improved since ACC Case is not involved. That it is better accords with the judgments of some analysts (e.g. Bošković) but not others (e.g. Martin), as discussed above.

(44)   ?Mary was conjectured to like Peter.

A second prediction is that if we put a propositionally interpretable DP in the exceptional Case marking position with *conjecture* (in place of *Mary* in (54)), this too should lead to improvement. This prediction seems right:

(55)   a. *John conjectured Mary to have upset Bill.
       b. John conjectured Mary's illness to have upset Bill.
       c. John conjectured Mary's having an illness to have upset Bill.

It seems to us that the DP following *conjecture* in (55b) and (55c), when interpreted propositionally, is more acceptable than the non-propositional DP *Mary* in this position.

Importantly, if such data is grammatical, then, *conjecture* does take infinitival complements and we no longer need to rely solely on the grammatical status of the infinitival passives, about which there exists disagreement in the literature. Thus, the central EPP-motivating case under discussion (namely (43) *John has conjectured __ to seem Peter is ill*) cannot be excluded simply by saying that *conjecture* verbs do not take infinitives.

A third prediction is that the same propositionally interpret*able* DP in the same position, but with non-propositional interpretation, should be comparatively degraded. Judgments yet again are unclear, but the following does indeed seem worse:

(56)   *?John conjectured Mary's illness to be influenza.

Here, *Mary's illness* cannot be interpreted as 'that Mary was ill', but rather is forced by the equative environment to bear non-propositional interpretation; thus, under the analysis considered here *Mary's illness* can't be ACC Case-checked (if *Mary's illness* is interpreted non-propositionally) or, if this DP is interpreted propositionally, there is a semantic anomaly, i.e. it would be interpreted as something like *John conjectured that Mary is ill is influenza*.

This then suggests that, contra Bošković, *conjecture* (or the little *v* selecting it) can indeed value ACC Case, but differs from ECM verbs such as *believe* in requiring that the infinitival subject have propositional content.

Given this curious property, *conjecture* is now importantly consistent with Burzio's Generalization, i.e. if we are on the right track, *conjecture* not only assigns an external theta role, but can assign ACC Case, as shown by reconsidering the following examples.

(57)   a.   John has conjectured Mary's illness to have upset Peter.
       b.   *It was conjectured Mary's illness to have upset Peter.
       c.   Mary's illness was conjectured to have upset Peter.

To summarize, recall that Lasnik (2002) argues that examples like (43) motivate the EPP.

(43)   *John has conjectured [__ to seem Peter is ill]

Specifically, following Bošković (1997), the assumption is that such examples cannot be excluded by appeal to undischarged Case on *conjecture* since, as we noted, Bošković argues that *conjecture* lacks Case altogether. In this section, we have called into question the data supporting and the analysis under which *conjecture* is assumed to lack Case. We have suggested, contra Bošković, that *conjecture* bears

ACC Case and thus example (43) is excluded without appeal to the EPP, on a par with *I believe __ to seem Peter is ill. More generally, with Martin (1999:9) we suggest that it might be the case that there do not exist any BELIEVE-type verbs. We stress again that the data from the literature as well as our own data presented here are unclear. But, to the extent that the data are clear, an analysis without the EPP seems feasible. We now confront at least three problems. First, we believe there may be a contrast between the following:

(58) a. ±John has conjectured Mary's illness.
      b. John has conjectured Mary's illness to have upset Fred.

Our impression is that (58a) is worse than (58b). But (58a)'s status is unclear – consider, for instance, the analogous

(59)   The doctors had conjectured Mary's illness long before she became symptomatic.

This seems better than (58a). But if (58a) is worse then (58b), we have no explanation thus far: *conjecture* can assign Case to *Mary's illness* and *Mary's illness* is a DP that can receive propositional interpretation. Our speculative hypothesis is that for some reason the DP *Mary's illness* in the direct object position of *conjecture* can't receive the requisite propositional interpretation; so, the reading one gets is not unlike 'John has conjectured influenza.' Notice that this seems to be true with *believe* too; i.e. the following seems to us anomalous: *I believe Mary's illness* (cf. *I believe that Mary is ill*). One might hypothesize a general law that when in direct object position NPs of this kind[19] are unable to receive a propositional interpretation. However, this seems false in light of examples like *I regretted Mary's illness* which can mean 'I regretted that Mary is ill' (not: 'I regretted influenza'). Thus, it seems that some verbs resist the propositional interpretation of apparent direct objects, while others don't. We leave the matter to further research.

The second and third problems with our tentative proposal that *conjecture* assigns ACC Case concern our attempted elimination of the EPP. While the ACC assigning hypothesis allows us to handle (43) without appeal to the EPP, at least two other kinds of data evade this Case discharge account. Namely, nominal forms of *conjecture*:

(60)   *[the conjecture [__to seem that Bill left]] upset me

---

19. By this kind, we mean as contrasted with 'anaphoric' NPs of the sort that occur in (51) above.

and passives. We turn to the nominal cases below. As for passives, consider

(61)   ±It was conjectured __ to seem that Bill left.

yet again the data is unclear. If such cases are ungrammatical, as this seems to be, we have no obvious way to exclude them: since it's passive, *conjecture* bears no undischarged Case, nor can we appeal to the EPP; recall that for us *to* has no features to check, thus we do not analyze these as expletive raising. The analysis we've proposed thus predicts that the examples are well formed: no ACC is assigned and thus the requirement that ACC recipients be propositional is inapplicable, as is the requirement that *conjecture* discharges ACC. Interestingly, certain passives are, as predicted, grammatical (or at least substantially improved in our view). Consider the following, where the raising predicate, unlike bare *seem*, allows a sentential subject as a lexical property. We think these are much improved:

(62)   It was conjectured to be likely that Bill left.

(63)   It was conjectured to be easy to finish this project.

(64)   It was conjectured to seem weird that Bill left.

Notice further, as we noted in a different context above, that perfective aspect arguably improves the examples still further:[20]

(65)   It was conjectured to have been likely that Bill left.

(66)   It was conjectured to have been easy to finish this project.

Some speakers detect further improvement with modals downstairs:

---

20. This is an effect already documented with agentive infinitival complements to 'standard' ECM Verbs like *believe*:

   (i)   *I believe John to kick Bill (right now).
   (ii)   I believe John to have kicked Bill.

   See Enç (1991) and Pires (2001).

(67)   It was conjectured to have been likely that Bill would leave (under those circumstances).

Even with *seem* itself, there are ways to improve grammaticality. Consider the following

(68)   It was conjectured to have seemed as if Bill would leave.

(69)   It was conjectured to have seemed weird that Bill left.

Notice that the latter case, *seemed weird*, allows a sentential subject; see Moro (1997). Thus, passives do not seem to present clear counter evidence to our predictions. Before returning to ACC-less nominal cases, we first consider theta marking and certain additional semantic properties of *conjecture*.

3.4.2.3 A note on conjecture *and* theta   Consider next theta marking. Recall that the following is predicted good (or at least improved) by our analysis.

(70)   I conjectured Mary's illness to have upset Bill.

(70) does *not* entail that I was the one who conjectured Mary's illness; i.e. the following is non-contradictory:

(71)   I conjectured Mary's illness to have upset Bill, but I was not the one who conjectured that Mary was ill.

By contrast, the following examples from Pesetsky (1991), as discussed in Bošković (1997:55), do seem to involve a semantic relation of some kind between *declare* and *March* and between *estimate* and *Bill's weight*:

(72)   I declared March to be National Syntax Month.

(73)   I estimated Bill's weight to be 150 lbs.

If true, then I *did* declare something (of) March and I *did* estimate Bill's weight. On this matter, citing Pesetsky (1991), Bošković (1997:55) notes what he calls:

> ...a rather surprising fact concerning the relation between theta-role assignment and ECM with agentive verbs noted by Pesetsky (1991). Pesetsky observes that in some cases [unlike *Peter wagered Fred to be crazy*, SDE, TDS] an agentive verb can exceptionally Case mark a lexical NP, in particular when it theta marks the NP...Consider
>
> (13)   Congress declared March to be National Syntax Month.
>
> Pesetsky notes that the matrix verb in (13) affects the embedded subject. The act of declaring changes the property of *March*. March becomes National Syntax month by virtue of the declaration. Pesetsky interprets this as indicating that the matrix verb theta marks the embedded subject across the embedded clause boundary...

The hypothesized generalization is that

(74)   Pesetsky's Generalization:
An agentive verb can exceptionally Case-mark, i.e. across a clause boundary, only if the agentive verb theta marks the exceptionally Case marked constituent.

But if we are correct that *conjecture* can indeed ECM a (propositional) NP, then unlike with *declare/estimate*, it seems that such ECM can occur in the absence of theta assignment. That is *I conjectured Mary's illness to have upset Fred* seems to us to involve no theta marking of *Mary's illness* by *conjecture*. (Although we have indeed suggested a semantic relation between the ACC-marked DP and *conjecture*; namely that the DP is required to have propositional interpretation.) To summarize we conjecture the following, namely that:

(75)   CONJECTURE
    a. s-selects a proposition
    b. CAN assign ACC to DP, and even to ECM subject that it fails to theta mark, provided the DP can be propositionally interpreted.

The next question is: what kind of Case assignment is *conjecture* engaged in, when it exceptionally Case marks a DP that it fails to theta mark, as in the following?

(76)   John conjectured Mary's illness to have upset Fred.

If inherent Case assignment requires theta marking, then this can't be inherent Case; *conjecture* does not (by hypothesis) theta mark *Mary's illness*. If structural is the only remaining possibility, then structural it is. This is interesting and unclear, since there does seem to be a semantic restriction on the ECM subject (it must be propositionally interpretable) but the relation between *conjecture* and the DP does not appear to be a theta relation. Now notice that if *conjecture* assigns the agent theta role to the subject, as we assume it does,[21] then these examples suggest that the generalization that Pesetsky postulated and Bošković elegantly sought to explain might be descriptively incorrect (see also Pesetsky (1991) and Bošković (1997:192–3, fn. 2) for discussion of other possible counterexamples). This too requires further investigation.

3.4.2.4 Conjecture *and expletives* Notice that the analysis tentatively outlined above would seem to predict that an expletive cannot occur in the ECM position with *conjecture*. This is because an expletive, being semantically vacuous, does not receive propositional interpretation. Thus, the ACC case of *conjecture* cannot be assigned, leading to ill-formedness. Thus we predict that all of the following are ungrammatical (due to the presence of undischarged Case on conjecture):

(77)   a.   John conjectured it to seem (that) Peter is ill.
          b.   John conjectured there to be a man outside.
          c.   John conjectured her to be crazy.
          d.   John conjectured Peter to be crazy.

The (77a) case seems pretty good to us (see below for ways to improve it), the others seem worse – with (77b) perhaps better than (77c) and (77d), yet still worse than (77a). It is interesting to digress here for a moment and compare *conjecture* with Bošković's judgments regarding *wager*-class verbs, which are similar to *conjecture* in that they are agentive verbs which bear ACC. Bošković claims that *wager*-class verbs are grammatical with an ECMed expletive or pronoun, but not an R-expression. This is similar (but not identical) to our tentative judgments regarding *conjecture*. *Conjecture* and *wager* pattern together in allowing an expletive and barring an R-expression. Bošković provides the following examples of *wager*-class verbs:

---

21. Conjecture is agentive according to standard diagnostics.

    (i)   What John did was conjecture Mary's illness to have upset Fred.
    (ii)   What John did was conjecture that Mary was ill.
    (iii)   *What John did was receive a summons.

(78)   He acknowledged it to be impossible to square circles.   (1997:58, ex. 21c)

(79)   Mary never alleged him to be crazy.   (1997:59, ex. 21h)

(80)   *John wagered Peter to be crazy.   (1997:52, ex. 5a)

Note, however, that Bošković does not use *wager* itself in (78) and (79), using instead *acknowledge* in (78) and *allege* in (79). The substitution of *wager* in these cases seems to yield a marginal result (we think):

(81)   He wagered it to be impossible to square circles.

(82)   Mary never wagered him to be crazy.

Bošković argues that *wager* has ACC, but in (80) *Peter* is, by locality, unable to 'shift' out of the agentive recursive VP and vP shells (induced by agentivity) and is thus unable to move to an Agr_O Spec, above the vP and VP; thus, structural Case requirements are unmet. However, Bošković argues, with an expletive or pronoun, incorporation of such non-branching X^0s is possible, in which case the Case Filter requirement is avoided via incorporation (Baker 1988).

Again, the status of such data has been documented as unclear. For example, Collins (2002:130) in his review of Bošković (1997) finds the following array of data, in which wager takes various infinitival complements, 'very unclear':

(83)   a. *Peter wagered the students to be crazy.   (Bošković 1997:49)
       b. John was wagered to be crazy.   (Bošković 1997:49)
       c. Who did Peter wager to be crazy?   (Bošković 1997:49)
       d. John wagered there to be a stranger in that haunted house. (Bošković 1997:58)

Collins writes the following regarding this data:

> I must admit that I find this data very unclear. For example I do not find a clear difference between (a) and (c). Furthermore, (d) does not seem particularly good to me (see Rooryck 1997:9 for related discussion).

Thus, there seems to be a relation between *wager* and *conjecture* but the data isn't clear to us. Returning to the central theme, recall that under our tentative proposals regarding *conjecture*, the following is predicted ungrammatical since *it*, being an expletive, cannot be interpreted propositionally.

(77)   a.   John conjectured it to seem (that) Peter is ill.

Recall we have claimed that (77a) is pretty good. Interestingly, Lasnik discusses the following, related example:

(84)   *John has conjectured it to seem Peter is ill.   (Lasnik 2002, ex.11)

For Lasnik, (84) is out since *conjecture* lacks Case, and expletives require Case. We agree (84) is ungrammatical. However, it doesn't constitute a counterexample to our proposals here, we would argue, since its unacceptability is in part due to the absence of a complementizer introducing the finite clause. For reasons we don't entirely understand, the complementizer seems to become obligatory in the complement of *infinitive* forms of raising predicates (see Epstein, Pires, and Seely 2004 for discussion).

(85)   It seems John left.

(86)   It seems that John left.

(87)   *I believe it to seem John left.

(88)   I believe it to seem that John left.

Now, in addition to the improvement made by adding the overt complementizer, suppose, as discussed earlier, we add perfective aspect and an overt experiencer, modify the tense of the finite clause, and change *that* to *as if*. The results seem fine:

(89)   John conjectured it to have seemed to the doctors as if Peter was ill
        (and that explains why they prescribed the medication).

Finally, let's also change the predicate to one that, unlike bare *seem*, allows an overt sentential subject as a lexical property, e.g. *likely*.

(90)   John conjectured it to have been likely that Peter was ill.

This seems to us to be acceptable (or only slightly marginal). It seems fairly clear to us that *it* in (90) is better than in the following, clearly Case-less environments:

(91)　　It seems [IT to have been likely [that John left].

(92)　　(*for) [IT to have been likely that John left] disturbs me.

This would indicate that *it* can be Case-assigned by *conjecture*, consistent with our proposal that *conjecture* is indeed a Case-assigner.

But our analysis now seems to confront a problem. As an expletive, *it* is not interpretable propositionally, and thus our proposal that *conjecture* can case-check only a DP that is propositionally interpreted is apparently not fulfilled. We would seem to wrongly predict that the examples we have just argued to be good are in fact bad (or no better than *John conjectured Peter to have left*). This raises the long-standing issue of the relation between the expletive *it* and the *that*-clause,[22] which it is important to note here *is* propositional as *conjecture* 'requires'. Without

---

22. For example, at least as early as Rosenbaum (1967) the association was postulated. For Rosenbaum, it was expressed by generating *it* and the *that*-clause together (along with a Determiner) all inside the subject NP, as in the following:

(i)　　[NP DET IT That John left] [PredP is likely]

From Deep Structures like this, there were two possible derivations. In one, Extraposition of the *that*-clause applies yielding

(ii)　　IT is likely that John left.

Alternatively, indefinite pronoun deletion can apply, generating sentences like:

(iii)　　That John left is likely.

Thus, the relation between construction types is captured in part by expressing an abstract (never surfacing as such) underlying relation between *it* and the *that*-clause, such that they are sisters (who must ultimately be 'separated') initially generated within the subject NP mother.
　　But crucially, notice that *seem* (in contrast to *likely*) disallows this configuration:

(iv)　　*That John left seems.

Interestingly, exactly this fact leads Moro (1997) to exclude such examples by postulating precisely an underlying sisterhood relation between the *that*-clause and *it*, which we discuss momentarily. See also Chomsky (1981:215) for binding-theoretic evidence for the *it*-to-*that*-clause association formally expressed in that framework by co-superscripting (a device now barred by inclusiveness).

going into detail, one can imagine an expletive replacement analysis,[23] whereby the propositionally interpreted *that*-clause endows it with the propositional content necessary for ACC Case checking.[24] Thus, the fact that the data is improved by using *likely* and degrades with *seems* may be related to their differences in 'overt replaceability' of, or association with, the expletive, as in

(93)   *That John left seems.

(94)   That John left is likely.

We leave the development of this somewhat speculative hypothesis to future research.
What about *there*-expletives with *conjecture* as in (95)?

---

23. See Bošković for arguments in favor of LF *it* replacement, and McCloskey (1991) for arguments against. (See also den Dikken 1995 for arguments against LF *there* replacement.)

Agreement phenomena have constituted the driving force for expletive-associate relations in existentials:

(i)   There is/* are a man outside.

McCloskey (1991) (ingeniously) argues that there is no such agreement in the case of an *it*-expletive and its clausal associate. McCloskey's argument is based on the following kind of data involving contradictory coordination:

(ii)   That he'll resign and that he'll stay in office SEEM(pl.) at this point equally likely.

(iii) *It SEEM(pl.) at this point equally likely that he'll resign and that he'll stay in office. (from Bošković 1997:91)

McCloskey argues that the failure of plural agreement in the second case supports the hypothesis that the clausal associate (in this case a plural coordinate) does *not* replace the expletive *it* at LF. This is in contrast to the expletive replacement that by hypothesis does occur with *there*-constructions, which *do* display agreement with the associate.
However Bošković argues that McCloskey's analysis does not go through. Bošković notes that even *there*-constructions fail to display agreement with the associate, when the associate is conjoined:

(iv) There is/*are [a man and five women] in the garden.

Thus Bošković (1997:91–2) argues that *there* and *it* are identical in their associations, both failing to agree with a plural coordinate associate. Bošković argues that in both cases what is in fact going on is first conjunct agreement. In both (ii) and (iv) the first conjunct is singular, hence plural agreement is barred.

24. Postulating a *relation* between *it* and the CP associate is *not* tantamount to proposing representational chains as syntactic objects.

(95) John conjectured there to be a stranger in that haunted house. (Adapted from Bošković 1997:58, which uses *wager* in the position of *conjecture*.)

Recall, with *wager*, Bošković judges it grammatical, yet Collins says it '...does not seem particularly good.' We're not sure. Our analysis predicts it's bad. *There* is not propositional nor by hypothesis is its associate (*a stranger*). Thus LF replacement shouldn't 'save' it. Suppose we use a DP associate that is propositionally interpretable, appropriately adjusted to control for the definiteness effect:

(96) ±John conjectured there to be someone's illness documented in the file.

We're not sure of the status of this example, nor of its interpretation, and leave the (potentially quite interesting) matter for further research.

Before turning to the next topic, an alternative analysis of the expletive cases considered above, on the assumption that they are well formed, is worth speculation. Rather than saying that *conjecture* can assign ACC to DP... provided the DP can be propositionally interpreted, we say instead the following:

(97) *Conjecture* can assign ACC provided the DP lacks non-propositional content.

This allows in the expletive cases since the expletive does lack non-propositional content by virtue of lacking all semantic content. Alternatively, we might argue that *conjecture* assigns ACC Case only to non-referential DPs, but we leave the matter here.

Consider finally *wh*-movement. We are unclear about the status of *wh*-movement examples such as the following:

(98) ±Who did you conjecture to have upset Peter

See Bošković (1997:61) for an analysis of arguably analogous cases with *wager*; if these are improved, then (following Kayne 1984) the right approach seems to be that Case is somehow acquired through the process of overt *wh*-movement, a process unavailable to a DP like *Peter*. Notice also that to the extent that these are good, we make the wrong prediction (we predict they are bad), since *wh*-elements are not interpreted propositionally (but note that *wh*-elements are non-referential; hence the alternative analysis briefly considered above would seem to predict that (98) is well formed).

This brings us finally to the central example with which we began. Suppose there is no EPP and the expletive is thus omiss*able*, and is omitted:

(84)   *John conjectured [__ to seem Peter is ill]

What rules this out? Recall, if there is no expletive, and (if, following Bošković) *conjecture* altogether fails to assign ACC, then it is unclear how to exclude such cases. However, by appeal to the EPP, an expletive is forced, then excluded by Case requirements on it. This is one of Lasnik's arguments for EPP. But if, as we have argued, *conjecture* bears ACC and ACC must be discharged, then this example is excluded, in the same manner as the following:

(99)   John believes [__ to seem that Peter is ill]

That is, Case is uninterpretable on V/v, or to put it more contemporaneously, unless *v* as a probe successfully locally matches and values Case on a DP, the uninterpretable phi features remain in *v*, where they are uninterpretable at LF, thereby inducing crash.

Before turning to the nominal case where we can't rely on Case discharge, we briefly consider an alternative approach, one which we do not pursue here, but which is, interestingly, independently motivated, and excludes Lasnik's example without appeal to the EPP.

3.4.2.5 An alternative to the Case analysis, an unnoted consequence of Moro (1997)   Suppose, for the purposes of this section, that we are wrong and that, as Bošković claims, *conjecture* does *not* have ACC Case to assign. It may still be that we can exclude (84) without appeal to the EPP. The basic idea runs in this way.

Under Moro's (1997) analysis, expletive *it* is a type of *predicate* when co-occurring with *seems*, in for example,

(100)   It seems that Bill is smart.

Thus, for Moro *it* is not an expletive. What we would like to note here is that this has interesting implications for the central example,

(84)   *John conjectured [__ to seem Peter is ill]

Under our application of the Moro story, there is no predicate predicated of the finite CP *that Peter is ill*. This omission of *it* results in a violation of predication (or theta) theory. Thus appeal to the EPP, at least in this case, is unnecessary. In what follows we briefly review, and reveal the consequences regarding the EPP of relevant aspects of Moro's 1997 analysis.

To begin, Moro (1997) notes the following paradigm with *seem*:

(101)   a. *That John left seems.
           b. That John left seems weird/true/to be the case.
           c. *John is.
           d. John is weird.

The ungrammatical (101a) and (101c) are each rectified by the addition of a predicate. This type of fact leads Moro to unify the copular data and the *seem* data, by analyzing them both as small clause complement constructions underlyingly:

(102)   SEEM   [$_{sc}$ that John left   WEIRD]

(103)   BE   [$_{sc}$ John   WEIRD]

In each case the subject of the small clause predication undergoes raising (in our view, for Case checking).[25]

As Moro notes, the ungrammaticality of

(101)   a. *That John left seems.

indicates that a predicate (e.g. *weird*) is required. However, this now raises a problem. If *it* is a pure expletive, then the following should be ungrammatical, due to the lack of the required predicate:

(104)   *it* seems that John left.

Thus we have an apparent contradiction:

(105)   A predicate is required (**That John left seems*).

---

25. Again, we assume CPs can but need not check Case.

and

(106)   (if we assume *it*=expletive) It is not the case that a predicate is required (*it seems that John left*).

Moro's solution is to propose that in fact a predicate is required, and *it* is in fact a predicate (not a subject-expletive), what Moro calls a 'propredicate placeholder'. Thus, consistent with the small clause complement analysis for *seem*, Moro hypothesizes that *it* can appear underlyingly as the small clause predicate

(107)   *seem* [$_{SC}$ that John left *it*]

Here then we have a formal 'association' between *it* and the finite clause; they are, we presume, Merged and the so-called 'subject-predicate' relation is thereby formed.

Moro now faces at least 2 questions:
1. Why must *it* raise in this example, with the *that*-clause obligatorily remaining in situ, even though the *that*-clause can and must raise in (102) with *weird*? That is, what excludes

(108)   *That John left seems *it*
         (cf. *That John left seems weird.*)

2. What exactly is meant when Moro calls *it* a propredicate placeholder? And what exactly is the 'subject-predicate relation'? That is, if not the EPP, what formal principle of grammar forces the propredicate *it* into the structure?

As concerns the first question, Moro (1997:177) notes that one possible way of requiring that *it* raise in this example is to assume that *it* requires Case, whereas a *that*-clause does not. Thus, if the *that*-clause raises, leaving *it* in situ, the Case on *it* remains unchecked.[26]

---

26. Moro explores a second possible analysis couched in terms of Full Interpretation, under which propredicate *it* is likened to the raising verbs *have* and *be*, in that it is 'semantically underspecified'. Following Chomsky's (1993) analysis of these auxiliary verbs, Moro (1997:179) suggests that *it* is not visible to LF rules, and by Full Interpretation, it must be raised overtly (see Moro 1997:178 for discussion). Again, we have a redundancy, perhaps three-fold, between the EPP, Case and Full Interpretation.

(109)   *[That John left]$_j$ seems [t$_j$ it]

Although unnoted by Moro, this predicate analysis gets us some distance toward our goal of excluding (43) without appealing to the EPP. Recall that the problem illustrated in (43) is created precisely by omitting the expletive from the derivation/numeration.

(43)   John has conjectured [__ to seem that Peter is ill]

But this example is in fact excluded, under Moro's assumption that the *it* omitted from (43) is a predicate and as such is required (see below for further discussion). That is, this example is excluded for the same reason that the following is excluded

(110)   *That Peter is ill seems.

The idea is that (43) is excluded not by the EPP but by a requirement on predication. Thus, underlyingly, we must satisfy the 'predication requirement'; and one way of doing so is by merging *it* as the predicative sister of the finite clause:

(111)   John has conjectured [__ to seem [$_{sc}$ that Peter is ill *it*]

Crucially under Moro's analysis *it* appears in the underlying representation, and is, we presume, within contemporary implementation, First Merged with the *that*-clause. Then we could appeal to Case to exclude *it* in this position.[27]

This brings us to the second question posed above: why precisely is this 'propredicate placeholder' forced into the predicate position? We're not sure what formal principle within Moro's analysis bars the omission of propredicate *it*. But to address the problem raised by (43) we need to explain why a predicate, such as *it*, is forced into the structure. As concerns *it*, we'd like to tentatively suggest an answer, by slightly modifying a suggestion made by Moro (1997:195).

---

27. If *it* raises to the, by our hypothesis, ACC-assigned ECM position of *conjecture*, the result seems to us radically improved. Recall, however, that we have claimed that the ECM ACC recipient must receive propositional interpretation and it isn't transparently the case that '*propredicate*' *it* is interpreted propositionally. Nonetheless, above we alluded to the association between *it* and the *that* clause as a possible approach to allowing such cases (104). Within Moro's analysis the association is directly expressed (by First Merge); what remains is a fully formal account of the manner in which *it* is propositionally interpreted.

As Moro notes, citing Ruwet (1982), the following are synonymous:

(112)   IT seems that John is sad.

(113)   It seems TRUE that John is sad.

We suspect the following is also synonymous.

(114)   That John is sad seems TRUE.

Moro (1997:195) suggests that this is not coincidental and is a 'syntactically codified' phenomenon:[28]

> ...the configuration with the propredicate IT...is assigned by default the interpretation which we have in the case of the associated sentence that actually has the word 'true'...[fn. deleted]

As Moro proposes, this might well explain, by appeal only to s-selection, not c-selection, why the following is ungrammatical

(115)   *It seems [for John to be sad]

Under Moro's analysis, the underlying structure is

(116)   SEEMS [$_{sc}$ for John to be sad IT]

In this configuration *it* assigns by default the *true* theta role to the infinitive CP. But as Moro notes, there is independent evidence that true cannot be predicated of such infinitives (which seem to receive a conditionally irrealis interpretation at least here), as evidenced by

(117)   *For John to be sad is true.

This is presumably due to s-selectional properties of *true* barring an irrealis from receiving the theta role assigned by true. This then s-selectively accounts for the anomaly of *seem* with a *for*-infinitive complement, without appeal to c-selection.

---

28. See Moro (1997:195, fns. 20 and 21) for further discussion of this matter.

Slightly modifying Moro's analysis here in which he proposes that a *configuration* is assigned a *default interpretation*, we'd like to suggest instead that *it* in such cases is not a propredicate placeholder, but rather assigns a theta role, the same one that is assigned by *true*.

Thus, as discussed, in examples like

(104)   It seems that John left.

The argumental *that*-clause must be assigned a theta role and it is assigned a theta role by *it* (under Merge) and *it* assigns the same theta role that is assigned by *true*.[29] Under this analysis, it is the theta criterion that bars (43) – i.e., a predicate is required to theta-mark the finite clause. If *it* serves as the theta assigner, Case requirements then force *it* to raise. If *it* is omitted (**that John left seems*) a theta criterion violation results, since the *that*-clause lacks a theta role, a hypothesis supported by the fact that the addition of a theta assigner which theta-assigns the *that*-clause remedies the anomaly.

(101)   a.   *That John left seems.

(118)   [That John left]$_j$ seems [t$_j$ WEIRD]

(119)   IT$_j$ seems [that John left t$_j$]

Note finally that in suggesting that the 'theta role' *true* is assigned to the *that*-clause by *it*, we are not committed to the view that the speaker asserts the truth of

---

29. Perhaps independent evidence for our analysis of *it* as assigning the *truth* theta role, is found in the following

     (i)   *I consider John it.

vs.

     (ii)   a.   I consider that analysis it.
                   b.   That analysis is it, I'm sure.
                   c.   That John left the scene of the crime is it.

Example (i) is out, meaning anomalously that John is true, but (iia) is allowed, and means something along the lines of 'this analysis is true.' Notice that there is a felicitous reading of (i), as in I consider John to be 'the right one'. If *it* is indeed a predicate, its theta assigning properties require further research.

the *that*-clause, rather only that it *seems* true. Thus, as predicted, the following is not self-contradictory:

(120)   It seems that John left is false.

Rather under our analysis, it means

(121)   Seems [that-John-left =TRUE] is false.

In summary, more research is required to explore our suggested theta theoretic extension of Moro's independently-motivated analysis. If viable, we have a way of excluding (43) without appeal to the EPP; rather, the theta criterion is violated and we exploit a previously unnoted partial redundancy between the theta criterion (or predication within Moro's analysis and the EPP).

Note finally if *there* is 'predicative' as Moro also argues, then perhaps the following analog of (43) can also be reduced to the theta criterion as well:

(122)   John has conjectured [__ to be a man outside]

Again, under the Moro analysis, this is excluded due to the omission of a required predicate.

3.4.2.6 Some limits of Moro and some new problems Adapting Moro provides an EPP-independent analysis of (43), but there are limits to its coverage. First, under our adaptation of Moro's analysis as traced above, there is no way to exclude the following modification of (43) in which a predicate theta-assigning the *that*-clause *does* appear, but the predicate is not *it*, and being adjectival doesn't require Case.

(123)   John has conjectured [__ to seem [that Bill left WEIRD]

Here, the theta criterion is satisfied: *weird* theta marks the *that*-clause. Thus, Moro, coupled with the assumption that *conjecture* lacks Case, appears to drive us back to the EPP to exclude such examples. (However, if *conjecture* bears ACC Case, as we suggested above, then the example is excluded due to a failure of Case discharge (the inverse Case Filter).)

Similarly, it is important to note that Moro does *not* analyze all so-called *it*-expletives as predicates. Consider the following:

(124)   It is obvious that John left.

As Moro notes, in contrast to the *seem* case there is already an overt predicate present in this construction, namely *obvious*, indicating that in this case *it* is not predicative. Another difference between *seem* and *obvious*, as mentioned above, is the following:

(125)   *That John left seems.

(126)   That John left is obvious.

Given these differences, Moro analyzes the latter as

(127)   BE [$_{SC}$ that John left   obvious]

The surface form is derived by raising the *that*-clause to Spec, TP. The question now is how does Moro analyze the following?

(124)   It is obvious that John left.

Here, Moro (1997:180) proposes that (i) *it* is generated as the subject – not the predicate – of the small clause; (ii) *obvious* is the predicate of the small clause; (iii) the *that*-clause appears as a right adjunct to S; and (iv) *it* undergoes raising to subject position.

(128)   [$_S$ [$_S$ It$_j$ [$_{VP}$ V=BE [$_{SC}$ t$_j$ obvious]]] [$_S$ that John left]] (Moro 1997:183)

Nonetheless, the exact derivation isn't entirely clear to us. Moro (1997:183) writes

> As for the position of the finite clause...we can simply follow the standard account and assume that it is in an adjunct position (technically 'extraposed')...

We are not sure whether Moro intends that the *that*-clause is base generated in adjunct position or is moved from some unspecified position ('extraposed') to the adjunct position. What is clear is that Moro intends that *it* is *not* base generated in the matrix Spec, TP position, but is instead base generated as the subject of the SC whose predicate is *obvious*. (For Moro (p. 183), under Full Interpretation, *it* must raise, otherwise FI excludes the derivation; hence, base generation in Spec, TP is precluded.)

The question we now confront is: What formal principle P of the grammar (P $\neq$ EPP) forces *it* to be generated as the subject of *obvious*?

Thus, directly relevant to our analysis is the question: what excludes the following analog of (43) where *obvious* replaces *seem*?

(129)   *John conjectured [__to be obvious [that Peter is ill]

Here, unlike with our analysis of *seem*, it is difficult to reduce the presence of *it* to the Theta Criterion. If we were to postulate that *obvious* assigns a theta role to the 'subject' position of the small clause (as it seems to in *that John left is obvious*), one could perhaps argue that *it* is forced into the structure by the Theta Criterion; *it* would be needed to receive the theta role of *obvious*. However, this analysis might be unmaintainable as it would overgenerate any argument in this position, for example:

(130)   *John is obvious that Fred left.

Therefore, without the EPP it is not clear how Moro's analysis forces *it* into the structure. An intimately related question (we suspect) is this: within Moro's analysis (128) how does the adjoined CP acquire a theta role? Ultimately, the question reduces to the enduring one (which we too have by no means fully answered): what exactly is the association between *it* and the finite CP, and for us, does that arguably independent association render appeal to the EPP unnecessary in this domain?

As mentioned at the outset of this section, although we ultimately do not adopt the Moro analysis here, we believe it merits further research as it may provide another means of or aid to eliminating the EPP, since, as we have shown here, this independently motivated analysis induces yet more redundancy with the EPP.

3.4.2.7 Some residue of the EPP   Notice that our proposed Case discharge analysis, whereby *conjecture* bears ACC Case, covers all of the examples that were problematic for the analysis considered in the last section. Thus, (129) repeated here

(129)   *John conjectured [__to be obvious [that Peter is ill]

is correctly disallowed since *conjecture* cannot discharge its uninterpretable ACC Case.[30]

Under our proposed elimination of the EPP, however, certain cases still elude our Case discharge proposal. First, suppose that we simply remove *conjecture* from (130). The result is still ungrammatical, yet there is no undischarged ACC Case:

(131)   [__to be obvious [that Peter is ill]

Here we cannot appeal to undischarged ACC Case. However, this example is arguably excluded by a prohibition barring matrix infinitives. In order to satisfy this prohibition, suppose we embed the example, as follows

(132)   *It is dangerous [__ to be obvious [that Peter is ill]]

(See Martin 1999 for an analogous example.) As Martin notes, if PRO appears in the underscored Spec T position, the example can be excluded since PRO is an argument but lacks a theta role here. But, as Martin also notes, suppose we entirely omit PRO (the same EPP-motivating technique under which expletives are simply omitted). Martin (1999) would disallow this as a null Case violation, i.e. *dangerous* selects null Case checking *to*, and with no Spec of *to* present, this uninterpretable Case is undischarged.

---

30. One question confronting our analysis is why *conjecture* can't discharge its ACC Case on the embedded CP in situ, under Chomsky's Probe-Goal analysis. Recall that we suggested above (see footnote 25) that sentential subject CPs can check NOM on T. In fact, however, we'll suggest in Chapter 4 that Case can be checked only in the spec-head configuration, and thus probe-goal checking of the ACC of *conjecture* with the CP in (129) is prohibited. Notice that raising the embedded CP to the ACC case position of *conjecture* improves the example, we think:

   (i)   John conjectured that Peter is ill to be obvious.

   Note that if (i) is relatively well formed, then the word string in (129) is potentially grammatical under the rightward extraposition of the finite CP. We've assumed that (129) is ungrammatical, but on the non-extraposed analysis. Intonational factors seem relevant in distinguishing the structures associated with (129).

We would extend the same analysis to the sentential subject analog,

(133)   *[__ to be obvious [that Peter is ill]] is dangerous

That is, we would suggest that the infinitival subject originates as a complement of *dangerous*, hence here too *to* is selected by *dangerous*, and contains undischarged null Case, thereby excluding this example as well.

But finally, suppose we change *dangerous* to a raising predicate, i.e. a predicate that fails to select null Case to, as in:

(134)   *[__ to be obvious [that Peter is ill] is likely
          (cf. the grammatical: *For it to be obvious that Peter is ill is likely.*
                    It is likely to be obvious that Peter is ill.)

Here we cannot appeal to the following to exclude the example:

   (i)   Undischarged null Case, since we've used raising *to*.
   (ii) Undischarged ACC, since we've omitted an upstairs ACC-assigning verb.
   (iii) The ban on matrix infinitives, satisfied here.
   (iv) Morovian requirements on predication. (Recall the *it* co-occurring with *obvious* (and the *it* is omitted here) is, for Moro, an underlying small clause subject, and it is not clear to us what forces its presence for Moro, as discussed in the previous section.)

Thus here we seem to be compelled to appeal to the EPP, although we hope to have suggested that such an appeal is no solution to the problem. We would hope people would not respond as follows: 'no further research is necessary; the example is readily explained by the EPP.' In the following section we explore a redundancy between null complementizer theory and the EPP. Although our primary focus will be on infinitival complements to nominals, we will suggest that the problematic example above is excluded because sentential subjects require overt complementizers; hence (134) above will be argued to be analogous to

(135)   *Peter is ill is likely.

We will attempt to derive this from independently motivated theories of null affixal complementizers.

3.4.2.8 A note on Bošković's (2002) dual activation approach There is yet another analysis of the ungrammaticality of (84), repeated here,

(84) *John conjectured [__ to seem Peter is ill]

(and, more generally, of the BELIEVE class of elements) that does not appeal to the EPP. Bošković (2002) observes in a footnote that (84) is correctly disallowed under the following two assumptions of Chomsky's (1999, 2000) probe-goal system:

(136) a. non-control *to* bears a proper subset of the phi features (specifically, the person feature)
       b. The operation Agree (X,Y) requires that both X and Y are 'active' (i.e. that both contain unchecked, unvalued features; let's refer to this as the 'dual activation' condition)

Since non-control *to* bears certain of the phi features, and since phi features are uninterpretable on T, it follows that *to*'s feature(s) must be checked. However, since non-control *to* is phi defective (i.e. since it does not bear the *full set* of phi features person, gender, and number), it follows that *to* itself cannot check Case. Under Chomsky's probe-goal system, agreement feature checking can take place in situ. Thus, for example, in a typical existential structure as in (137)

(137) there T is a man outside *vs.* there T are men outside

Agree applies between T and *a man* resulting in the checking (valuation) of T's phi features (and resulting in the checking of *man*'s Case feature), but there is no movement relation (overt or otherwise) between T and *a man*. It is *there* that checks T's EPP feature, for Chomsky.

As Bošković points out, (84) is excluded under Chomsky's system: *to* probes down in order to find an element that can check its feature, but since the only potential candidate, namely *Peter*, is 'inactive' since all of its features, specifically, its Case feature, have been checked, it cannot participate in Agree given (136b). There is, in short, no 'dual activation' between *to* and *Peter* and hence Agree(*to,Peter*) cannot apply thereby causing crash by virtue of *to* having unchecked features. Note further that if this analysis is right, there is yet a further redundancy between the EPP and independently motivated mechanisms; namely between the EPP and in situ probe-goal combined with 'dual activation'.

However, there is an interesting, and unnoted, negative consequence of the analysis reviewed above. Consider (138)

(138)   I believe [it to have been likely that Bill left]

If there is no EPP, then nothing forces *it* to merge into the spec of *to* position. Thus, it would appear to be the case that *it* could merge directly into the ACC position (i.e. spec of Agr_O) of *believe* checking *it*'s Case feature. The problem now though is that since the only potential candidate for checking *to*'s person feature is *Bill*, then since *Bill* is inactive, the structure should be out since Agree(*to*, *Bill*) cannot apply. Thus, it would appear that the EPP-less probe-goal 'dual activation' analysis of (84), undergenerates (138).

We could allow (138) if we could somehow force the expletive to 'start' below *to* and then move up to the ACC Case position. In this regard, consider the abstract representation in (139)

(139) $to_{defective}$ ... DP

Suppose, as in Chomsky (2000), that non-control *to* bears the person feature. Then, *to* must find some matching element to check its person feature, but since it's phi-defective this *to* cannot check Case. The DP in (139) is a potential person checker for *to*. However, if DP has its Case checked, as in (84), then this DP is 'inactive' and cannot participate in Agree(*to*, DP). On the other hand, if the DP *is* active by virtue of not having its Case feature checked, it can participate in Agree with *to* (resulting in *to*'s person feature being checked), but the DP cannot get its Case feature checked by this defective *to*. Thus, the DP would have to get its Case feature checked by some element other than *to*. If *it* in (138) starts low, as in, say (140),

(140)   I believe to have been likely it that Bill left

the 'right' configuration would exist: *to* checks its person feature with *it* (since *it* has not yet checked its Case feature and thus is still 'active') and then *it* moves up to the ACC position of *believe* in order to check its Case feature (and checked *to* would not block this *believe*-to-*it* relation).

But the question is: what forces the *it* to start low? It's not the EPP (we're assuming there is no EPP). We might appeal to Moro's analysis according to which *it* in

(140) would start low given that *it* is a predicate that must associate with the *that*-clause. Interestingly, the Moro analysis would force the representation in (140). However, even for Moro, *it* is not forced to start low in (141)

(141)   I believe it to have seemed weird that Bill left

In (141) it is *weird* that serves as the predicate of the *that*-clause and *it* is a non-predicational expletive that presumably could merge directly into the ACC Case position of *believe*. Furthermore, Bošković (2002) presents evidence that in fact expletives *don't* move. Thus the problem we raised for (138) above remains.

Overall, Bošković notes an interesting possible account of (84) that does not appeal to the EPP. If that analysis is right, there is yet a further redundancy with the EPP. However, there is a potential problem with the approach, represented by the undergeneration of (138). We note in closing that (138) does not represent a problem for the analysis of (84) that we have developed. (84) is out since the ACC features of *conjecture* are not checked. (138) is in, on the other hand, since we're assuming that *to* has *no* features at all to check, and hence the 'dual activation' issue does not arise.

3.4.3   A new problem: nominal conjecture

We have suggested a possible reanalysis of the VERB *conjecture*, one in which *conjecture* is a Case-assigner that requires propositional interpretation of its Case recipient. Importantly, it would seem that our overall Case discharge account cannot be extended to the nominal form of *conjecture*. Thus to begin consider

(142)   *[the conjecture [it to be possible that Fred left]] turned out to be false

The NOUN *conjecture*, bearing inherent Case if any, cannot assign inherent Case exceptionally to the infinitival subject. This example can then be excluded since it lacks Case. Similarly for the propositionally interpretable DP *Mary's illness*, as in (143).

(143)   *The conjecture [Mary's illness to have upset Fred]] turned out to be false

But if there is no EPP, and nouns do not assign Case exceptionally, what rules out the following – in which a subject is simply omitted from the expletive position?

(144)   *[The conjecture [__ to be possible that Fred left]] turned out to be false

In the case of the VERB *conjecture* we sought in the previous section to reduce such phenomena to undischarged ACC Case on the verb, an option that does not seem available with the NOUN *conjecture*. This seems to motivate the EPP in this domain. In the remainder of the current chapter we will explore a number of different independently motivated approaches to this problem, none of which appeal to the EPP.

3.4.3.1 Failure to select non-control to One possible way to exclude examples like (144) above, without appeal to the EPP, is through the following generalization

(145)   Descriptive generalization:
        Nouns cannot take on infinitival complements of the non-control type (see, e.g., Lasnik 2002:5).

However, Lasnik (2002) argues that if this descriptive generalization is true, then it would be preferable to explain it. With regard to the example he discusses, namely

(146)   *The belief [__ to seem [Peter is ill]]

Lasnik writes:

> The only obvious explanation... must rely on the EPP; the infinitival clause lacks a subject. One might object that for some independent reason, *belief* (and nouns in general) simply cannot take an infinitival complement of the non-Control type.

Lasnik continues:

> Descriptively, it is certainly true that nouns never take such complements. But in the absence of a better account of the fact, it seems most principled to rely on the combination of the Case Filter and the EPP.

We agree entirely with Lasnik's commitment to going beyond what may seem to be empirically adequate descriptive generalizations, and seeking to deduce them from deeper principles. If nouns don't take non-control infinitival complements, then we, like Lasnik, would like to ask *why* that it is, and want to explain it. Where we disagree concerns the nature of explanation, an admittedly delicate matter. Specifically, we disagree that 'the only obvious explanation... must rely on the EPP.' We think it is preferable, at least for the time being, to rely on the admittedly descriptive trans-lexical generalization, which avoids all the problems associated with the EPP and has the merit of focusing future efforts on explaining why the generalization might be true. In the following sections, we explore analyses under which the descriptive generalization, or at least the parts of it relevant to the elimination of the EPP, is derived by appeal to independently motivated lexical properties. We end this section by noting that, in fact, the descriptive generalization may not be true. Consider the following examples:

(147) My preference for it to be likely that my horse will win is clear.

(148) My desire for it to be obvious that he is smart pleased them.

These are well formed and if the *for*-phrase is a complement, the examples would violate the descriptive generalization. The analyses presented below allow (147) and (148), correctly so in our view.

3.4.3.2 Is inherent Case on Ns interpretable?   Again, suppose we have no EPP and suppose that there is no selectional prohibition against N taking a non-control infinitival complement. Then, the question becomes what disallows

(149)   *[the conjecture [__ to be likely that Fred left]] was false

One possibility is that, likening the nominal case to the verbal case, this example too is bad because the N bears undischarged, and by hypothesis uninterpretable, Case. The difference is that the verb bears structural, while the nominal bears inherent, Case. This requires that inherent Case on the noun is uninterpretable, as is structural Case on the verb. (The fact that inherent Case is associated with theta role assignment does not necessarily entail that inherent Case is itself interpretable on the nominal head.) We leave the implementation of this idea to future research.[31]

---

31. While the specifics of inherent case are unclear (see Chomsky 1986, see particularly p. 193, and Bošković 1997), one possible implementation of this is that the nominal head bears unvalued phi features which become valued only under phi feature matching with an inherent Case bearing DP, adapting the probe-goal analysis of structural Case (Chomsky 2001a).
    If inherent Case must indeed be discharged from the noun, questions emerge regarding, at the very least, four types of construction: one with no apparent complement to the noun (ia); one with

3.4.3.3 A stranded, null, affixal C Another approach to (149), repeated here,

(149) *[the conjecture [__ to be likely that Fred left]] was false

is based, in part, on analyses in Martin (1999) and Bošković and Lasnik (2003), which in turn borrow from and extend key ideas of Pesetsky (1991) and Ormazabal (1995). Essentially, we seek to derive the descriptive generalization that such nouns do not take non-control infinitives as in (149) from the idea that these non-control infinitives are full CPs with an affixal null C head. (By contrast, the CPs in (147) and (148) are headed by the overt C^0 *for*.) This affixal null C requires an appropri-

---

an overt propositionally interpretable DP complement to the noun (as in (ib)); one with a finite CP complement ((ic)); and the ECM configuration with a noun (as already discussed).

(i) a. The conjecture upset me.
 b. *?The doctor's conjecture of Mary's illness upset me.
 c. The doctor's conjecture that Mary was ill upset me.

To begin, (ia) is grammatical. However, if the inherent Case is obligatorily discharged, as our account requires, the question is: why is (ia) grammatical? A possible answer is that it's grammatical because inherent Case is discharged onto a phonetically null recipient (for a related discussion see Martin 1999, fn. 13). Notice in this regard that indeed (ia) is interpreted consistent with the view that *conjecture* theta marks a null propositional argument. Of course this raises widespread and notoriously difficult issues regarding lexical, semantic, syntactic, vs. discoursal mental representations of 'transitivity'. The correct division of labor is especially unclear within DPs and we leave the matter here, as exploring it would take us too far afield in the present context.

Consider next (ib). It may be predicted good under our analysis. Suppose that the hypothesized inherent Case of the N *conjecture* can be discharged only on a propositionally interpreted recipient (analogous to the verb *conjecture*). In (ib), the DP *Mary's illness* can be interpreted propositionally and hence the inherent Case of *conjecture* might be appropriately discharged. But (ib) seems as bad to us as the corresponding verbal case: *that the doctor conjectured Mary's illness upset me*.

Consider next (ic). If *conjecture* must discharge inherent Case, then one possible recipient is the embedded CP. Let's suppose that the CP can check the inherent case of *conjecture*. But this raises a new question about how to exclude our central example,

(ii) *The conjecture [__ to seem that Bill left] upset me

Why can't the inherent Case of *conjecture* be discharged with the complement CP here, just as we speculated it is in the finite case (ic). Suppose, along the lines of Case and phi feature checking with DPs, the CP goal like a DP goal must be phi complete to effect inherent Case checking. Then the contrast between (ic) and (ii) would emerge. But again, this raises a serious problem: why not probe 'through' the *to seem* just as we argue you do with 'successive cyclic' A-raising:

(iii) That Bill left is likely __ to seem __ to have upset Mary ate host, which, by hypothesis, it cannot find in examples such as (149). Thus, such examples are excluded as 'stranded affix' violations, without any appeal to the EPP. Moreover, the components of this EPP-less analysis are each independently motivated. The approach is developed in Epstein, Pires, and Seely (2004); we review that analysis and extend it below.

3.4.3.4 Martin (1999) derives only a proper subset of the nominal cases We begin by noting that Martin (1999) provides an analysis, without any appeal to the EPP, of a nominal case similar to (149). Consider

(150)   *The belief [__ to seem that [Peter is ill]] upset Mary. (see Bošković 1997, Martin 1999)[32]

Martin (1999) suggests that (150) is excluded as it ultimately violates 'Myers' Generalization' (Myers 1984).

(151)   Myers' Generalization:
... if zero derivation is a kind of inflection, we predict that no zero-derived word could [can] appear inside a derivational suffix, i.e. no such suffix could [can] be added to a zero-derived word. (Myers 1984:62)

Martin's basic analysis runs as follows: (i) a nominal like *belief* is derived (in the syntax/morphology) from its verbal root, and that root takes a full CP complement, which in this case has a null complementizer; (ii) following Pesetsky (1991), Martin assumes that this null complementizer is an affix; (iii) the affix incorporates into the verb *believe*; and (iv) the [*believe* + null affix C] element is then input to nominalizing affixation (so as to derive the N *belief*). However, by Myers' Generalization, a zero-derived element (like *believe* + null affix C) cannot host a derivational affix

---

32. Bošković (1997) is the first to argue for the EPP on the basis of examples like (150) and he provides a more comprehensive paradigm than the one we present here; see Bošković (1997) for further discussion. Bošković (2002), on the other hand, argues against the EPP but presents (150) as problematic for the elimination of the EPP. He argues that the cases, besides (150), that purportedly motivated the EPP are redundantly ruled out by independently motivated principles of the grammar and hence that the EPP 'should' be eliminated. Bošković, in fact, points out that 'the EPP seems to be the only formal requirement on the target that is apparently not allowed to drive movement,' and thus that 'it simply does not make sense.' See also Martin (1999) for important discussion. Bošković (personal communication) points out to us that (150) is disallowed under the 'Activation Condition' of Chomsky (2001a); the defective EPP probe *to* Matches with the local DP *Peter* but Agree cannot operate since the goal *Peter* has already had its Case feature checked and hence is 'inactive'.

(see also Allen 1978). Hence (150) is correctly disallowed by the independently motivated Myers' Generalization, and there is no need to appeal to the EPP.

Notice that Martin's (1999) Myersian analysis of (150) derives a proper subset of the cases that support the descriptive generalization that 'nouns never take infinitival complements of the non-control type.' For Martin, in any case equivalent to (152), the null complementizer (assumed to be an affix) must incorporate into the verb (otherwise the 'stranded affix constraint' will be violated):

(152)   verb [$_{CP}$ null C [$_{TP}$ to$_{non\text{-}control}$ ...]]

but then the verb+null C is a zero-derived word which cannot be nominalized, since the nominalizing affix is derivational and derivational affixes can't take a zero-derived word as host, according to Myers.[33]

3.4.3.5 Martin (1999) does not account for underived nominals
Interestingly, Martin (1999) does not consider another possibility. Suppose that the N head taking the CP complement is *not* a *deverbal* nominal, but is instead an underived nominal:

(153)   underived-noun [$_{CP}$ C [$_{TP}$ to$_{non\text{-}control}$ ...]]

In this case, as Bošković (1997: 43) points out, there is no violation of Myers' Generalization; rather, the null C incorporates into the non zero-derived noun, and the result is (ceteris paribus) predicted well formed.[34] In fact, however, it is not well formed. This situation is precisely what arises relative to the example that started this section, namely,

---

33. Ormazabal (1995:128, fn. 45) notes that Lasnik (personal communication) observes that the success of the analysis rests on rule ordering: first the null C incorporates, then subsequent derivational affixation of the nominalizing affix is blocked by Myers' Generalization. However, the opposite ordering is not blocked. See Ormazabal 1995 for analyses blocking a derivation in which Nominalization precedes zero-affixation.

34. Ormazabal (1995:136) (citing Bošković, personal communication, and Chomsky 1970) notes that underived nominals are also incompatible with the null complementizer, yet being underived they escape Myers' Generalization, as in

(i)   *Their hypothesis [∅ neural nets are not connected].   (Ormazabal 1995:ex. 108b)

Cases like (i) in which we have an infinitival raising complement, and their relevance to the EPP, are to the best of our knowledge not noted in Ormazabal (1995).

(149) *[the conjecture [__ to be likely that Fred left]] was false

The Martin (1999) analysis fails to exclude (149). In order to illustrate this, note to begin with that Martin (1999) argues that (154) (a verbal case not equivalent to (149))

(154) *Bill conjectured [__ to seem that Fred left]

is excluded since the verb *conjecture* is derived from the noun *conjecture*; thus, according to Martin (1999), in (154) the null C incorporates into the noun *conjecture* to yield the zero-derived word [[*conjecture*]$_N$ +C]; but this zero-derived element is then, by Myers, not accessible to the verbalizing derivational affix. Thus, for Martin, it is required that the verb in (154) is derived from the noun, ultimately leading to a violation of Myers' Generalization in this case. Crucially then, Martin clearly assumes that the noun *conjecture* is *not* derived from the verb. But, unnoted in Martin (1999) is that (149) above is ungrammatical; and it is unclear why it is so. Specifically, (149) does not violate Myers' Generalization. This is because it is the VERB *conjecture* (as in (154)) that is zero-derived from the noun, hence we assume the noun *conjecture* is not zero-derived. Thus, in (149) the null C incorporates into the *un*derived noun *conjecture* and there is no violation of Myers' generalization.[35]

So even with Martin's analysis of (150), it would seem that (149) is an important remaining argument (a 'loophole') motivating appeal to the EPP. *With* the EPP (149) is out since the spec of the lower TP (spec of *to*) is empty.

3.4.3.6 Toward a solution: adapting Bošković and Lasnik (2003) and Ormazabal (1995) We suggest here that an approach to null complementizers as affixes, as proposed by Pesetsky (1991) and adopted with modifications by Bošković and Lasnik (2003), supplemented with a proposal in Ormazabal (1995), each motivated

---

35. Bošković and Lasnik (2003) note an empirical problem for the Pesetsky (1991) null C analysis (using Myers' Generalization) of examples like (**the belief [__ to seem that Peter is ill] upset Mary*); specifically Bošković and Lasnik argue that the analysis does not extend to *non*derived nominals like **the fact C Mary left*. Since the noun *fact* is not derived, there is no possibility of violating Myers' Generalization. Bošković and Lasnik state that to account for **the fact C Mary left* there would have to be appeal to the 'complicating assumption that all nouns are derived when taking a clausal complement' (p. 534–5). What (i) above shows, however, is that it's more than a complicating assumption; in fact it's impossible to derive all cases under that assumption, (149) being the case in point, since here we have a noun from which the verb is derived; hence the noun itself is by hypothesis underived, immunizing this data from a Myersian account.

on entirely independent grounds, actually excludes (149). Thus, even this apparent 'loophole' can be correctly excluded without appeal to the EPP.

Bošković and Lasnik (2003) (henceforth B&L) propose a theory of null complementizers that assumes the principles in (155):

(155)   a.   The English lexicon contains null complementizers that are (PF) affixes and require a lexical host.
           b.   Affix hopping is PF merger.
           c.   PF merger requires adjacency at PF.

Under these assumptions, B&L account for the ill-formedness of structures such as (156), lacking the complementizer *that*, as a 'stranded affix' violation: the null C, which in this case is by hypothesis an affix that requires a lexical (+V) host, is not adjacent to a +V category at PF.

(156)   *it seemed at that time [$_{CP}$ C [David had left]]

Now, consider again our central case (149),

(149)   *[the conjecture [__ to be likely that Fred left]] was false

One unnoted consequence of the B&L analysis is as follows. First, following Ormazabal (1995), suppose the infinitival complement to the noun *conjecture* in (149) is a CP projection, headed by a null C. Assuming that the null C in this case is an affix which requires a +V host, then (149) is out since the N *conjecture* can't host the C. Indeed, in relevant respects (149) is similar (except for the [−tense] of the lower CP) to B&L's example (157) (p. 534):

(157)   *I heard about the fact C Mary did it.   (=B&L 2003:534, ex. 13)

In (157) the affixal null C is assumed by B&L to require a +V host and so can't take the adjacent N *fact* as its host, and thus the null affix C is stranded.

Under this approach, (149) is excluded not because we 'need to have a subject', but because we have +affix null C that can't find an appropriate host. This provides an independently motivated account of the critical example (149) *without appeal to the EPP*.

In fact, B&L don't note it, but it seems their analysis can (be made to) derive the descriptive generalization that there is no N that can take a raising (non-control) infinitival as its complement.[36] In earlier work, as discussed above, Lasnik (2002) claimed that this descriptive generalization follows in part from the EPP; i.e. in (149) above, *to* requires a Spec, TP so (149) is out as an EPP violation (and if we fill the Spec, TP with an overt expletive *there* will be a Case Filter violation). But, given that the null affix C account is independently motivated (as B&L argue), and was proposed independent of EPP-related issues, then we have yet another redundancy between the EPP and independently motivated principles. One obvious path to follow, then, is to 'eliminate' the EPP's utility in this loophole case as well – as we've shown, we can account for (149) without the EPP. Note further that regardless of the EPP, B&L need the null affixal C analysis to account for the ill-formedness of:

(158)   * the conjecture [C [it seems that Fred left]] is ludicrous
        (cf. *the conjecture [that it seems that Fred left] is ludicrous*)

Presumably, what blocks (158) is the fact that the null affixal C can't affix to the N *conjecture*; but our point is that the very same analysis cannot be prevented from automatically extending to (149) (if indeed there is also a CP complement here, according to Ormazabal's proposal), rendering the EPP unnecessary to exclude even this loophole in the Martin (1999), Myers-based, analysis.

3.4.3.7 Does B&L subsume Myers?   Adapting independently motivated proposals of Bošković and Lasnik (2003) and Ormazabal (1995), we have suggested that we can derive the generalization that Ns do not take (subjectless) non-control

---

36. Recall that we have argued that the descriptive generalization might be false given such examples as *my desire for it to be obvious that he is smart pleased them*. What's important for present purposes is that we derive the relevant part of the descriptive generalization, namely, that if a N takes an infinitival raising complement, the subject of that complement must be realized. Thus, we need to block not only (149) in the text, but also **my desire to be obvious that he is smart pleased them*. The null C analysis presented above can do just that.
    What about 'control' complements to nouns:

    (i)   the desire C to win

    Why is (i) good? If there is a null C here – as in (149) above – and if that null C can't take N as its host, then (i) should be out. Note, however, there is extensive evidence (see Ormazabal 1995, Bošković 1997, Pesetsky 1991) that control infinitives are bare IPs, not CPs, and thus there is in fact no C at all, hence no null C, in (i).

infinitives and can do so without appeal to the EPP. Instead, what disallows examples such as

(159) *the conjecture [__ to be likely that Bill left] upset us

is the fact that the null, affixal C can't find an appropriate host.

For Martin (1999) what counts as an 'appropriate host' is a non zero-derived element (Martin crucially relies on Myers' Generalization as we have seen). Our extension of B&L claims that what counts as an 'appropriate host' in (159) is the categorial status of the potential host; specifically, that the null C of the non-control infinitival complement can't take a +N element as host. It would seem, then, that B&L subsume Martin: specifically, with respect to nominals, we need not appeal to Myers' Generalization. However, the matter becomes more complicated when we return to complements to verbs. Some of the relevant issues are considered in what follows.

Notice first that (160) below is bad:

(160) *I conjectured Bill left   (cf. *I conjectured that Bill left.*)

Suppose the V *conjecture* is derived from the N *conjecture*, as Martin argues. Then, it would seem that we need Myers to disallow (160). We would assume that the finite complement of the derived verb *conjecture* is a CP with a null affixal C head. Then, this null C can't affix to the derived V *conjecture* by Myers.

However, we might exclude (160) by instead saying that the null, affix C can't affix to the verb *conjecture*, not by virtue of the fact that this V is derived, but simply by virtue of the fact that it is a verb. Thus, the claim is that the null C can't take a +V as host, essentially adopting the B&L account.

If we use the B&L approach for (160), i.e., if (160) is out since the null C can't attach to +V, then we would be claiming, in effect, that the null C can take neither V nor N as a host, which leaves open the question of whether it can take *anything* as its host. Presumably the null affixal C in (160) is the same null affixal C that occurs in *the conjecture Bill left (vs. *the conjecture that Bill left*). But, regardless of whether we adopt Myers or B&L to exclude (160), we apparently need to say that with *infinitival* complements to the verb *conjecture*, the complement is a bare IP and not a CP. If it were a CP headed by a null C that can't take the verb *conjecture* as host, then we incorrectly exclude examples such as the following, which we have argued to be relatively good:

(70)   I conjectured Mary's illness to have upset Bill.

If the infinitival complement here is a bare IP, we correctly allow (70) above. But, we need to be sure that we don't incorrectly also allow:

(161)   I conjectured [__ to be likely that Bill left]

Fortunately, even if this is a bare IP, we can get it out under our earlier hypothesis that *conjecture* has ACC Case, which goes undischarged in this example; see section 4.2.

If this is on the right track, then perhaps we can avoid appeal to the EPP given our ACC Case analysis, combined with independently motivated null affixal C analyses.

There is a further previously unnoted consequence of the null C analysis, as adapted above. Consider again the example in (162a), which was presented as a 'residue of the EPP' in section 4.2.7:

(162)   a. *To be obvious that Peter is ill is likely.
        b. *It to be obvious that Peter is ill is likely.
        c. *For to be obvious that Peter is ill is likely.
        d. For it to be obvious that Peter is ill is likely.
        e. It is likely (for it) to be obvious that Peter is ill.

As we noted earlier, (162a) is not excluded by appeal to undischarged null Case, undischarged ACC Case, or the ban on matrix infinitives, nor is it clearly excluded by Moro (1997). Hence, the EPP appears to be implicated. Notice, however, that the null affixal C analysis, as explicated above, seems to directly extend to these cases. That is, if, as has been independently argued, the infinitival here is (i) a CP projection headed by the null, affixal C, and (ii) originates as the complement to *likely*, then the example is correctly excluded since the null C is 'stranded'. Thus, the example is out for the same reason that a finite sentential subject lacking a complementizer is out:

(163) a. *Peter is ill is likely.
       b. That Peter is ill is likely.
       c. It is likely (that) Peter is ill.

Specifically, the null C can't find an appropriate host. Note that we adopt the B&L PF merger analysis of the affix. Thus, a derivation whereby the null C affixes to *likely* before the CP preposes (and thereby avoids being stranded) is impossible.

Note finally that control complements must (at the least) have the option of being bare IPs, as is independently argued by Bošković (1997). That is, if control complements were obligatorily CPs, with a null, affixal C, we would wrongly exclude such cases as:

(164) To go now would upset Mary.

Alternatively, we need to ensure that the infinitival in (163a) does not have the option of being a bare IP, since then the null affix analysis could not be appealed to.

Thus, in effect, we've postulated another property of non-control *to*, which we might state in this way: phi defective (i.e. non-control *to*) must be selected by C. This guarantees that non-control *to* will be contained within CP; and if there is a null C it is, by hypothesis, affixal.

4 *More challenges to the elimination of the EPP: some movement cases*

4.1 Introduction

In this chapter, we consider further challenges to our proposed elimination of A-chains, the EPP, and at least some cases of successive cyclic A-movement. The data examined here all involve evidence that a DP has moved *through* the spec of a non-control infinitival *to* position. Since the spec of non-control *to* is not a Case-checking position, it can't be that movement is motivated by Case.[1] The EPP, then, is implicated in such cases.

We will first review, in Section 2, the basic phenomena to be dealt with. Next, we consider one recent analysis of it, that of Bošković (2002). Like our own, Bošković's approach rejects the EPP. But, interestingly, Bošković's approach may not be compatible with our hypothesis that there are no A-chains, and it is not compatible with our contention that there is no movement to, or through, spec of this non-control *to*. After reviewing Bošković, we consider potential problems with his analysis, in Section 3. In Section 4 we consider, rather speculatively, a set of alternative proposals that reject the EPP and that also reject successive cyclic A-movement, while accounting for core data with independently motivated mechanisms. Finally, in Section 5 we briefly consider some of the arguments (not dealt with in earlier discussion) for the EPP based on work by Lasnik, in a series of important recent papers.

---

1. Bošković (2002) refers to such cases as 'intermediate EPP' effects.

4.2 Evidence for successive cyclic A-movement as evidence for the EPP

We argued in Chapters 2 and 3 above that raising *to* has no formal checking features. Specifically, raising *to* has no 'EPP' feature, and therefore, assuming that syntactic operations are purposeful (i.e., an operation applies only if interface-uninterpretable features are checked as a result), there is no 'A-movement' to or through spec of raising *to* in classic cases like (1).[2]

(1)   Bill seems to sleep a lot.

In deriving (1), we motivated one-step movement as in (2), with nothing in the spec of *to*,

(2)   Bill seems to Bill sleep a lot
        ▲_____|

rather than having standard EPP-driven successive cyclic A-movement, as in (3).

(3)   Bill seems Bill to Bill sleep a lot
        ▲_____|▲_____|

In the previous chapters, we argued for this EPP-less, non-successive cyclic A-movement approach on both 'conceptual' and empirical grounds.

In a number of recent works,[3] problems for this type of EPP-less, one fell swoop approach have been presented. There appear to be cases providing evidence that in fact successive cyclic A-movement through spec of raising *to* has taken place. These include:

(4)   Condition A
        *Bill appears to Mary$_1$ [__ to seem to herself$_1$ to like physics]

---

2. For related analyses, see also Castillo, Drury, and Grohmann (1999), Chomsky (2001a), Hornstein (2001), and Manzini and Roussou (2000).
3. See, among others Boeckx (2000, 2001), Bošković (2002), and Lasnik (2003).

It is argued that *Bill* needs to move through spec of *to* (marked '__') to block the binding of *herself* by *Mary*.[4]

(5) Q-float
The students$_1$ seem [__$_1$ all] to know French

In this case, the DP *the students all* is argued to have moved to spec of *to*, as indicated by the floating quantifier *all* that is 'left behind' by subsequent movement of *the students* to the matrix (under the Sportiche 1988 analysis of Q-float).

(6) Reconstruction
    a. *His$_1$ mother's$_2$ bread seems to her$_2$ __ to be known by every man$_1$ to be the best.
    b. His$_1$ mother's$_2$ bread seems to every man$_1$ __ to be known by her$_2$ to be the best.

The DP *his mother's bread* (it is argued) needs to move through the lower spec IP position, marked as '__', to create the necessary structural relations to allow the indicated binding in (6b), which is not possible in (6a).

In addition, Lasnik, in a series of recent papers, has argued for the EPP on the basis of optional object shift in ECM constructions, which it is argued involves movement through the lower Spec, IP position, as evidenced by a range of interesting scopal, binding, ellipsis and other phenomena.

What the cases above have in common is the abstract configuration in (7), indicated informally here:

(7)   DP$_1$ ...[$_{IP}$ t$_1$ to ... DP$_1$ ...]

There is evidence that DP$_1$ moved through the spec of *to* position (indicated by the 'trace' t). The DP does not have any of its own features checked in this spec of *to* position. Since *to* is defective, it in fact can't check the (only) feature of the DP that is in need of checking, namely its Case feature. Why then does the DP move through the spec of *to* position? One argument is that it is because of a feature of

---

4. It is argued that in (4), *Mary* c-commands *herself* (for reasons that we'll consider below) and hence *Mary* is a potential binder of *herself*; *Bill* in spec of *to* then serves as the (crucial) blocker of the *Mary* to *herself* binding relation.

to, specifically, *to*'s 'EPP' feature. Note the form of the reasoning: the evidence supports successive cyclic A-movement; i.e. movement through spec of raising *to*. This *to* does not check the Case of the mover. Thus, it must be that *to* has some other feature that it needs to check, which the moving DP can in fact check. The EPP is then implicated as the relevant feature of *to*. Alternatively, the EPP might be construed as a 'structural requirement', which, as discussed in Chapters 1 and 3, seems to us problematic.

We have argued that there is no successive cyclic A-movement in such cases, and no EPP feature of *to*. Thus, (4)–(6), and Lasnik's cases, constitute a serious challenge to our approach. Indeed, Bošković (2002) suggests that such 'intermediate EPP effects' provide even 'stronger evidence for the EPP' than the BELIEVE-class of cases considered in Chapter 3 above.

In the next section, we review and examine Bošković's (2002) approach to the problems represented by (4)–(6) above. As we'll see, he also adopts the idea that the EPP 'should be eliminated'. He does provide an extremely interesting EPP-less analysis of (4)–(6). However, unlike our proposals above, Bošković does assume that there is successive cyclic A-movement; and he further assumes that there are A-chains (and thus a chain-formation operation). Thus, for Bošković, in (7) there *is* movement through spec of *to*; it's just that this movement is not motivated by the EPP. We consider Lasnik's cases in section 5. Overall, the claim is that with successive cyclic A-movement the facts are covered, and without it, they are not. We challenge both; i.e. it may be unclear how even with successive cyclic A-movement the facts are covered, and we speculatively suggest that without successive cyclic A-movement perhaps we have not lost empirical coverage.

4.3 The Bošković approach

We first briefly review the approach of Bošković (2002) (subsection 4.3.1). We then consider a number of potential problems with it (subsection 4.3.2).

4.3.1 Bošković: successive cyclic A-movement without the EPP

Following a number of researchers,[5] Bošković argues that '...the EPP should be

---

5. In particular, Boeckx (2000), Castillo, Drury, and Grohmann (1999), Epstein & Seely (1999), and Martin (1999); and earlier work by Borer (1986) and Fukui & Speas (1986).

eliminated.' There is assumed to be no EPP feature (e.g. the D-feature of Chomsky (1995)) that, under Attract, drives successive cyclic A-movement. Nor is the EPP a 'structural requirement', namely, the phrase-structure stipulation that IPs need specifiers at some level.

However, contrary to what we have argued in Chapters 2 and 3, Bošković does assume that successive cyclic A-movement occurs through spec of *to* in cases like (8), whereas we have argued that there is one step movement from the θ-position directly to the Case position.

(8)   Bill seems Bill to Bill sleep a lot

If there is no EPP, what motivates the movement through spec of *to*? For Bošković (2002:183),

> the intermediate...[Spec, IP] in the constructions in question [like (8)] [is] filled as a result of the property of the movements involved. We do not need to invoke a property of the embedded...Infl to drive the movement...

More specifically, Bošković assumes the Minimize Chain Links Principle (MCLP) of Chomsky and Lasnik (1993) and Takahashi (1994). The idea is that *Bill* moves through spec of *to* in (8) since only via this movement will the chain links (associated with the movement of *Bill*) be as short as possible, as required by the MCLP.

The deeper theoretical point is that Bošković treats 'movement through intermediate [Spec, IP]s ...on a par with movement through intermediate [Spec, CP]s' (p. 186). In short, the successive cyclicity of *wh*-movement is extended to 'NP-movement'. In neither case is the movement to the intermediate spec position driven by a feature of the head of that spec position; rather, it is driven by certain overarching locality requirements on movement (and/or on chains). Interestingly, and almost paradoxically, movement is nonetheless hypothesized to be feature-driven in the sense that the operation Move is *initiated* by the need of a feature to check (there is not the completely gratuitous 'Move anything anywhere' of GB theory; though see subsection 4.3.2.3 below for further discussion). In order to see how this seeming contradiction is resolved (movement to spec of *to* is *not* feature-driven, yet the 'movement sequence' is initiated in order to check features), consider:

(9)   [__ X ...[__ to ... DP ...]]

In (9), X, bearing an uninterpretable feature, attracts the DP. A necessary condition on X attracting DP (and the subsequent move of DP) is that X has an uninterpretable feature. Movement, then, is purposeful in that it applies in order to create the conditions under which an uninterpretable feature is eliminated. But, for Bošković, what is 'built into' Move is a locality condition, which forces the DP in (9) to first move to spec of *to*. To reiterate Bošković's central point, this is not because of a checking feature of *to*, but because of a property of movement itself. Although we find Bošković's approach extremely insightful and attractive in exploiting another apparent redundancy between the EPP and other principles (locality in this instance), we address a number of potential problems with this approach in Section 4.3.2.

First, however, let us briefly consider how the approach fares with respect to the phenomena represented by (4)–(6). According to Bošković, the problematic cases considered above are accounted for. In (4)–(6) there is movement through spec of *to*, marked '__'. In fact, these cases are treated in relevant respects just as they would be if there were an EPP: for Bošković, the key is to get the mover to pass through the spec of *to* position, and Bošković's approach does just that. Thus, in (4), repeated here and annotated (letter subscripts used to indicate occurrences of *Bill*), *Bill* moves to the indicated intermediate positions due to a 'locality constraint' on movement.

(4)   *$Bill_d$ *T* appears to Mary$_1$ [$Bill_c$ to seem to herself$_1$ [$Bill_b$ to $Bill_a$ like physics]

The *collective* movements indicated above are driven by the need of the matrix T to check its features, but *Bill* stops off at the intermediate positions (where no features of any category are checked) in order to satisfy the 'shortest links' requirement. A positive consequence of this is that without the EPP, *Bill* is nonetheless forced to move through the spec of the embedded *to*, and in that position, the copy $Bill_C$ desirably blocks the binding relation between *Mary* and *herself*; in effect, the example '...exhibits a Specified Subject Condition effect' (Bošković 2002:179).[6]

Regarding Q-float, as in (5), repeated here,

---

6. Notice that the necessary and sufficient conditions for satisfaction of Condition A, including 'timing of application', are crucial here. So may be obligatory copy-creation in spec of *to*, which however is argued against in Lasnik (1999) and Epstein *et al.* (1998). This is discussed further below.

(5)   the students₁ seem [__₁ all]₂ to __₂ know French

assuming the Sportiche (1988) analysis of Q-float, under Bošković's approach the DP, *[the students all]* moves to Spec, *to* and can 'drop off' the *all* in this position. Finally, in (6)

(6) a. *his₁ mother's₂ bread seems to her₂ __ to be known by every man₁ to be the best.
     b. his₁ mother's₂ bread seems to every man₁ __ to be known by her₂ to be the best.

there is again movement through spec of *to*, such movement being induced by the requirement that chain links be as short as possible. In (6a), for *his* to be interpreted as a variable bound by *every man*, it is assumed that the DP *his mother's bread* must 'reconstruct' to a position lower than (i.e. c-commanded by) *every man*. That position is the theta position of *his mother's bread* in the lower clause. But in that position, *her* c-commands *mother* thereby yielding a Condition C violation. (So, in this case movement through spec of *to* is not relevant.) But in the grammatical (6b), since *his mother's bread* moves through spec of the indicated *to*, this DP can get out of the scope of *her* (avoiding the Condition C effect) yet still stay within the scope of *every man*, thereby allowing the bound variable reading of *his*. Only relative to this spec of *to* position, the argument runs, can we have *his* bound by *every man*, but not have *his mother* bound by *her*.

Further details of this analysis, and certain problems with it, will be considered in a moment. Again, we stress here that for Bošković this successive cyclic A-movement is not motivated by the EPP but rather is 'a result of the property of the movements involved.' Recall that these examples are problematic for us, since we have claimed (contra Bošković) that there is no movement through spec of *to*. Of course, it should be noted that analyses forcing movement through spec of *to* don't automatically account for the facts at hand. Intricate issues concerning level of application of binding theoretic principles to chains, copies, and reconstructed representations must be sorted out (by all of us). But, for the purposes of the discussion at hand, we assume that movement through spec of *to* is sufficient to account for these cases; however, we will suggest later that it is not necessary.

4.3.2 Potential problems with the Bošković approach

Before turning to our alternative analysis, recall that in a case like (10),

(10)   the students seem [the students to [the students like French]]

Bošković proposes that *the students* moves through the spec of *to*, not because *to* has an EPP feature, but rather the spec is filled as a result of the property of the movements involved. But we will suggest in this section that each of the various implementations that Bošković considers leads to various problems. Furthermore, Bošković's approach has interesting, and we believe largely unexplored, consequences regarding the driving force of movement. We stress from the outset that we fully support Bošković's attempted elimination of the EPP. His work presents an extremely interesting set of proposals to deal with important challenges to the elimination of the EPP. But we also see in the proposals a number of potential shortcomings, raising further issues of interest.

4.3.2.1 Does Bošković have both chains and movement?

As noted, Bošković (somewhat tentatively) adopts the Minimize Chain Links Principle (MCLP) of Chomsky and Lasnik (1993), further developed in Takahashi (1994). Bošković explicates the application of the MCLP as follows:

> ...successive cyclic movement is not a result of feature checking. Rather, it is a result of the requirement that all chain links be as short as possible. The requirement forces element X undergoing movement of type Y to stop at every position of type Y on the way to its final landing site, independently of feature checking. Bošković (2002:183)

For the moment, suppose we embrace this MCLP approach. Then, a potentially serious problem emerges. To the extent that the approach in fact incorporates appeal to chains and chain formation, then the arguments developed in Chapter 2, against chains, re-emerge. Under the MCLP analysis, one seems to be able to maintain what looks like an EPP-less analysis. But, if the MCLP is adopted, one associated price is that we would seem to bring back an ill-understood, and empirically inadequate, chain-formation operation (see our extensive discussion in Chapter 2). Moreover, if movement is concomitantly appealed to, then the long-noted, massive (but perhaps only partial) redundancy between chains and Move returns. Interestingly, we will suggest below that the MCLP approach might be forced into the position that Form

Chain is required, and thus the problems we present for A-chains cannot be avoided by such an approach. We will return to this point in a moment, but we first address a number of related issues.

4.3.2.2 Two different types of locality One issue is that there seem to be, in effect, two types of locality associated with movement under the Bošković approach. Recall that in a typical raising structure like (10),

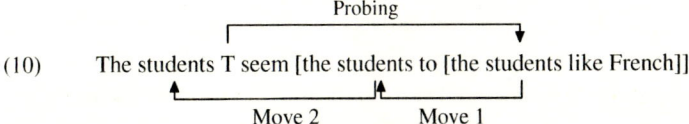

(10)   The students T seem [the students to [the students like French]]

the matrix T probes down 'in search' of an element to check its features. There is one type of locality associated with this probing; namely, T takes 'the first' matching goal, which in this case is the DP *the students*. The DP *the students* ULTIMATELY raises up to spec of the matrix T. But for Bošković this ascension is constrained by 'locality', stated either in terms of shortest chain links (as briefly reviewed above) or else in terms of 'bounding nodes' on movement (which we'll consider below). Either way, *ascension is subject to a different locality condition than probing down*. Thus, Attract has locality built into it: X probes down to find a matching goal and X takes the *first* matching Y found, where X and Y match if they share the same φ-feature set. But, crucially, there is another type of locality, that of shortest chain link, which can be interpreted as 'move to the first available position.' That these are different types of locality associated with the same derivation (and associated with the single relation, that of feature checking, between the matrix T and *the students*) is nicely represented by (10). Recall that for Bošković, Move is initiated by a probe, i.e. an element with an unchecked feature. Crucially, operations are purposeful in the relevant sense. Thus, in (10), initially the matrix T probes down, but it probes *through* the intermediate spec of *to* position. This 'position' crucially does not block the probing of *the students* by T.[7] However, this intermediate position *does* count for the movement of *the students* up (ultimately) to the matrix T. In short, in probing down, the intermediate position is not relevant; however, in moving up, this very same position crucially is relevant.

---

7. Of course spec of T is presumably not a position yet (there is no sister of T′ before the movement of *the students*); but the point is that neither the infinitival T head nor its projection interferes in any way with the probe-goal relation between T and *the students*.

Of course, it may be that two different notions of locality are required, one for probing and one for moving (or Form Chain). But optimally this would be avoided, as seems to be sought in, for example, CT, where Move and Attract are unified; i.e., Attract replaces Move, the latter eliminated from the grammar. Such unification would appear to be impossible under the above approach.

4.3.2.3 The foundational issue of 'purposefulness'? There is the further, and we believe fundamentally important, issue of how to carry out the derivation associated with (10), and it raises foundational issues concerning the central role of 'purposefulness' and its explanatory properties within the architecture of the minimalist system seeking to eliminate descriptive filters of the GB type. Bošković assumes that it is the matrix T that triggers the movement of *the students*. Recall the foundational minimalist assumption that operations are 'purposeful'. *The students* moving through the intermediate positions is thus, at the 'global' level, not gratuitous (in the GB Move-α sense); it is driven by the uninterpretable features of the matrix T and the hypothesized locality constraint on movement (where this locality constraint, according to Bošković, can be stated in various ways). Indeed, not having *purely* gratuitous movement (the 'free Move' of GB) is crucial for Bošković, and for us (see our discussion in Chapters 2 and 3), to disallow

(11)   *there seems a student to be __ outside

without appealing to Merge over Move, which in part following Epstein and Seely (1999), Bošković too rejects. Thus, for Bošković the indicated movement in (11) is disallowed, not by Merge over Move, but by the fact that such movement is not feature-driven and hence not purposeful in the relevant sense. As Bošković (2002:189) notes, 'there is no reason to move the indefinite *[a student]* to the embedded Spec, IP, hence the movement is blocked by the Last Resort Condition.'

But now the question arises regarding the reason for the very same kind of movement in the derivation of (10). Assuming a bottom-up derivation in (10), what happens at derivational point (12)?

(12)   to [$_{vP}$ the students like French]

By our (1999) hypothesis (assumed in Bošković), *to* has no features to check and hence Move of *the students* is not, at this point in the derivation, triggered by anything. And, if it's not triggered by a probe, then, as we've just seen relative to (11), such movement is disallowed. In fact, movement of *the students* in (10) will not be triggered *until the matrix T (the probe) is introduced*, i.e. at the later derivational point (13):

(13)   T seem __ [to [the students like French]]

But, at this point in the derivation, movement to spec of *to* would appear to be counter-cyclic (at least in the sense of involving tree-infixation). (See Kitahara 1995, 1997 for an elegant explanation of the Extension Condition in terms of a derivational economy condition on targeting categories.)

There are a number of approaches we might take here, but they yield their own additional problems. First, we could assume look-ahead. Thus, at point (12) it is presumed that it is somehow possible to look ahead and 'see' that there *will be* a trigger for movement *later* in the derivation. Thus, moving now (in (12)) but not in the derivation-internally identical (11) is permitted. However, such look-ahead is at best computationally costly and at worst unimplementable.

Another approach to the counter-cyclicity issue just raised is to adopt Chomsky's (1995) reduction of cyclicity to the Extension Condition. Specifically, under Extension we could adopt the 'monolithic' 'Form Chain' as a single operation, as in Chomsky (2000). Thus, we wait to raise *the students* until the derivational point in (14):

(14)   T seem [to [the students like French]]

Then, to satisfy cyclicity, and particularly the Extension Condition, we *instantaneously* form the entire chain (a single operation) thereby mapping (14) directly to (15):

(15)   the students seem [the students to [the students like French]]

Cyclicity is satisfied by the instantaneous operation Form Chain, which does extend the tree in the required way (specifically, extension at the root). However, we are now back to having (A-) chains, with many of the problems associated with them from our Chapter 2 above; for example, the redundancy between Form Chain and Move; the specification of the chain formation algorithm; chains as non-syntactic objects; chains as arguably unspecifiable given X′-invisibility; and chain deletion given the semantic vacuity of intermediate links. Finally, instantaneous, unbounded chain formation would seem to be entirely inconsistent with the derivational approach.[8] As pointed out in Epstein and Seely (2002:83), '...simultaneous rule application seems nonderivational. For example, a theory seeking to explain syntactic relations (as in Epstein 1994, 1999, Epstein *et al.* 1998) in terms of the step-by-step derivation cannot be maintained since the iterative steps of the derivation are necessarily eliminated under simultaneity.' Instantaneous Form Chain, as in the mapping of (14) to (15), to the extent that it fails to 'care' about its substeps (i.e. each local move) is, likewise, non-derivational, again, in that it ignores individual rule applications.

Moreover, under Instantaneous Form Chain (IFC), there can be no 'timing' solution to (6b): *his$_1$ mother's$_2$ bread seems to every man$_1$ __ to be known by her$_2$ to be the best*. That is, one cannot analyze (6b) by saying e.g.

(16)   Apply Condition C and Pronominal Variable Binding (to *[his$_1$ mother's$_2$ bread]*) when this DP occupies spec of *to* and before it raises to the matrix Spec, TP.

Under IFC, there is no such derivational point. How then would (6b) be accounted for, given IFC? It seems a certain copy must be selected as the copy to which Condition C and Pronominal Variable Binding applies. But it is not clear to us how to formally specify the correct copy. We return to this problem, as it concerns copy selection and/or timing of application, below.

As concerns EPP, the issue at hand is that (by hypothesis) there needs to be an intermediate spec of IP position; i.e., it is necessary if there is to be any hope of accounting for the facts (like (6b)). Recall, we claim there is no such position, while Bošković (also seeking to eliminate the EPP) says that there *is* such a position, forced by movement locality.

Suppose, then, that we pursue our program from Chapter 2 of eliminating the EPP *and* eliminating (A-)chains, adopting instead the arguably independently necessary structure-building operations of Merge/Move (rather than Form Chain). Can successive cyclic movement be generated in (10) without the EPP and Chains, and without IFC? Bošković (2002) briefly notes a number of ways that it might be done,

8. On different problems confronting simultaneity vs. derivationality relevant to the Form Chain discussion above see Epstein and Seely (2002), Section 5.3.

but we would argue that they entail the abandonment of feature-driven movement and a return to a GB-type 'free' move system, which in turn raises certain serious, foundational issues regarding the central Minimalist attempt to explain transformational rule application.

First, let us suppose that there is a locality constraint built into Movement such that movement across an IP (or CP) is disallowed, but movement to Spec, IP (CP) licenses subsequent movement out of these domains.[9] Such a locality constraint would apparently force successive cyclic movement in (10). However, the derivational problem raised above emerges now in a particularly problematic way. Consider again (10):

(10)   The students T seem [the students to [the students like French]]

At the derivational point (12), repeated here,

(12)   to [$_{vP}$ the students like French]

the question emerges: what motivates movement of *the students* to Spec, IP *now*? The answer cannot be that there is some attracting feature (*to* has no such features by our hypothesis, adopted by Bošković) and we haven't introduced the matrix T yet. And, again, if we wait to move until we introduce the matrix T, i.e., wait until (13), repeated here;

(13)   T seem __ [to [the students like French]]

although we do have the attracting T to motivate movement, the application of Move to the intermediate position, as in (17),

(17)   T seem the students [to [the students like French]]

violates the Extension Condition (as this local instance of Move has affected only a proper subpart of the object undergoing the operation). To avoid this problem, we might try to modify the definition of Extension to incorporate some form of look-ahead: apply Move as in (17) but only if there will be another instance of Move

---

9. As Bošković (2002: fn. 26) notes, '...this analysis would be close to the Barriers system, with "relativized barriers" CP and IP being voided through adjunction.' See also Grohmann and Boeckx (2004) for insightful comparison of Barriers and phase-based approaches. How to derive such a locality condition is an open question. But see below for further comment.

immediately applied to the same DP (*the students*)[10] which applies in such a way as to (ultimately) extend the root of the object that contains the attracting feature.

The problem seems to reduce to this: in (10), in order to maintain the foundational minimalist tenet of feature-driven (i.e. non-gratuitous) rule application, we must wait until we reach the derivational point (13), introducing (the matrix T) attractor. The derivational point (12) is *too early* since there is no relevant attracting feature yet. But, derivational point (13) is *too late* in that the derivational point (12), with respect to which *the students* can raise to Spec, *to* and thereby satisfy the Extension Condition, has already 'passed' by.

Note that we can 'solve' the counter-cyclicity problem (again assuming that there is no EPP and no chains) by giving up 'purposefulness'. Interestingly, if we return to a GB-type 'free Move' system, then from derivational point (12) we (may) move *the students* to Spec, IP, generating (18).

(18)   the students to [~~the students~~ like French]

If we do so move it, then there is no counter-cyclicity in ultimately deriving (10) from (18).

(10)   The students seem [~~the students~~ to [~~the students~~ like French]]

But, now we seem to have given up the central minimalist thesis (operations apply for a reason, namely, to check uninterpretable features and thereby to create interface-interpretable objects). Furthermore, we now have to deal with the empirical motivation for purposefulness. For example, what now rules out[11]

(19)   there seems a man to be __ outside

---

10. See Collins (1994) for an interesting analysis barring the 'interruption' of Form Chain by other operations. Notice that the statement in the text of look-ahead won't work in the case of Q-float. Thus in *the students seem all to sleep* the DP *the students all* moves to the intermediate Spec, *to*, but only a proper subpart of it moves higher. So, it's not *the same* DP that moves higher.
11. Bošković (2002) disallows example (19) by maintaining a form of 'global purposefulness'. With us, Bošković assumes that raising *to* has no features and hence 'there is no reason to move the indefinite to the embedded [Spec, IP]...' The higher T apparently does not count as a prober since *there* is in its Spec; i.e. since the higher T doesn't (ultimately) attract *a man* up, then there is no reason for *a man* to move; and hence it can't. But our points above about local gratuitous movement hold.

Note that Chomsky's (2000) system assumes the EPP in part in order to retain purposefulness. Thus, for Chomsky *the students* moves to spec of *to* at derivational point (18) since *to* has an EPP feature that must be checked (via the spec-head relation). But, an important issue arises, as Bošković (2002) briefly points out, relative to successive cyclic 'A'-movement', as in

(20)   who do you think that Mary likes

If the intermediate C bears the EPP feature, then successive cyclic A'-movement, i.e. movement of *who* to spec of CP at derivational point

(21)   [who [that Mary likes who]

is locally feature driven – by the EPP feature in C. But, what happens in

(22)   you think that Mary likes someone

where there is no *wh*-movement at all? There had better not (obligatorily) be an EPP feature in C, since given that there is nothing in Spec, CP, this EPP feature can't be satisfied. Chomsky (2000) then assumes that the EPP in C is optional. The EPP's presence in (20) forces movement to Spec, CP; and its (possible) absence in (22) entails that there need not be movement at all.

But, without the EPP we would seem to be back to gratuitous movement. Curiously, Chomsky's phase-based system yields yet another problem with the EPP; namely, that the EPP is in fact redundant with a fundamental mechanism of the phase system. Consider again (20). For Chomsky, successive cyclic *wh*-movement is induced by the architecture of his multiple Spell Out system. Given the Phase Impenetrability Condition (PIC), the *wh*-phrase moves to the 'edge', i.e. to spec of CP since, by the PIC, the IP that contains the *wh*-word will be 'shunted' to the interfaces at the point that C is reached. If *who* did not move to the edge, it would be shunted along with the IP and hence would be inaccessible. So at derivation point (21) we can ask, under the phase system, 'Why does *who* move to Spec, CP?' And the answer is 'if it doesn't move there, then it will not move at all since it will be "gone" (i.e. inaccessible by the PIC).' But, interestingly, what seems to be adopted by Chomsky is a kind of 'inverse EPP'. That is, if C has an EPP feature, then Spec, C must be filled. And, if Spec, CP is filled (and here it's filled given the PIC); then

C must have an EPP feature. It is the very architecture of the phase-based system that attempts to *derive* the locality condition on movement. That is, it is the PIC as outlined above that forces *who* to move to Spec, CP. But, in order to *actually* move to the Spec, CP, it seems to be assumed that the CP must be headed by a C^0 bearing a feature in need of checking by *who*, namely, the EPP feature. But if there is an EPP in C, then that EPP feature is *also* driving the movement to Spec, CP. Thus, there seem to be two answers to the question, 'why does the *wh*-word move in (21)?' 'It moves given the PIC,' *and* 'it moves to check the EPP feature.' We have attempted to avoid such a redundancy.

Interestingly, if we eliminate the EPP, we would seem to be forced back to gratuitous free movement (of the GB type), giving up the foundational minimalist thesis of feature-driven movement. Suppose there is no EPP, but there is the phase-based PIC. Then, *who* moves to the intermediate Spec, CP in cases such as (20) not because it is attracted by any feature of this intermediate C but because of the PIC. But, this in turns entails that there is free Move. *Who* moves to Spec, CP because it can (there is free Move). We don't need to stipulate that it obligatorily moves there: its apparent obligatoriness follows from the PIC. It may move because it can. In order to yield convergence, it must move, because if it doesn't, it will not be available (by the PIC) and hence it will not be available to (ultimately) check the higher +Q feature.

To sum up subsection 3.2.3, Bošković (2002) states that 'the details of the analysis... are not essential here.' We agree, in that his essential contribution might well be the highly insightful recognition of redundancy between intermediate EPP effects and the subtheory of movement locality. But, what we have suggested above is that the different implementations that Bošković briefly considers each have important consequences for certain deep and foundational tenets of minimalism and that they reveal certain of the difficulties in the transition from the freely-derive-and-filter GB system to the (partially; see Epstein 2003) constrained-rule application and interface-conditions of minimalism. The options considered above for motivating successive cyclic movement without appealing to the EPP, along with their potential problems, can be summarized as follows:

(23) If we adopt Form Chain subject to the Minimize Chain Links Principle, then:

Problems:
a. The theory may have the Move plus Form Chain redundancy.
b. The theory will have global, instantaneous Form Chain, which yields the problems associated with chains laid out in Chapter 2, and further may not be derivational and/or implementable.

(24) Suppose we eliminate the EPP and chains (and Form Chain), adopting instead Merge and Move, where Move is subject to a Locality Condition, then:

Problems:
a. It is not clear how to state (and more specifically to derive) the Locality Condition.
b. We seem to require a return to a GB-type gratuitous Move, hence retreating from the foundational minimalist notion of feature-driven purposefulness.

(25) Suppose we attempt to derive locality, as in Chomsky's phase-based system, via the PIC, but we also eliminate the EPP and a separate locality condition on movement. Then:

Problems:
a. Recall Chomsky maintains the EPP within his system. But a problem here is that there is a redundancy between the EPP and PIC-driven 'edgification'.
b. If we eliminate the EPP, then we seem to again require nothing more than GB-type gratuitous Move, thereby sacrificing feature-driven 'purposefulness'.

Thus, we believe

(26) Contemporary Minimalist theory displays potentially serious redundancies between EPP and:
a. Movement-locality theory
b. Phase-based 'edgification'
c. Cyclicity

In our view, more research is needed to determine the optimal implementation of 'computationally efficient *satisfaction* of the interface conditions', and the concomitant existence of crashing derivations which do *not* in fact satisfy the interface conditions (see Epstein 2003 for further discussion).

4.3.2.4 Eliminating the EPP (but not bringing it back?): a theory of landing sites?

Bošković (2002) states: '...*the students* in [(10)], whose final landing site is [Spec, IP], passes through the embedded [Spec, IP] as a result of successive cyclic movement, not a property of Infl...' But, notice, crucially there must be some property of I (it must be a property of I in an EPP-free, lexically based approach) that allows movement to its specifier. [Spec, IP] is assumed to be a *possible* landing site for NP movement and thus by the MCLP requirement, it is a necessary landing site for such movement. Thus, under this approach there is still clearly something about the spec of I, (and not the spec of, say, AdjP, or PP, or VP) which allows (successive cyclic) A-movement to it. A critical difference between what we have argued in Chapters 2 and 3 above, and what Bošković argues for, is this: for us, there is movement to spec of I only if there is a feature of I that needs to be checked. For Bošković there is movement to spec of I because you *can*, and there is something about I that allows you to move there (if you are e.g. a DP). Bošković (2002:183) writes, 'We do not need to invoke a property of the embedded C and Infl to drive the movement to these positions [= Spec, CP and Spec, IP].' But this is not clear to us. We agree there is not a *feature* of I that attracts the element to Spec, IP; but there is *property* of I that must allow the movement to its spec (where the spec of IP position is created by the movement). This property of I is 'a possible landing site for a DP,' or, in GB parlance, the property is 'spec of IP is a (theta-less) A-position; i.e. a possible landing site.' And it is not clear to us whether and in what way this is distinct from the 'EPP property'.[12]

4.4 Some alternative solutions

In this section we consider a number of alternative approaches to the problematic cases with which this chapter began, the problems, specifically, of binding and Q-float – what Bošković (2002) refers to as 'intermediate EPP effects'. The approaches that we speculatively develop here do not appeal to the EPP nor to successive cyclic A-movement, but rather to other independently motivated mechanisms that are consistent with the methods and goals of the framework we have developed.

---

12. As suggested to us by Acrisio Pires (p.c.), one difference is that the EPP forces movement to Spec of IP, while the property of I discussed above, allows, but does not force an element in its Spec. The Spec of IP position (for raising I) is a possible landing site, but movement through this spec of I is motivated by a higher probe and a locality condition on movement.

4.4.1 Getting into (and out of) a bind

As we mentioned above, (27) represents a challenge to our EPP-less, no successive cyclic movement account of A-movement.[13]

(27) a. *Bill appears to Mary$_1$ to seem to herself$_1$ to be ill.
  b. Bill$_1$ appears to Mary to seem to himself$_1$ to be ill.

(Note that indices are used for expository convenience to indicate intended anaphoric relations; they have no theoretical status.)[14]

There is a contrast between (27a) and (27b) on the indicated readings. (27b) is relatively[15] well formed on the reading 'it appears to Mary that Bill seems to himself to be ill.' But (27a) is ill formed; the relevant reading is something like 'it appears to Mary to seem to herself that Bill is ill.'

There is independent evidence, from Condition C effects, that the object of the preposition *to* in (27) c-commands out of the PP headed by *to*.[16] For example, (28) is standardly argued to be out on the indicated coreferential reading, and this can be accounted for on the assumption that Condition C is violated since *Mary* is A-bound by *her*:

(28) *Bill appears to her$_1$ to like Mary$_1$.

The natural assumption, based on (28), is that *Mary* c-commands *herself* in (27a). Note further that *Mary* does seem close enough to the reflexive to satisfy Binding

---

13. The examples were originally brought to our attention by Howard Lasnik in his response to our LSA Summer Institute paper in 1999. Lasnik, in turn, attributes the examples to David Pesetsky and Danny Fox. This type of example is also considered in Castillo, Drury, and Grohmann (1999), who attribute it to Danny Fox.
14. Indeed, the indexing (or linking, see Higginbotham 1983) system of GB violates Inclusiveness. We are instead assuming the general interpretive binding theory outlined by Chomsky and Lasnik (1993). See also Freidin (1994) for important discussion of binding theory under Minimalist assumptions.
15. Certain pragmatic considerations might intrude somewhat on judgments of examples like those in (27). Thus (27b) entails the truth of 'it appears to Mary that Bill seems to himself to be ill'; and one's seeming to oneself is perhaps somewhat odd. Furthermore 'Bill seems to himself to be ill' can presuppose 'interpersonal' mind-reading. But, abstracting away from such considerations, the data in (27) – and much of what follows – is reasonably robust. The grammatical status of some related cases, however, as we'll see, is quite unclear.
16. See Lasnik and Saito (1992) and Chomsky (1995). See also Boeckx (1999) which includes an insightful review of the history and recent analyses of this phenomenon; see also Kitahara (1997).

Theory.[17] Consequently, *Mary* is a potential binder of the reflexive. The central problem then becomes: Why is *Mary* not a legitimate antecedent in (27a)? The further question is: just how is (27b) allowed? That is, if, as we have proposed, *Bill* moves in one step from the lowest IP to the matrix, how can *Bill* be 'close enough' to bind *himself*, without *Mary* (illicitly) intervening between them?

The standard analysis is that (27) involves successive cyclic A-movement of *Bill*; *Bill* must move through the spec of each intermediate *to* in order to satisfy the EPP. Thus, (27a) involves the movements represented in (29):

(29)   Bill$_d$ appears to Mary$_1$ [Bill$_c$ to seem to herself$_1$ [Bill$_b$ to be Bill$_a$ ill]

In this case even though *Mary* (apparently) c-commands *herself*, *Bill$_c$* is a subject that intervenes between *Mary* and the reflexive (presumably at the relevant point of the derivation; see Kitahara 1997, Epstein *et al.* 1998 and Boeckx 1999) and hence a Condition A violation results. Note that this analysis requires a number of important assumptions which may not be entirely clear. Under a bottom-up derivational approach, and critically, assuming that movement of *Bill* leaves behind a copy, particularly in the position marked *Bill$_c$* in (29), it follows that there is no point in the derivation where *Mary* locally binds *herself*. At the point where the PP containing *Mary* is introduced into the derivation and at all points thereafter (assuming copies), *Bill$_c$* will intervene between *Mary* and *herself*. It is important that there be no point in the derivation where *Mary* binds *herself* given that, as Lebeaux (1988, 1991, 1995) points out, for reflexives it appears that if there is any point in the derivation where a reflexive is locally bound, Condition A is satisfied (Condition A is, in effect, an 'anywhere' condition). Thus, we get the well known:

(30)   Which pictures of *herself* does Mary think Tom likes ~~which pictures of herself~~ best.

At an early point in the derivation, relative to the lower clause for example, there is no 'properly' agreeing local binder for *herself* (*herself* is certainly not locally bound by *Mary* at that early point in the derivation since *Mary* hasn't yet en-

---

17. A reflexive may be bound inter-clausally, as in *Bill said pictures of himself were on sale*. We'll consider this matter in more detail below, but the assumption in the literature is that *Mary* is a potential binder of *herself* in (27a). But, see Lasnik (2002) for a 'clause-mate' condition on binding.

tered the derivation). However, *herself* can, by virtue of the successive cyclic *wh*-movement of its container *which picture of herself*, move into the local domain of *Mary* (specifically, into the embedded spec of C; see DASR). Thus, there is a point in the derivation where *herself* is bound in (30); but our point is that, critically assuming copies and successive cyclic A-movement, THERE IS NO POINT WHERE *herself* IS LOCALLY BOUND BY *Mary* IN (27A), AND HENCE THE STRUCTURE IS CORRECTLY DISALLOWED AS A CONDITION A VIOLATION. (Importantly, notice that under Instantaneous Form Chain, as discussed in the previous section, one waits until the φ-complete matrix T probes the first-merge site of *Bill*, and only then is a multi-link chain instantaneously formed, satisfying Extension. But under this approach, notice that there is (incorrectly) a point where *Mary* does licitly bind *herself*.)

Under our approach, on the other hand, (27a) is problematic. For us, *Bill* does not, and cannot, occupy the relevant intermediate spec of *to* position, and hence there is no obvious reason for the ill-formedness of (27a): *Mary* is argued to c-command (out of the PP) and to be close enough to the reflexive to satisfy Condition A, as indicated below, and hence we would seem to incorrectly predict that the structure is well formed:

(31)   *Bill appears to Mary$_1$ [__ to seem to herself$_1$ [to be Bill ill]]
       ↑_____|

Indeed, the relation between *Mary* and *herself*, (31) is, for us, the same as the relation between these two elements in (32), where there is no movement of *Bill* from the lowest to the matrix clause:

(32)   It appears to Mary$_1$ [to seem to herself$_1$ that Bill is ill]

The status of (32) is not entirely clear to us. It does, however, contrast with (31). What is clear is that (31) is out and, so far, we would seem to have no account of this.

Consider next (27b), repeated here.

(27)   b.   Bill$_1$ appears to Mary to seem to himself$_1$ to be ill.

This too is an apparent problem for our one fell swoop movement approach. Suppose that there is successive cyclic movement, driven by the EPP or by movement locality (the latter as in Bošković 2002), yielding

(33)   Bill_c appears to Mary Bill_b to seem to himself Bill_a to be ill

There is a point in the derivation where *Bill*_b locally binds *himself*, thereby satisfying Condition A. It is important to note, however, that (27b) might not *require* such successive cyclic movement. Thus, for us, (27b) involves one-step movement as in (34).

(34)   Bill appears to Mary to seem to himself to be __ ill.

But given that Mary is not a 'subject', it does not necessarily induce a Condition A intervention effect. Indeed in relevant respects (34) might be arguably similar to, e.g., (35).

(35)   a.   *Bill* talked to Mary about *himself*.
            (cf. *Bill* talked to Mary about *herself*.)
       b.   *Bill* said to Mary that pictures of *himself* were over there.
            (cf. Bill said to *Mary* that pictures of *herself* were over there.)

Here *Mary*, the object of *to*, also does not count as an intervener between *Bill* and *himself*, even though *Mary* (apparently) c-commands and is close enough to the reflexive. So, (27b) is not necessarily problematic for us, depending on how, exactly, locality and intervention are to be specified in the statement of Condition A. It is (27a) that is the more difficult case.

4.4.2   Does the experiencer c-command into the lower clause?

There are a number of assumptions that are critical to the argument that (27), repeated below, requires successive cyclic A-movement (with, potentially, copy theory inducing a Condition A intervention effect):

(27)   a.   *Bill appears to Mary_1 __ to seem to herself_1 to be ill.
       b.   Bill_1 appears to Mary to seem to himself_1 to be ill.

What is essential to the successive cyclic (and EPP) proponent is that *Mary* in (27a) qualifies as a potential binder, i.e. a c-commander, of *herself*. Evidence for such c-command is supported by BT-C effects, as in (28), repeated here:

(28)   *Bill appears to her₁ to like Mary₁.

We agree that (28) is not perfect. (For us, however, it is significantly better than such Condition C effects as *she appears to Bill to like Mary*.) But let us assume that it is bad, following for now the recent literature. The argument is that *her* binds (and hence c-commands) *Mary* in violation of Condition C in (28). Other evidence for the experiencer c-commanding into the lower clause, however, at least on one set of judgments, is unclear. It is perhaps the case that it is only Condition C effects that argue for the experiencer c-commanding into the lower clause; in other cases it looks as though the experiencer does not c-command down. And, if this is true it eliminates (27) as a problem induced by our approach seeking to eliminate the EPP and successive cyclic A-movement. That is, if *Mary* in fact fails to c-command *herself* in (27a), the example is independently excluded as a Condition A violation, and the presence of movement through (or a copy in) spec of *to* is rendered irrelevant. It does, however, raise a number of other problems, but ones which also plague analyses which assume the EPP (and successive cyclic A-movement). Thus we are not arguing that our analysis confronts no problems. We are suggesting that problems thought to be unique to or engendered by our EPP-less hypothesis are in fact encountered even with the EPP (or locality-driven successive cyclic A-movement). We briefly trace some of the details below.

Note first that with respect to the locality condition on Attract, the experiencer does not c-command down. Thus examples like (36) were discussed by Chomsky (1995) as a problem for Attract in that if *her* c-commands *Mary* then it also c-commands *Bill* at the point where the matrix T 'attempts' to attract *Bill*, namely:

(36)   T appears to her to Bill like Mary

But, then *her* should block the Attraction of *Bill* by T (just as in, say, **Bill appears it seems to like Mary*). Indeed, this paradox was addressed derivationally by Ferguson (1994) and Epstein *et al.* (1998), with an analysis according to which *her* does *not* c-command into the lower clause at derivational point (36), perhaps solving the locality condition on Attract (but then *her* does c-command down at a later point in the derivation – after T has attracted *Bill*).

The full range of other phenomena should be explored. In the abstract, with such raising predicates containing experiencers we have the configuration in (37):

(37)   T seems to X [. . . to . . . Y . . .]

The argument based on (27) for the EPP and successive cyclic A movement crucially involves the claim that X c-commands Y. But, if X c-commands Y in (37), then (depending on the timing of the application of the relevant principles) we expect the following:

(38)   Condition A Satisfaction:
        If X c-commands Y in (37), we would expect X to be able to bind Y where Y is an anaphor (assuming that Condition A locality can be satisfied).

In this regard, consider (39), an analog of the schema in (37), but with a finite CP complement.

(39)   *?It appears to the artists that each other's paintings got the most attention.

Example (39) seems marginal to us (granting that the judgment is unclear), suggesting that *the artists* does not c-command *each other*[18] (note that we do get *the artists said that each other's paintings got the most attention*).[19]

Next, consider

---

18. However, consider (i) ((ia) from Boeckx (1999); and (ib) modeled on Lasnik (1998); Belletti and Rizzi (1988) attribute a similar example to K. Johnson):

    (i)   a.   Pictures of himself seem to John to be ugly.
           b.   Each other's paintings seem to the artists to be ugly.

    If we assume that the experiencer does not c-command into the matrix subject position, then it apparently must be the case that the experiencer c-commands into the lower clause and can bind the reflexive before the reflexive's container moves up to the matrix subject position. Hence, (i) could be seen as arguing that in fact the experiencer does c-command into the lower clause. However, it is then entirely unclear why (ib) is relatively ill-formed (see also footnote 19 below). See Lasnik (1998) for further comment about the unclarity of these data; with respect to an example structurally parallel to (ib) Lasnik writes '. . . I must confess that I am no longer confident that [(ib). . .] are as good as they are always claimed to be. . . ' We consider the examples in (i) in greater detail in section 4.4.2 and 4.4.3.

19. Note that the lower clause is tensed in (39), thus to that extent it is different than (27)/(28). But the infinitival case is hard to test. Consider (i):

    (i)   Bill appears to the boys to [__ like themselves]

    This seems clearly ungrammatical. Now, if *Bill* leaves a copy in the VP-internal position marked __, it could be argued that *the boys* does c-command down, but that *Bill* blocks the binding relation. See

(40)   Negative Polarity Item licensing:
        If X c-commands Y in (37), then X should be able to license Y where X is a
        Negative element and Y is a Negative Polarity Item.

With regard to NPI licensing, consider (41).

(41)   ?*Bill seems to no linguist to like any recent theory.
        (cf. *No linguist seems to Bill to like any recent theory.*)

Example (41) seems quite bad to us, again suggesting that the experiencer does not c-command down.[20] Next, consider

(42)   Bound variable interpretation for a lower pronoun:
        If X c-commands Y in (37), then we expect that X can bind Y where X is a QP
        and Y is a pronominal interpreted as bound by the QP.

With regard to bound variable interpretation, consider (43).

(43)   *?Mary seems to no man/every man to like him a lot.
        (cf. *No man seems to Mary to like his theory.*)

Judgments are unclear here,[21] but the bound variable reading of the pronoun seems

---

Huang (1993) regarding the role of the VP-internal subject hypothesis in explaining why there is no intermediate reconstruction with fronted predicates containing an anaphor, as in (ii).

(ii)   [$_{VP}$ t how proud of himself$_{*i/k}$] does John$_i$ think [[Bill$_k$ is]]

However, if Condition A is an 'anywhere' condition, and if there is no A-reconstruction, as argued in Lasnik (1999), then (i) could be evidence that the experiencer does not c-command into the lower clause; thus (i) is out since *the boys* does not bind *themselves*.

20. Boeckx (1999) and Bošković (2002) present examples like (i)

(i)   pictures of any linguist seem to no psychologist to be pretty

as evidence that the experiencer can license (hence c-commands) the negative polarity item. However, for us (i) is ill-formed. We'll consider further unclarities regarding this, and related, data below.

21. Interestingly, independently negative quantifiers seem to resist being experiencers. Thus (i) and (ii) below

(i)   it seems to no man that Bill left
(ii)   Bill seems to no man __ to have left

marginal, yet again, suggesting the absence of c-command.[22]

The data above are not clear to us, and hence conclusions drawn from them are by no means conclusive. However, we can tentatively hypothesize that, across a range of relevant structures, the experiencer behaves as though it does not c-command into the lower clause. The idea then is that it is only Condition C effects which argue that the experiencer c-commands into the lower clause. With respect to other relevant phenomena, the experiencer does not seem to c-command down. And note that if the experiencer does not c-command down, particularly with respect to

---

are somewhat odd to us, perhaps (playing some role in) confounding judgments of (43) and (41).
22. Relevant also are (assuming the abstract structure in (37)):

(i) Superiority Effects:
X and Y, where both are *wh*-expressions, should display Superiority Effects.
(ii) No Weak Crossover:
If X is a *wh*-variable ('trace') and Y is a pronoun bound by a *wh*-element, there should be no WCO effect.
(iii) No Parasitic Gap Licensing:
X can't license Y if X is a variable and Y is a parasitic gap.

Superiority and PG licensing are difficult to test given the independent, and we think not well understood, constraint against *wh*-movement of the experiencer without pied piping the *to*, another oddity regarding the experiencer position. Thus, even simple *wh*-movement as in (iv) is relatively ill-formed.

(iv) a. *?Who does it seem to __ that Mary left the party
b. *Who does Bill seem to __ [to be ill]

The relevant PG licensing structure would be (v).

(v) a. *?Who does it seem to t that Mary likes PG
b. * Who does Mary seem to t to like PG

(v) is ill-formed; but this does not allow the conclusion that it's ill-formed because the variable t c-commands the PG, and therefore the PG is not licensed, since it appears that independently, *wh*-movement is disallowed.

Consider next the Superiority context of (vi).

(vi) *Who does it seem to t that Mary likes what

Again, if t c-commands *what*, we expect Superiority, forcing *who* and not *what* to move. But (vi) is ill-formed, and arguably for independent reasons. Interestingly, (vii) is arguably relatively well formed.

(vii) What does it seem to whom that Mary likes best?

This suggests that *whom* does not c-command *what*, thereby avoiding the Superiority Effect violation.

Condition A, then (27a), the central case arguing for successive cyclic A-movement is unproblematic for us. Of course, there is still a problem. It's just that the problem shifts from (27) to (44).

(44)   *Bill seems to her to like Mary.

Specifically, we now have the question: if the experiencer does not c-command into the lower clause, then why does (44) seem to exhibit a Condition C effect?[23] We consider one approach to this 'new' problem in a moment. Note, however, that the 'standard' successive cyclic approach to (27) also now has a problem: it is crucial to the argument associated with (27a) that the experiencer c-commands into the lower clause; however, the evidence above (unclear though it may be) raises another question: if there is c-command, why aren't the further predictions associated with this assumption borne out?

4.4.3   Toward a solution: Torrego (2002) on experiencers

Below, we trace another possible approach to the problem raised by (27a) that involves neither the EPP nor successive cyclic A-movement. The idea is that the experiencer, for independent reasons, raises to a position higher than the matrix subject and it is the subject (the DP that has raised to the matrix TP for Case) that then constitutes an intervener blocking the binding relation between the experiencer and the embedded reflexive. Our approach is in the spirit of recent proposals regarding conflicting c-command requirements associated with experiencers. There is evidence, as discussed above, that the experiencer does c-command into the lower clause, but there is also evidence that it does not. This apparent contradiction can be resolved by appealing to the derivation, and specifically to different derivational points, arguably the oldest form of transformational evidence. There is no single representation that suffices, but the apparent conflict can be resolved by exploiting the (independently required) steps in the derivation (see Boeckx 1999, DASR, Ferguson 1994, and Kitahara 1997; and also the foundational work of Belletti and Rizzi 1988 and Lebeaux 1988, 1991). Our approach is in the spirit of these, but also

---

23. Another important question has to do with (i), from our earlier discussion

   (i)   it appears to *Mary* to seem to *herself* that Bill is ill

   Again, the status of this example is unclear to us. But, if it's well formed, then it provides evidence that the experiencer, *Mary*, does c-command down (at the relevant point of the derivation).

appeals to certain independently motivated aspects of the recent analysis of Torrego (2002), specifically with regard to a proposed covert movement of the experiencer.

First, we assume (with e.g. Kitahara 1997, DASR, Torrego 2002), that

(45)   The experiencer PP of raising predicates *is* in fact a PP.

Thus, in (27), repeated below, *to* is Merged with *Mary* to create the PP *to Mary*; and this PP is then merged into the larger structure.

(27)   a. *Bill appears to Mary$_1$ to seem to herself$_1$ to be ill.
        b. Bill$_1$ appears to Mary to seem to himself$_1$ to be ill.

With Torrego (2002), we assume that

(46)   The experiencer PP is merged into a spec position outside the VP headed by *seems*; thus:
        [T [[to XP] v [seems . . .]]]
            vP   VP

(See Torrego 2002,[24] and for a related proposal see Kitahara 1997:64 and references therein.)

Next, following Torrego (2002), who in turn develops important insights of Boeckx (2000), we adopt the idea that

(47)   There is a functional category, call it P, associated with 'point of view,' that checks the Case of the experiencer. We adopt from Torrego the ideas that: (i) the functional category P bears an interpretable [person] feature (it is interpretable since it is linked to point of view) and the (Dative) Case feature and (ii) the functional category P is higher than T.

It follows from (45)–(47) that a basic case like (48)

(48)   It seems to Mary that Bill sleeps.

is represented (after multiple merges) as

---

24. Torrego (2002) states that 'I will assume that the experiencer merges as a subject...' Interestingly, we'll see below that the experiencer does have certain 'subject' properties, but that it is not an 'unadulterated' subject, for reasons that will be discussed momentarily.

(49)   P [$_T$ [$_{vP}$ to Mary [seems [that Bill sleeps]]]]

Assume finally, and again following Torrego (2002), that

(50)   P attracts the experiencer to its spec, and the 'Case-checking relation [between P and the experiencer] renders the experiencer a DP.'

At the point in the derivation represented by (49), *Mary* is contained inside the PP headed by the preposition *to*. Consequently, *Mary* does not c-command out of the PP (we assume the derivational definition of c-command proposed in DASR and Epstein 1999) and hence can't bind an element in the lower CP/TP at this point in the derivation. However, for Torrego, after Experiencer-Raising to [Spec, P], P checks the Case of the experiencer, yielding (51):

(51)   P-Mary [$_T$ [$_{vP}$ __ [seems that Bill sleeps]

At this point in the derivation, *Mary* does c-command downward into the TP. Note that (50) is one implementation of the idea, developed in a number of recent works, that the object of the experiencer PP does not c-command at one point in the derivation, but that the object of *to* (or else a feature of it) raises to a higher position, and that movement is hypothesized to extend the object's c-command domain (i.e. the object DP does c-command into the lower clause at a later point in the derivation).

What we would like to point out now is that the assumptions above, motivated by Torrego (2002) on grounds independent of (27), repeated here, allow a potential solution to the problem raised by such examples for our approach.

(27)   a.   *Bill appears to Mary$_1$ to seem to herself$_1$ to be ill.
        b.   Bill$_1$ appears to Mary to seem to himself$_1$ to be ill.

Let us begin with (27a). Why is it excluded? The first relevant point in the derivation of (27a) is represented in (52):[25]

---

25. Note that the experiencer of *seem*, namely *to herself*, also raises to the P above *to seem* in the intermediate clause; thus, we would have:

(i)   P-Mary Bill ~~to Mary$_1$~~ appears [herself to seem ~~to herself$_1$~~ to Bill like physics

(52)   T [$_{vP}$ [$_{PP}$ to Mary₁] appears [to seem to herself₁ to be Bill ill]]

Recall that since *Mary* is within the PP *to Mary*, it does not c-command out of this container, and hence can't bind the reflexive at this point in the derivation. In (52), we assume that *Bill* raises directly to spec of the matrix T for Case checking. Since *Mary* doesn't c-command *Bill* at this point and hence is not an 'intervener', T can attract *Bill* under attraction locality (again, for us each intermediate *to* has no attracting features, so attraction of *Bill* is in one fell swoop):

(53)   Bill [$_{PP}$ to Mary₁] appears [to seem to herself₁ to be ~~Bill~~ ill]
        ↑_____|

Mary still does not c-command *herself* and hence can't bind it. Next, the functional category P is merged in, following Torrego (2002):

(54)   P [Bill [$_{PP}$ to Mary₁] appears to seem to herself₁ to be Bill ill]

P then attracts the experiencer to its specifier, and 'converts' the PP to a DP under Case-checking:[26]

(55)   P-Mary Bill ~~to Mary~~₁ appears [to seem to herself₁ to be ~~Bill~~ ill]
        ↑_____|

At this point in the derivation, *Mary* does c-command *herself*.[27] But crucially *Bill* is now a subject that intervenes between *Mary* and the reflexive, and thus Con-

---

We don't show this added detail mainly for exposition; the arguments go through as indicated in the text.

26. It could also be that the DP itself raises (not the whole PP) and thus the DP would c-command down after it is merged with P. Furthermore, as we'll see in chapter 5, our system does not allow covert movement of a category with phonetic features. Thus, to implement the Torregovian analysis, we may have to adopt feature movement as in Chomsky (1995); thus 'experiencer raising' in (55) is raising of just the relevant features.

27. Chomsky (1995) raises a question regarding attraction relative to (i).

    (i)   T seems to Bill to be John ill (yielding: *John seems to Bill to be ill*)

Specifically, how can the matrix T attract *John* when *Bill* is closer to T? Attraction states that the attracting probe takes the first matching goal. Torrego's analysis reviewed here raises a similar question: how can the attracting P (above T) attract the experiencer 'over' the subject (which has raised to Spec, T). We leave the issue open here.

dition A is never satisfied.[28] To sum up, the ungrammatical example is excluded as follows under a Torregovian analysis: before experiencer movement, *Mary* fails to c-command *herself* and so is not a licit binder at an 'early' point in the derivation; after experiencer raising to Spec, P (i.e. the 'point of view' position), although *Mary* now c-commands *herself*, *Bill*, having raised to spec of matrix T, functions as an intervening specified subject. Thus, at no point is *Mary* a licit antecedent for *herself*, and (27a) is correctly excluded with no appeal made to either the EPP nor to successive cyclic A-movement.

Within the classic, EPP-based analysis of (27a), it follows that there is a (crucial) point in the derivation where *Bill* (or its trace) is closer to the reflexive than is *Mary*; namely, the point where *Bill* occupies the intermediate spec of raising *to*, as forced by the EPP. So, even though *Mary* c-commands and appears to be close to *herself*, *Bill* (or its trace) in fact remains the closer binder and, being a subject, blocks the binding relation between *Mary* and *herself*.

What is suggested here, as in the standard EPP-based analysis, is that *Bill* is in fact the closest binder for the reflexive; it's just that the point in the derivation where this 'happens' does not involve spec of *to*. Thus, both the present analysis and the standard EPP-based analysis have the structure (56) in common:

(56)   ...Mary ...Bill ... -self

i.e. where *Bill*, a 'subject', c-commands and is closer to *-self* (and *Mary* c-commands but is 'blocked' by *Bill* from binding *-self*). But, within the standard account, (56) emerges since *Bill* moves through the relevant lower spec of *to*. By contrast, in the present account, this configuration emerges when *Mary* is attracted by P (after *Bill* is attracted by matrix T). It is important to stress here too that the crucial components of this analysis, specifically the point-of-view functional projection P and its location higher than T, and the special role of the experiencer, are all motivated independently of consideration of (27) (for the role of P, see particularly Torrego 2002).[29]

---

28. There are various characterizations of the binding principles that could be adopted here, all compatible with the basic approach assumed. For concreteness, we assume the interpretive theory of Chomsky & Lasnik (1993); see Epstein *et al.* (1998), Chapter 2, for detailed discussion. An open question with this account is why *Bill* does not intervene for probing between P and *Mary*, but does intervene (after movement of *Mary*) between *Mary* (now in Spec, P) and *herself* for binding.
29. The analysis suggested here, even if correct, applies only to experiencers. If there exist similar

Before considering a number of challenges to this approach, let us further explore some of its consequences. Recall (27b), repeated here.

(27)   b.   Bill₁ appears to Mary to seem to himself₁ to be ill.

Arguably, *Mary* is not a 'subject', and by hypothesis does not block the binding-theoretic relation between *Bill* and *himself* (parallel to, say, *Bill talked to Mary about himself*). If *Mary* doesn't count as 'a subject', then it won't block the indicated binding relation. And, even if *Mary* in (27b) does count as a subject, (27b) still does not involve a Condition A violation. In relevant respects, (27b) has the same derivation as that for (27a). The key difference is that unlike in (27a), in the derivation of (27b) there is a point in the derivation where *himself* is locally bound by *Bill*, namely the point after the higher experiencer has raised to P (above T).

(57)   Mary Bill appears __ [himself to seem to be __ ill

Again, *Bill* has moved to the matrix in one step. And *Mary* (or just its relevant features) has moved to Spec, P (covertly). After *Mary* moves, *Bill* locally binds *himself*, by hypothesis satisfying Condition A, provisionally assuming, as we noted in Chapters 2 and 3, that there are no 'A-traces' (or in more recent terms, no 'A-reconstruction'; see also Lasnik 1999).

Under this account, the standardly noted Condition C effects follow – on one set of assumptions regarding the 'timing' of Condition C. Consider (58):

> phenomena, but without experiencers, we don't account for them. In this regard, the following might well be an instantiation of the phenomenon but with no experiencer PP in the matrix, but rather an agentive by-phrase.
>
> (i)   Bill is believed by Mary [__ to seem to himself/*herself to be sick]
>
> If *[by Mary]* is not an experiencer (as seems correct), then perhaps this PP cannot undergo experiencer raising. Moreover, perhaps *herself* can be licitly bound by *Mary* (indicating a c-command relation), as evidenced by
>
> (ii)   It is believed by every man₁ that he₁ is attractive.
>
> Thus we confront the question, 'if there is no EPP, hence nothing in the embedded spec of *to*, why can't *herself* appear grammatically in (i)?'

(58)   a. ?*It seems to her$_1$ that Mary$_1$ is smart.
        b. ?*Bill seems to her$_1$ __ to like Mary$_1$.

Here, *her* will bind *Mary* (in violation of Condition C) after checking by P, i.e. at the point in the derivation represented in (59):

(59)   a. *P-her$_1$ it seems to her that Mary$_1$ is smart
        b. *P-her$_1$ it seems to her to like Mary$_1$

Following Lebeaux (1988, 1991)), we could assume that a reflexive must be locally A-bound at some point in the derivation, but that an R-expression must not be A-bound at any point in the derivation. At the derivational point in (59), *her* binds *Mary*, violating Condition C by hypothesis.[30]

Notice further that the present proposal offers an account of a contrast between Condition C and Condition B effects noted in Castillo, Drury, and Grohmann (1999). They note that while (58) exhibits a Condition C effect, (60) does not seem to exhibit a Condition B effect:

(60)   Mary seems to John$_1$ to appear to him$_1$ to be in the room.

We've seen how (58) is disallowed. As for (60), under the proposal suggested here, there is no point in the derivation where the pronoun *him* is locally bound by *John*. At an early point in the derivation, *John* is contained inside the PP *to John* and hence does not c-command *him* (hence there is no Condition B violation at this early derivational point). After *John* is attracted by P, *Mary* (already attracted by

---

30. A potential problem with this assumption (see section 4.4.2.1 below for further comment) is that it seems to predict, incorrectly, that (i) is ill-formed:

(i)   Mary's father seems to her to be __ ill

After experiencer raising we have

(ii)   her Mary's father seems to be ill

and here *her* binds *Mary* in apparent violation of Condition C. As we mentioned above, examples like (58), at least for some speakers, are marginal, and contrast with the completely ill-formed *she seems to Bill to like Mary's dog*. One approach to (i), then, would be that the 'point of view' position, spec of P is an 'A'' position and hence does not count for BT-C. This allows in (i) and (58). But it leaves unexplained the unacceptability of (58) for some speakers.

the matrix T) intervenes between *John* and *him* (thus, even though *John* does c-command *him* at this later derivational point, by hypothesis it does not bind *him* locally enough to violate Condition B).

(61)   John₁ Mary seems to appear to him₁ to be in the room.

Thus, the Condition B violation is (correctly) avoided.[31]

To summarize, following Torrego's (2002) independently-motivated analysis, we suggested that in a raising-with-experiencer structure like (62)

(62)   Bill seems to us to be nice.

Bill raises directly to the matrix T, for Case. At the point where *to us* is merged into the derivation, and at all points until the point where 'experiencer movement'

---

31. Consider next the related cases in (i).

(i)   a.   It seems to John to appear to him that Mary is in the room.
       b.   It seems to John to appear to himself that Mary is in the room.

As mentioned above, the status of these examples is not clear. We pointed out that (ib) is better than *Mary seems to John to appear to himself to be in the room*.
We predict that (ia) is ill-formed while (ib) is well formed. After experiencer raising, we have:

(ii)   John₁ it seems to appear to him/himself that IP

Under the assumption that expletive *it* does not count here as a subject that can block a binding relation, *John* locally binds *him/himself*. An EPP account forces *it* to start low and raise up, as in (iii):

(iii)   It seems to John ~~it~~ to appear to him/himself that IP

If *it* doesn't block binding relations, then *John* locally binds *him/himself* (allowing (ib), and disallowing (ia)). Note that Bošković (2002) argues that expletives don't move, but rather are first-merged into their surface positions. Thus, he also would make the same prediction. The status of such examples, however, is not entirely clear. It seems to us that (ia) is in fact worse than (ib) (at least one informant reports that (ia) seems better than (ib)); however, both examples are accepted in Grohmann *et al.* (2000:161). We still disallow (iv), correctly, we think:

(iv)   Mary₁ seems to John to appear to her₁ to be in the room.

See Chomsky (1981) and Lasnik and Uriagereka (1988) for analyses within which *it* sometimes does but sometimes does not count as an accessible subject for X, depending on the relative positions of *it* and X.

applies, *us*, as an oblique, does not c-command into the lower clause. When *us* (covertly) raises to the spec of the 'point of view' projection P, which is hypothesized by Torrego to be above T, it does c-command the lower (and the higher) clause (but *Bill* now functions as an intervening subject):

(63)   us Bill seems to be nice

We've speculated that this analysis might account for the basic (and some 'new') cases of binding that have been presented as problematic to the one fell swoop analysis of A-movement that we have proposed.

One potentially serious problem with this account is that it involves covert movement (of the experiencer to the 'point of view' position). As we'll see in Chapter 5 (see in particular section 5.5.3), covert movement is not possible in our model of grammar. Given that, by hypothesis, PF and LF interpret an object at all points of a derivation, movement of an element with phonetic content will necessarily have PF consequences; under our architecture it is not possible to spell-out X to PF and then continue X to LF wherein further movement takes place without PF consequences. The only form of 'covert' movement would be movement of an element that does not have phonetic features; perhaps, for example, movement of just formal, or semantic features. To allow for 'covert' experiencer raising, then, we might have to adopt the feature movement approach of Chomsky (1995). It's been argued (see Chomsky 1981 and more recently Lasnik 2001) that covert movement does not affect binding relations. Experiencer raising would be movement of features, then, and not movement of the entire category with phonetic features. Furthermore, we would apparently have to adopt the position that such feature movement (at least in the case of experiencers) can effect binding relations (as outlined above).

4.4.3.1   Further unclarities concerning experiencer binding   We note now that the analysis traced above has a number of further positive consequences and a number of negative ones. Let's consider its advantages, beyond the data above, first.

Boeckx (1999) presents (64) as evidence against the analysis of Kitahara (1997):

(64)   Pictures of himself$_1$ seem to John$_1$ [to be blurry]

Boeckx states that '. . .it is not sufficient to let the experiencer c-command [only

SDE/TDS] into the embedded clause after subject raising, for there is evidence that the experiencer c-commands into the raising subject...' [that evidence being example (64)]. Thus, for Kitahara's (1997) analysis, *John* does not c-command 'down' until after the subject *pictures of himself* has raised to the matrix T for Case. But even though *John* does c-command 'down' at LF, that is 'too late' since now the raised subject is out of *John*'s c-command domain (again, assuming no A-reconstruction). Note that under our analysis, (64) becomes (65) after (covert) raising of the experiencer:

(65) John pictures of himself seem __ to be blurry

And here *John* can (locally A) bind *himself*, satisfying Condition A. For the analysis under consideration, the point where *John* does c-command outside of its (previously) containing PP is not 'too late', since for us, following Torrego, the experiencer moves to a position higher than the subject (and hence can bind into the subject).[32]

A potential problem for our proposal (and for others), however, concerns the grammatical (66) (modeled on examples from Lebeaux 1991:228, (60)).

(66) Pictures of Mary seem to her to be blurry.
      (cf. ?*It seems to her that pictures of Mary are blurry.)

We've just seen that, under our adoption of Torrego, the experiencer c-commands into the raised subject after experiencer raising; and that was good news in the case of (64). But it's apparently undesirable in (66). After raising of the experiencer in (66), we have

---

32. Boeckx (1999) also presents (i) as evidence that the experiencer can c-command into the matrix subject:

   (i) Pictures of any artists appear to no critics to be revealing.

   The grammatical status of this example isn't altogether clear to us. The following seems ungrammatical, however:

   (ii) *Any artists appear to no critics to be very good.

   We leave the matter for future research.

(67)   her₁ pictures of Mary₁ seem to be blurry

and here we would seem to have a Condition C violation (*her* binds *Mary*), incorrectly predicting that (67) is ungrammatical on the indicated reading.

We should note that the well-formedness of (67) is also potentially problematic for Boeckx's (1999) analysis. For him, the experiencer '...c-commands (into) the embedded clause right from the start (upon merger).' Thus, before the DP *pictures of Mary* raises to the matrix T in (66), *her* would c-command *Mary*, violating Condition C at that point in the derivation. But, interestingly, for Boeckx's analysis, the R-expression is moving out of the domain of the binder; i.e. even though for Boeckx *her* c-commands *Mary* at derivational point (68).

(68)   T seems to her to be pictures of Mary blurry

Then, *pictures of Mary* moves out of the c-command domain of *her*, in raising to the matrix subject position, as in (66), repeated below:

(66)   Pictures of Mary seem to her to be blurry.

And, at the right level of abstraction, this is just what happens in (69)

(69)   Which picture of Mary does she like best

which, at least according to some researchers, is well formed on the indicated co-referential reading.[33] (Higginbotham 1983 accepts (69) on the indicated reading, while this same reading is rejected as ungrammatical in Chomsky 1993, Epstein *et al.* 1998, and others.)

---

33. Another potential problem for our analysis involves (i).

   (i)   Bill seems to himself to be blurry.

   At the point in the derivation where *Bill* raises to the matrix T for Case checking, it does locally bind the reflexive; thus, Condition A is satisfied. However, after raising of the experiencer, we have:

   (ii)   himself Bill seems __ to be blurry

   And here *himself* binds *Bill* in apparent violation of Condition C (at LF). It is not clear to us just how to deal with this case, but we note that a similar problem arises with topicalization.

   (iii)   a. Bill likes himself.
           b. Himself, Bill likes.

   Somehow this too avoids a Condition C violation. Perhaps this is A′ binding in the 'GB sense', thereby avoiding the BT-C violation.

To summarize, we find much of the existing data unclear. Moreover, the analyses, including our own, seem in many respects problematically underspecified. Given this state of affairs, it is not clear whether this domain of phenomena constitute a compelling argument for or against successive cyclic A-movement.

4.4.4 Experiencers and reconstruction

Consider again (6) (from Lebeaux 1991).

(6)   a. *his_1 $mother's_2$ bread seems to her_2 __ to be known by every man_1 to be the best.
       b. his_1 $mother's_2$ bread seems to every man_1 __ to be known by her_2 to be the best.

It is not clear to us, how, even with the EPP and/or successive cyclic A movement, these examples are handled. (Nor do we mean to claim that we have a clear analysis.) The question we address here then is the following; is there a compelling descriptively adequate account of these (complex) examples that relies on, hence motivates the existence of the intermediate spec positions? Only if there is, does the elimination of the EPP (and successive cyclic A-movement) represent a weakening of empirical adequacy.

Bošković (2002) uses (6) to motivate successive cyclic A-movement through spec of *to*. The general idea is clear enough: in (6) *his mother's bread* must have moved through the indicated intermediate spec of *to* position in order to allow 'reconstruction' to that position. As a result, in (6b), *every man* can bind *his* but *her* does not bind . . . *mother*. In (6a), what's critical is that to get low enough to be bound by *every man*, *his mother's bread* will be lower than *her*, and hence *her* will bind . . . *mother*. . ., thereby violating Condition C (assuming, as is 'standard', that BT-C applies throughout a derivation).

However, there is evidence against A-reconstruction (see Chomsky 1995 and especially Lasnik 1999).[34] Thus, as Bošković (2002) notes, he is using the term 'reconstruction' in an informal way in reference to (6). He states that 'the [reconstruction] process in question can either involve activation of lower copies of chains in LF or a derivational, online application of relevant conditions at the point when the intermediate positions are actually heads of chains' (Bošković 2002:180, fn. 14).

---

34. But see Boeckx (2001) for a critical assessment of the evidence against A-reconstruction.

For us, it can't be copies or chains (since there are no 'chains' nor A-traces).[35] But, if it's 'online' for Bošković, it's not clear just how the examples in (6) are accounted for, even with movement of *his mother's bread* through spec of the intermediate *to*. Bošković's specific assumptions about '... a derivational, online application of relevant conditions at the point when the intermediate positions are actually heads of chains...' are not clear to us. Let us consider some of the details.

Regarding (6), we can't evaluate the binding conditions only at the point where *his mother's bread* is in the intermediate position, marked '__'. At that point in the derivation, (6a) appears as in (70).

(70)   His$_1$ mother's bread to be known by every man$_1$ to be ~~his mother's bread~~ the best.

Even assuming that *every man* counts as binding *his*, there is no Condition C violation in (70), since *her* is not yet even introduced into the derivation. Consider, then, the derivational point depicted in (71):

(71)   T seems to her$_2$ his$_1$ mother's$_2$ bread to be known by every man$_1$ to be __ the best

Here *her*, by hypothesis, binds ... *mother*... thereby violating Condition C, correctly predicting that (6a) is ill-formed. But there now seems to be a problem with (6b). With respect to (6b), at the 'early' derivational point represented in (72),

(72)   to be known by her$_2$ to be his mother's$_2$ bread the best

her binds ... *mother's*... thereby violating Condition C. If Condition C cannot be violated at any point in the derivation (the 'standard' assumption from Lebeaux 1991, and see references therein), then it doesn't matter how we proceed from (72); (6b) will be incorrectly excluded (since we can't 'undo' the BT-C violation later in the derivation).

A critical component of Lebeaux's (1991) original analysis of (6) is the

---

35. In fact, Lebeaux argues that a chain-theoretic account of the contrast in (6) is empirically inadequate. The contrast in (6) '... goes strongly against a purely representational view of the chain, in which all positions are held as interpretively equivalent and the chain itself is interpreted as if it were a single interpretive entity...' And he continues '... it does not predict the interaction between positive [e.g. pronominal binding] and negative conditions (e.g. BT-C; TDS, SDE]... of the sort in (6)].' Lebeaux (1991:235).

hypothesized 'information increasing' character of the derivation, and specifically the idea that the DP *his mother's bread* can be added 'late' in the course of the derivation (just as adjuncts can be 'late inserted'). This solves one problem mentioned above, namely, the following: If BT-C can't be violated at any point in the derivation, it's hard to see how to distinguish (6a) and (6b) since if *his mother's bread* is present at its theta position and at all points thereafter, then BT-C will be violated in both (6a) and (6b). How Bošković (2002) deals with this issue is simply unclear to us. But Lebeaux avoids this particular problem by assuming that *his mother's bread* can be inserted late in the derivation. One, among many, of Lebeaux's fascinating insights is that (6a) and (6b), repeated here

(6)   a.   *his_1 $mother's_2$ bread seems to her_2 __ to be known by every man_1 to be the best.
         b. his_1 $mother's_2$ bread seems to every man_1 __ to be known by her_2 to be the best.

are parallel, in relevant respects, to the *wh*-movement cases in (73) below

(73)   a.   which paper [that he_i gave to $Bresnan_j$] did every $student_i$ think that she_j would like t
         b.   *which paper [that he_i gave to $Bresnan_j$] did she_j think that every $student_i$ would like t

Lebeaux argues that adjuncts, including relative clauses, can be inserted late in the derivation. Thus the bracketed relative clause in (73a) and (73b) can be built separately from the main clause, and then attached to the *wh*-phrase *which paper*, at the point in the derivation where *which paper* is in the intermediate Spec, CP position. For (73a), then, we have the derivation indicated in (74)

(74)   a.   . . . every $student_i$ think that she_j would like which paper
         b.   every $student_i$ think which paper that she_j would like t
         c.   that he_i gave to $Bresnan_j$
         d.   every $student_i$ think which paper that [he_i gave to $Bresnan_j$] that she_j would like t

Since the adjunct (the relative clause) containing the name *Bresnan* is inserted late in the derivation, at point 'd', it follows that there is no point in the derivation where *she* c-commands *Bresnan*, and hence BT-C is not violated in the derivation of (73a). But, crucially, there is a point in the derivation where the pronoun *he* is c-commanded by, and hence properly bound by, *every student*, again at the point 'd' above. Thus the indicated reading of (73a) emerges; crucially it is relative to the intermediate CP position where *Bresnan* can escape *she*, yet *he* can fall within the binding domain of *every student*. Not so (73b). In (73b), in order to avoid a BT-C violation, we must late insert the name-containing adjunct *that he gave to Bresnan*. But if we late insert this adjunct, then *he* contained inside the adjunct will not ever by bound by *every student*. And if we insert the adjunct early enough for *every student* to bind *he*, we will also be inserting *Bresnan* (*he* and *Bresnan* being contained in the same adjunct) and hence a ('everywhere') BT-C violation results. Overall, then, there is no well-formed derivation for (73b), just the right result.

Lebeaux's insight is that the DP *his mother's bread* behaves in (6) much like the adjunct *that he gave to Bresnan* does in (73). Specifically, Lebeaux notes that if *his mother's bread* can be late inserted in (6), the indicated contrast between (6a) and (6b) emerges. We simply don't know if Bošković would accept a Lebeaux-style 'online' analysis of the sort indicated above, but, at least on one view, what Bošković (2002) can be seen as stressing, is that for a Lebeauxian analysis to work, critically, there must be successive cyclic movement through the intermediate Spec, IP position. Consider first the well-formed (6b):

(6) b. his$_1$ mother's$_2$ bread seems to every man$_1$ ___ to be known by her$_2$ to be the best.

The idea is that *his mother's bread* is not present in its 'base' position (rather Lebeaux assumes that an empty element, pro, may occur there). Thus, early in the derivation we have (75)

(75) . . . to be known by her to be pro the best

Since *his mother's bread* is not present, *her* does not bind *mother* and hence BT-C is not violated (at this point, nor any point hereafter, in the derivation). If we late insert *his mother's bread* in the intermediate Spec, IP position, then we have derivational point (76):

(76)   seems to every man$_i$ [his$_i$ mother's]$_j$ bread to be known by her$_j$ to be pro the best

In (76) *every man* binds *his*[36] thereby securing the bound pronoun reading, but at no point is BT-C violated, thereby allowing coreference between *[his mother's]$_j$* and *her$_j$*. It's critical that *his mother's bread* not be inserted higher than the intermediate Spec, IP position, since otherwise (if, for example, *his mother's bread* is inserted in the matrix Spec, IP position), *his* will not be in the c-command domain of *every man* and hence the bound pronoun reading won't be secured. On the other hand, it's critical that *his mother's bread* not be inserted lower than the intermediate Spec, IP position (for example, in its 'base' position) since then *her* will bind *[his mother]* and thereby run afoul of BT-C. The only way to secure the bound pronoun reading of *his* and avoid a BT-C violation relative to *her* and *mother* is for *his mother's bread* to be inserted in the intermediate Spec, IP position.

Consider next (6a):

(6) a. *his$_1$ mother's$_2$ bread seems to her$_2$ __ to be known by every man$_1$ to be the best.

No well-formed derivation arises here. Essentially parallel to (73a), we need to insert *his mother's bread* low (in its 'base' position) in order to get *his* bound by *every man*. But then *her* will bind *[his mother's]*, thereby violating BT-C. If we late insert *his mother's bread* (in any position higher than the 'base' position, *every man* will fail to c-command (and hence can't bind) the pronoun *his*.

We see, then, the role that the intermediate spec of raising infinitival position is potentially playing in (6). But there are a number of potential problems with the 'late insertion' proposal. First, the interpretation and distribution of the 'pro' element in the derivation of (6b) and its presumably 'coindexed' relation to the 'late inserted' DP are unclear. A central question is how the predication relation between *his mother's bread* and *be the best* can be established 'at a distance'. Somehow without violating inclusiveness, the pronominal element pro must be obligatorily related to *his mother's bread* and some theta role transmission mechanism from pro to the full DP must also be developed. Second, it's unclear that the late insertion proposal is consistent with Bošković's notion of globally feature-driven movement; i.e. unlike in an example like *Bill seems to be happy* (where *Bill* is directly attracted

---

36. Lebeaux assumes that the experiencer c-commands into the lower clause.

by the matrix T but moves to the intermediate Spec, IP position because of movement locality), the DP *his mother's bread* in (6) never moves to spec of *to* under the late insertion analysis. That is, contra Bošković's theory *his mother's bread* is not moving to the crucial intermediate Spec, IP position and therefore it cannot be in this position as a result of locality constraints on the application of movement. Rather, *his mother's bread* is late first-merged into the crucial Spec, IP position. Importantly, this (see section 4.3.2.3) seems like a GB-style 'gratuitous' operation; we insert the DP because we can. But even this isn't clear; i.e. it isn't clear that we even can first merge into Spec, IP. The late insertion of *his mother's bread* in (6) runs afoul of Lebeaux's original idea that only adjuncts (i.e. non-theta marked) elements can be inserted in the course of the derivation. In Chomsky's (2001a) terms, such late insertion of the DP in (6) is not possible given the following, derivational residue of part of the theta criterion:

(77)   all and only arguments are first merged into a theta position

In (6), the DP *his mother's bread* would be inserted into a non-theta position, in violation of (77). Now, even if this crucial theta-based problem were resolved and such insertion into non-theta positions allowed, the question remains: what drives the operation; specifically, how can it be a locality-constrained, feature-based operation?[37]

We are not arguing here that we have an alternative analysis of these data. What we are suggesting is that Bošković's claim relative to (6) that 'the data in question can be easily accounted for if the matrix-clause subject passes through the embedded [Spec, IP]s, which can then serve as reconstruction sites' (p. 180) isn't altogether clear.

4.4.5   Q-float

4.4.5.1   The basic problem: Q-float appears to motivate the EPP   We begin by reviewing the basic problem represented by Q-float. We have argued that there is no movement to or through the spec of raising *to* in cases like (78):

---

37. Interestingly, this could be construed as an argument for the EPP. That is, the EPP is the feature that drives the operation (here then would be an instance of pure EPP checking). But, that leaves the problem of such examples as **John expected [__ to be discovered a proof]*; i.e. the examples that originally motivated (77); see Chapter 3, section 3.3.3.

(78)   Bill seems [to be ~~Bill~~ sick]

However, under the Sportiche (1988) analysis of Floating Quantifiers, there is evidence that there is in fact movement through spec of raising *to*. Consider, for instance, (79):

(79)   The students seem [all to know French]

Under the Sportiche analysis, according to which the Q 'starts' adjoined to the NP it 'modifies' and then is strandable as the NP moves out, (79) would be represented as in (80).

(80)   The students seem [all ~~the students~~] to ~~all the students~~ know French

The floating Q is, in effect, a movement 'place-holder' and since in (79), *all* appears to be in Spec, IP, then the perfectly natural argument is that there must have been movement to Spec, IP, contrary to what we have argued. In short, the counter-argument to us is that in (80) *all* couldn't be in Spec, IP unless it was stranded there, and it could only have been stranded there if the NP *all the students* moved there; and its reason for moving there is (or, 'must be') the EPP.

Recall furthermore that Bošković (2002) accounts for these cases of Q-float without appeal to the EPP; rather, movement through the spec of the intermediate *to* is motivated by a locality constraint on movement. Thus, Bošković can adopt the derivation in (80); it's just that for him *all the students* moves to spec of *to* given movement locality; it doesn't check any features in this position. We've raised a number of potential problems for the Bošković approach. Let us then consider if there is an alternative account of these Q-float data, one that is consistent with our attempted elimination of the EPP, and also our attempted elimination of A-chains and successive cyclic A-movement.

4.4.5.2 Some notes on the data   While we agree that (79) above is fine, and while we agree that it represents a significant challenge to the central proposals we advanced in Chapters 2 and 3, we note that a different paradigm emerges (at least for some dialects) with raising adjectives. With adjectives, floating a quantifier in Spec, *to* is significantly degraded:

(81)	a.	The boys are all certain to like pizza.	(cf. *The boys all seem to like pizza.*)
	b.	The boys are certain to all like pizza.	(cf. *The boys seem to all like pizza.*)
	c.*?The boys are certain all to like pizza.	(cf. ?*The boys seem all to like pizza.*)

Even for raising verbs, the floating quantifier in apparent spec of *to* seems somewhat less acceptable than in the other available positions, as indicated in the parentheses next to each of the examples in (81). But the contrast between the (81c) vs. (81a/81b) examples with adjectives seems more pronounced than between (81c) vs. (81a/81b) with raising verbs. Notice next that ECM structures, as in (82),

(82)	I believe the boys all to like pizza.

also evidence movement through spec of raising *to* (again, contrary to our proposal). Essentially the same argument associated with (79) applies here. Thus, given the Sportiche analysis, (82) 'must' have been derived as in (83),

(83)	I believe the boys [$_{IP}$ [all ~~the boys~~] to [~~all the boys~~] like pizza

where *all* is a 'placeholder' for movement through spec of *to*. But, we note that the passivized ECM raising structure does not seem to allow the floating quantifier in Spec, *to*:

(84)	a.	The boys are all believed to like pizza.	(cf. *I believe all the boys to like pizza.*)
	b.	The boys are believed to all like pizza.	(cf. *I believe the boys to all like pizza.*)
	c.*?The boys are believed all to like pizza.	(cf. ?*I believe the boys all to like pizza.*)

Thus, (81c) and (84c) could be seen as evidence that, consistent with our EPP-less analysis of A-movement, there is *not* movement through Spec, IP.

We note too that there is some variation among the floating quantifiers, particularly in the intermediate position. To begin with, even the FQs that are licensed in intermediate spec of *to* position are slightly degraded relative to the other positions, as mentioned briefly above:

(85) a. The kids all seem to like apples.
 b. ?The kids seem all to like apples.
 c. The kids seem to all like apples.

And *all* is better than *each* or *both* in the intermediate position:

(86) a. The kids both/each seem to like apples.
 b. ??The kids seem both/each to like apples.
 c. The kids seem to both/each like apples.

The (b) cases in (86) seem somewhat worse than (85b), though still relatively acceptable.[38] And both (85b) and (86b) are best with a pause, giving a 'parenthetical feel' – almost a reduced form of, say, 'the kids seem, all of them, to like apples.'

But, overall, despite the data above (particularly (81c) and (84c)), we agree that (79) is well formed, and we agree that some response to the argument based on (79) against the EPP-less approach is needed.

Before considering a potential alternative analysis, we consider some further, curious data involving Q-float and raising.

In Epstein and Seely (1999), we present an argument that there is no EPP as feature checking based on certain ellipsis effects. In short, we argue that if Lobeck (1990) and Saito and Murasugi (1990) are correct that a functional head can license ellipsis of its complement only if that functional head has undergone feature checking, then there must not have been feature checking between *to* and its spec in (87).

---

38. We note too that with cases like (79), repeated here:

 (79) The students seem [all to know French]

 there seems to be a (loose) relation between the Q being acceptable in Spec, IP position and the Q occurring in a 'reduced' bare partitive. Thus, we get *all/both of the boys* and also *all/both the boys* and *all* and *both* are acceptable in what appears to be Spec, IP position of (79). But note that although *each* can float (we get *the boys can each eat an apple*), *each* does not occur in reduced partitives; thus we get only *each of the boys* and not *each the boys*. And, *each* is significantly worse than *all/both* in Spec, IP:

 (i) *?The students seem each to know French.

 We leave investigation of this possible correspondence for further research.

(87)   *John believed Mary to like pizza but Bill believed Tom to.

(See Martin 1996, Bošković 2002, and references therein.) For us, *Tom* in the second conjunct of (87) has raised directly to the accusative Case position of *believed* and has not moved through the spec of *to* (there being no features to check in this spec of *to*). Thus, (87) is out since the ellipsis conditions have not been properly met. Although the data are not entirely stable, we note that ellipsis is degraded in certain raising structures as well. Consider (88):[39]

(88)   *Bill doesn't seem to be happy, but Mary seems to.

(87) and (88) contrast with (89), where there is (arguably) null Case checking between *to* and PRO (recall that we've assumed, following Martin 1996, that control *to* does bear checking features, specifically, the null Case feature).

(89)   Bill (really) tries PRO to be happy, but Tom never tries to.

Hence, ellipsis of the VP in (89) is licensed since *to* has checked null Case with PRO.

Based on data like that in (90),

(90)   I believe the students all to know French.

Bošković (2002) argues that there is movement through the spec of *to*, thus accounting for the presence of *all*, but that this movement through the spec of *to* does

---

39. The ellipsis is particularly bad where the complement of raising *to* is copular. Thus, consider (i) vs. (ii):

(i)   *Bill doesn't seem to be happy, but Mary (certainly) seems to.
(ii)   ??Bill doesn't seem to like baseball, but Mary (certainly) seems to.

This contrast seems less pronounced with ECM:

(iii) *Bill believes Mary to be insincere, but he doesn't believe Tom to.
(iv)   *?Bill believes Mary to like baseball, but he doesn't believe Tom to.

And there is no contrast, at least for us, with control infinitives:

(v)   Bill tries to be happy, but Tom never tries to.
(vi)   Bill tries to grow beans, but Tom never tries to.

not result in any feature checking, thereby accounting for the ill-formedness of (87) above.

There are other curiosities concerning the Floated Quantifier data. Consider a proposal of Bošković (2001), arguing (in fact attempting to derive) that:

(91) A FQ can't be 'stranded' in a theta position.

Bošković uses (91) to account for the ill-formedness of (92):

(92) a. *The students were arrested [all ~~the students~~]
      b. *Mary likes the students [all ~~the students~~]
      c. *The students arrived [all ~~the students~~]

Consider now (93):

(93) The students seem to all like syntax.

If, for Bošković, (93) is derived as in (94),

(94) The students seem [the students] to [$_{vP}$ [all the students] like syntax]

then (91) is violated since we seem to be stranding the *all* in a θ-position. Bošković (2001) accounts for cases like (95)

(95) The students all like syntax.

by appealing to the (independently motivated) Split Infl Hypothesis. Thus, *all the students* first moves to Spec, TP, a non-θ position, and then *the students* moves out to Spec, AgrS, leaving *all* behind – and satisfying (91). Interestingly, (94) suggests that infinitivals too have a split Infl. Consider

(96) The students seem [the students [to [$_{AgrSP}$ all the students [all the students like syntax.

We would now like to note a rather curious set of facts regarding Q-float. Consider (97):

(97) a. The girls seem all to like baseball, and...
      b. ?*...the boys seem all to as well.
      c. *...the boys seem to all as well. (cf. *The boys seem to all like baseball.*)

While both are degraded, for some speakers there is a contrast between (97b) and (97c). If there is no feature checking between *to* and its spec (as we and Bošković suggest), then it's unclear why we should be able to elide the VP in (97b), but not in (97c); both cases, all else equal, should be ill-formed (see also Baltin 1995). The same seems true for ECM:

(98) a. I believe the girls all to like baseball...
      b. ...but Bill doesn't believe the boys all to.
      c. *...but Bill doesn't believe the boys to all.

Note an apparently similar effect from Sag (1978) (see also Bobaljik 2001):

(99) a. Otto has read this book, and...
      b. ...my brothers all/probably have, too.
      c. *...my brothers have all/probably, too. (cf. *My brothers have all/probably read this book.*)

Sag (1978) uses cases such as (99) as evidence that FQs pattern together with adverbs (and thus should be treated similarly, as adverbs).

4.4.5.3 Williams' argument extended: a potential solution? Williams (1982, 1989, 1994) rejects the Sportiche 'floating' analysis of FQ, arguing instead that FQs are adverbs adjoined to VP. Thus, in (100),

(100) The boys [both read the book]

both is adjoined to VP and it 'modulates the subject-predicate relation.' Thus, the FQ *both* 'says of the VP it is attached to that the VP will be true of the subject it applies to only if that subject denotes two individuals, and the VP is true of each of those individuals separately.' As a consequence, the FQ is related to the NP only indirectly – the FQ modifies the VP and the VP, in turn, is predicated of the NP.

Williams then argues that there are 'true' adverbs that do just the same thing as FQs, and for these 'true' adverbs an analysis like the one Williams proposes is independently necessary. But that adverb analysis of the 'true' adverbs carries over to the FQ cases 'rendering any analysis other than the VP-modifying adverbial one superfluous' (hence the 'floating' Q analysis is rejected). The relevant adverbs include *separately* and *jointly*. And, we might add *together*, *individually*, and others (see Seely 1993).

Consider now (101).

(101)   They [separately carried out the orders]

According to Williams, *separately* is adjoined to the VP and 'distributes' it (similar to, say, the FQ *each*). It is not plausible to treat *separately* (and like adverbs) as floating quantifiers a la Sportiche, since these adverbs occur in positions where an NP cannot occur. Thus, as Williams notes, we get:

(102)   They carried out the orders separately/jointly.

It is unlikely that *separately* in (102) was left behind by NP movement (there is simply no evidence, independent of the presence of the FQ, that the NP moved to such a post-verbal position). Thus the VP-modifier analysis is needed independently of Q-float, but that VP-modifier analysis, by hypothesis, carries over to the Q-float cases 'rendering the [Q-float story] superfluous.'

Williams does not examine the position of distributivizing adverbs in embedded clauses. But an argument based on Williams's analysis presents itself, one that offers a potential solution to the problem raised by (79). Our argument runs in this way: (79) does not necessarily evidence NP movement through Spec, IP. The alternative interpretation, assuming Williams, is that 'floating' adverbs can adjoin not just to VP but also to IP (or some projection higher than VP and lower than IP). In support of this, note that the 'true' adverbs, like *jointly* and *separately*, can occupy the same position as *all* – although the result is not perfect. Thus, we get

(103)   ?The boys seem separately/jointly/individually to have cleaned the room.

Since such adverbs are not plausibly derived from NP movement, it must be that they can adjoin to IP. But since the adverb analysis subsumes the quantifier 'stranding' analysis of Sportiche, we can derive (79) in the same way as (103); i.e., there was no movement to or through spec of *to*, but rather the adverb *all* is simply adjoined to the lower IP – in line with Williams.[40]

Independent support for the claim that distributivizing adverbs (a.k.a. floating quantifiers) can adjoin to IP is provided by such examples as:

(104)   Separately the boys cleaned the rooms.

Further support is provided by the fact that the data above is variable (with respect to the positions of the adverbs) and adverbs are well known to be variable in this regard (i.e. variation regarding which adverb can attach where).

Yet further support for the adverb analysis comes from the fact that examples like (79) improve as the FQ gets 'heavier', and such heaviness improving the acceptability of adverbs in certain positions is independently argued for in Jaeggli (1982):

(105)   a.   The boys seem all in their own way to be sick.
        b.   The boys seem each in a different way to like the wild.

Note also the 'parenthetical feel' of some of these examples.

(106)   a.   The boys seem, every last one of them, to know French.
        b.   The boys seemed, each in his own way, to have cleaned the rooms.

The above examples are not plausibly derived via stranding the quantifier (we don't have the NP *each in his own way the boys*, for example); but rather, the adverbial analysis is preferred, and yet we have the quantifier in the apparent Spec, IP position. Again, we argue that in fact it's adjoined to IP and not, despite appearances, a pronounced part of the Spec, IP 'copy' *[the boys all]*.

Interestingly, Bobaljik provides an extensive review of the relevant Q-float literature and concludes that the matter is far from settled. Thus, it's not conclusive that the Sportiche analysis holds; there are interesting pros and cons of each (movement vs. adverb) views.

---

40. To claim that *all* is an adverb is not to claim that its distribution is identical to, say, *separately*. It isn't:

   (i)   They carried out the orders separately/*all.

As Bobaljik (1999:13) notes, '...the hypothesis that FQs mark positions from (or through) which a DP has moved deserves close scrutiny. Such scrutiny reveals, however, that the evidence for this proposal is thin and that many crucial questions are still unanswered...'

Here, once again, we are simply arguing, as we have above, that all analyses are implicitly conditional; for example, '*if* Sportiche (1988) is correct, *then* it appears we have evidence for movement through spec of *to*.' We have suggested some possible reasons for rejecting a Sportiche-type analysis. To the extent that these reasons are suggestive or compelling, the (conditional) arguments for the EPP or successive cyclic A-movement forced by locality are reduced.

4.5   Lasnik's cases

4.5.1   Introduction

In a series of important papers,[41] Lasnik presents a number of arguments supporting the retention of the EPP. Some of those arguments we have already considered in some detail. Recall, for example, Lasnik's argument for the EPP based on raising infinitival complements of nominals, as in (107).

(107)   *the belief [to seem [Peter is ill]]

To account for such cases, Lasnik suggests that '...it seems most principled to rely on the combination of the Case Filter and the EPP.' The EPP forces the spec of the lower IP to be filled with an overt DP, but then that DP can't get Case checked. We argued, however, that (107) and the like can be accounted for by appealing not to the EPP, but rather to independently motivated assumptions regarding the embedded clausal structure (that the infinitival is a CP with a null head C) and null complementizers (that the null C is an affix that requires a +V host, and can't find such a host in (107)). In fact, we've suggested that the EPP is redundant with null complementizer theory in such cases (as discussed in Chapter 3). Lasnik also considers Bošković's (1997) cases involving *conjecture*, as in (108), where the EPP is again implicated.

(108)   *John has conjectured [to seem [Peter is ill]]

---

41. See, for example, Lasnik (1999) and (2003).

But we've suggested that *conjecture* is in fact an accusative Case checker and thus that (108) is excluded as an unchecked Case violation; indeed, we've argued that with respect to cases such as (108), the EPP is redundant with independently motivated Case checking mechanisms (see our discussion in Chapter 3).

In this section we focus on another of Lasnik's arguments for the EPP, using Lasnik (2002), which summarizes certain of his key earlier papers, as our point of departure. In the abstract, the reasoning is as follows. Consider the configuration in (109)

(109)   DP ...[$_{IP}$ __ [$_{VP}$ DP ...]
        a   *b*

Suppose the indicated IP is an embedded raising infinitival. The indicated DP 'starts' in the VP internal theta position and ultimately moves to the position marked *a*, which we assume is a Case checking position (either the subject of a raising predicate like *seem* or the accusative position of an ECM verb like *believe*). What Lasnik does is provide scopal and binding theoretic evidence that the DP *first* moves to Spec, IP. Only if the DP is in the Spec, IP position (at the key point in the derivation) can the attested scope and binding facts be accounted for, Lasnik reasons. Since this Spec, IP position is a non-Case position (nor an agreement nor any other standard morphological featural position), movement to (and through) it must be driven by something other than Case, leaving the EPP as the likely candidate. Thus, it is argued, the EPP must be retained. Let us turn our attention to the details of Lasnik's arguments, and to certain potential problems with them.

4.5.2   ECM verbs and the scope of the problem

One of Lasnik's major arguments for the EPP involves ECM verbs and certain scopal interactions between the universal quantifier and negation that occur within the constructions that contain these ECM verbs. Consider a standard ECM construction as in (110).

(110)   She proved him to be guilty.

Recall we have argued that in (110) there is one-step movement of *him* from its theta position to the Case position, which we've assumed is the spec of the Agr projection above, or in the outer Spec, *v* position of, the ECM verb *prove*. For us, there is no successive cyclic A-movement to or through the spec of the lower IP. Thus we have argued for the movement depicted in (111)

(111)   She proved him [$_{IP}$ to be ~~him~~ guilty]
              ↑_____|

With respect to (110), it is clear from the word order that *him* has moved out of its theta position. Before the development of the split VP hypothesis, however, Chomsky argued that *him* moved to Spec, IP, this movement being motivated by the EPP.[42] From the pre-minimalist perspective, the word order in (110) indicates that *him* has moved and the EPP gave an independently motivated landing site for the movement. But under Chomsky (1991), Johnson (1991), and Lasnik and Saito (1992), ECM ACC Case checking occurs in the higher spec of Agr$_O$. But if so, is there successive cyclic movement through Spec, IP? That is, is the movement as in (111) or as in (112)?

(112)   she proved him [~~him~~ to be ~~him~~ guilty]
              ↑_____↑_____|

In fact, Lasnik suggests that there is evidence that *him* has moved through Spec, IP on its way to the higher Case position and further that the need to move to Spec, IP motivates the EPP (i.e. it constitutes empirical evidence for the EPP).

As mentioned above, Lasnik's argument involves scopal interaction between a universal quantifier and negation. Consider (113) (from Lasnik 2003:13; also see Chomsky 1995).

(113)   a.   I expected everyone not to be there yet.
        b.   I believe everyone not to have arrived yet.

The factual claim is that the examples in (113) are ambiguous between the wide vs. narrow scope reading of the quantifier relative to negation. If true, this is interesting.[43] On independent grounds the following generalization seems to hold. Lasnik (2003:13), reviewing Chomsky (1995), states that

---

42. Interestingly, such movement was also 'motivated' by the need for the lower 'subject' to check Case overtly. Only by moving to the Spec, IP could the subject get close enough to the higher ECM verb to be exceptionally Case marked by that verb.
43. See Hornstein (1995) for certain challenges to the data; and see Lasnik (1999) for a response to Hornstein. See also Boeckx (2001) for discussion.

(114)   ...a subject universal quantifier can be understood inside the scope of clausal negation only if it has not raised away from subject (= Spec of IP position) ...

The idea is that there is no reconstruction into an A-chain. The independent evidence for (114) comes from examples like (115).[44]

(115)   a. It seems that everyone isn't there yet.
        b. Everyone seems [not to be there yet]
        c. Everyone is expected not be there yet.
        d. Everyone was believed not to be there yet.

The factual claim regarding (115b–d) is that the universal quantifier is unambiguously interpreted as having wide scope relative to negation, whereas (115a) is scopally ambiguous. Indeed, examples like (115b–d) are used by Chomsky, and by Lasnik, to argue that there is no reconstruction in an A-chain.

For Lasnik, it follows that in (113) the 'subject' *everyone* must not have moved to the higher clause (in other words, it must not have 'raised away' from the lower subject position when scope is computed; thus in relevant respects (113) and (115a) are equivalent). If in (113) the 'subject' has raised away (i.e. moved to the higher Agr_O position above the ECM verb), then the Negation-over-quantifier reading would be impossible (given (114)). But the word order shows that *everyone* HAS raised; at least that it has raised from its theta position. So, Lasnik reasons, *everyone* has raised, but it can't have raised into the higher clause. Thus, it must be in Spec, IP. But Spec, IP here is not a Case position. Movement to Spec, IP, then, 'must' be driven by the EPP. For Lasnik, it is the EPP that motivates movement to spec of the lower IP; and it is relative to this IP-internal position that *everyone* and *not* are scopally ambiguous. In (115b–d), on the other hand, *everyone* clearly has raised away (from the lower IP); and thus these examples are unambiguous (given that there is hypothesized to be no A-reconstruction).

The argument traced above does present challenges to our one-step movement approach to ECM constructions. If a universal quantifier and negation can scope over each other only if they are both in the same minimal clause at the point of scopal interpretation, then a potential problem does seem to emerge. Consider again (113a) and (115c), as representative examples:

---

44. The literature assumes that (115a) is ambiguous, i.e., a universal quantifier in subject position of a negated finite clause is sufficient for scopal ambiguity to occur.

(113) a. I expected everyone not to be there yet.   = scopally ambiguous

(115) c. Everyone is expected not be there yet.   = only wide scope universal

If, as we've assumed, *everyone* in (113a) moves overtly to the higher accusative Case position in one step, then in relevant respects (113a) and (115c) are identical: in both *everyone* has 'moved away' from the lower IP and hence we incorrectly predict that both are scopally unambiguous (with only the quantifier over negation readings). Note that, in large part, it's a problem of the timing of scopal interpretation.[45] If we allow scopal interpretation before overt movement of *everyone* in (113a), i.e. if we allow scopal interpretation relative to the pre-movement object in (116),

(116)   ...not to be everyone there yet

then we'd correctly predict that (113a) is ambiguous, since at the relevant derivational point, *everyone* and *not* are in the same minimal clause. Of course, the problem then is we could do the same thing in (115c) since the derivational point represented in (116) is precisely one that leads to (115c).[46] That is, if we do scopal interpretation relative to (116) and if we have a 'memory' of the result (i.e. that *not* and *everyone* scope over each other), then continuing (116) to (115c) predicts a scopal ambiguity that in fact does not hold for (115c). But if we wait until after overt movement of *everyone*, then, for us (but not for Lasnik), *everyone* is outside the lower IP in both (113a) and (115c); and all else equal (and specifically if we adopt (114)), we would seem to predict, incorrectly, that both are therefore scopally unambiguous.

What we'd like to suggest now is that Lasnik's argument for the EPP is potentially problematic in certain respects. It does involve interesting and important questions regarding the architecture of the grammar and it does present challenges

---

45. See Lasnik (2001) for important discussion of the derivational approach, including the point that such interpretive issues as scope seem to take place 'late' in the derivation, whereas thematic information is 'early'. This was captured in the GB framework under the idea that the theta criterion holds at D-structure, while scope and binding take place at S-structure or later (perhaps with Reconstruction). The problem for *any phasal approach*, and in particular for our approach following DASR, is how to incorporate in a natural way a 'delayed' interpretive mechanism. Our claim is that LF and PF 'look in' at all points in the derivation, not just certain, 'special' points of the derivation.
46. We assume throughout this discussion a 'bottom up' derivation as envisioned in Chomsky (1995) (and subsequent work), along with the standard minimalist tenet that there are no syntax-internal 'levels' of representation.

for our derivational approach, as we have just pointed out. But we suggest that these same questions hold over and above the question of the EPP, i.e. they arise for Lasnik as well. It's not that we have any 'better' analysis of the data. Rather, our analysis, without the EPP, is no better but we tentatively suggest here that it is, perhaps, no worse.

One issue regarding Lasnik's argument for the EPP relative to (113) vs. (115b–d) concerns the timing of the interpretation of scope, and the larger issue of the architecture of the grammar. Indeed, on one view, an apparent contradiction emerges. To illustrate, consider again the representative examples (113a) vs. (115c), repeated here

(113) a. I expected everyone not to be there yet.   = scopally ambiguous

(115) c. Everyone is expected not be there yet.   = only wide scope universal

As we saw above, scopal interpretation can't be done before movement of *everyone*, i.e. scopal interpretation must not be allowed to take place relative to the point in the derivation represented by (116) – common to both (113a) and (115c) – repeated below:

(116)   . . . not to be everyone there yet

(To state the matter in GB terms: scopal interpretation had better not be allowed at D-structure; cf. Lasnik and Saito 1991.) The argument is essentially the same as what we saw a moment ago: Suppose scopal interpretation could take place at this early derivational point, and suppose, as Chomsky (1995) suggests, that the quantifier and negation can scope over each other only if they are contained in the same minimal clause. The good news is that (113a) would correctly be predicted ambiguous. Scope would be determined relative to (116), and we can continue on from (116) to produce (113a). But as we mentioned earlier in our discussion, the bad news is that we can continue from (116) to (115c).

(115) c. Everyone is expected [not to be there yet]

which is precisely the type of case that is scopally *un*ambiguous. Before overt movement would be 'too early' for scopal interpretation, as we'd predict that both (113a) and (115c) are scopally ambiguous.

Rather, what Lasnik assumes is that in (113a) *everyone* moves to Spec, IP, and it moves to Spec, IP because of the EPP. Thus from (116), we derive

(117)   [$_{IP}$ everyone not to be there yet]

It is (crucially) with respect to this representation that scopal interpretation takes place: since *everyone* and *not* are in the same minimal clause, then they can scope over each other. Thus, we continue (117) to (113a), but we do not for Lasnik move *everyone* to spec of Agr$_O$ overtly; and (113a) is correctly predicted to be scopally ambiguous. Then, after Spell Out, there is covert movement of *everyone* to spec of Agr to check Case (in order to have LF convergence). (Note further that it is important that scopal interpretation not be allowed only at LF since then (113a) is predicted to be unambiguous, given that at LF (117) is mapped to an object where *everyone* has raised away to the higher Spec, Agr$_O$).

But interestingly, an apparent contradiction now emerges relative to (115c). In fact, the derivation of (115c) involves precisely the derivational stage (117), where *everyone* has moved to spec of the lower IP to satisfy the EPP. If scopal interpretation takes place relative to (117) to get the scopal ambiguity in (113a), then that interpretation should also be able to take place relative to (117) when (117) continues on to yield (115c). But then (115c) is *in*correctly predicted to be scopally ambiguous.

What then is assumed, for Lasnik's analysis, regarding the timing of scopal interpretation? Scopal interpretation *before* overt movement is too early. We've just seen that scopal interpretation after *any* instance of overt movement is also too early: (117) is the result of overt movement, but if scopal interpretation takes place relative to it, then we (incorrectly) predict (115c) as ambiguous.

The descriptive generalization, stated heuristically in GB terms (see Lasnik and Saito 1991), is that scopal interpretation takes place at S-structure, but not before S-structure. Stated in terms of the level-less minimalist architecture, Lasnik could say that scopal interpretation takes place at all overt movement, i.e. at Spell Out. Scopal interpretation at spell-out does seem to yield the desired result. Thus, in the case where (117) continues to the ambiguous (113a), there is no further overt movement of *everyone*. At Spell Out, then, *everyone* and *not* are in the same minimal clause.

But in continuing (117) to (115c), there *is* further overt movement of *everyone*; namely to the matrix Spec, TP. Thus, with the convergent derivation, at Spell Out, *everyone* has raised away from the lower IP and hence can't scope under negation. But to say that scopal interpretation can take place only at (or later than) Spell Out would seem to reincorporate into the architecture of the grammar a level of representation somewhat like GB's S-structure. It is a level (the level at which Spell Out applies) defined by application of a particular operation (scopal interpretation) that is not available at an earlier derivational point.

Note further that we can salvage our direct (non-successive cyclic movement) approach, one that rejects the EPP, by modifying (114) along the following lines.

(118)   A universal quantifier and negation can scope over each other if they are not separated by +tense.

For Lasnik, the universal quantifier can't raise away from the lower IP. For us, the universal quantifier can't raise away from the lower Agr_O (and 'cross over' a +tense element). Consider yet again (113a) and (115c), repeated here.

(113)   a.   I expected everyone not to be there yet.   = scopally ambiguous

(115)   c.   Everyone is expected not be there yet.   = only wide scope universal

We assume one-step movement in (113a) of *everyone* to the higher Agr_O position. But since *everyone* has not gone beyond the higher +tense head, it 'counts' as being in the same scopal interpretation domain as the negation. In (115c), on the other hand, *everyone* has raised higher than the +tense head (to Spec, IP) and hence 'counts' as being outside the relevant domain. Granted, this is a stipulation. But substituting our stipulation (118) for the stipulation (114) may (if empirically sustainable) facilitate elimination of the EPP.

Note that one immediate problem confronting (118) involves Lasnik's (2001 and 2003) cases below:

(119)   the mathematician made every even number out not to be the sum of two primes

(120)   the mathematician made out every even number not to be the sum of two primes

The claim is that (119) is unambiguously wide scope universal, while (120) is ambiguous (allowing both the wide and narrow readings of the universal quantifier relative to negation). Lasnik argues that (119) involves overt movement of the lower 'subject' *every even number* to the higher ACC position, while in (120) *every even number* is (crucially) in the spec of the lower IP ('EPP') position, thereby allowing the attested scopal ambiguity (since only in (120) are the quantifier and negation in the same minimal clause at the point of interpretation). Extending our analysis mechanically to this data, for us, there would presumably be direct overt movement of *every even number* to the higher ACC position in both (119) and (120), and in neither case are the quantifier and negation separated by +tense. This contrast then is not accounted for by (118), and we have no immediate response to it, leaving the matter for future investigation.[47]

Note finally, that for both Lasnik, and for us, there is the issue of reconciling the conflicting evidence regarding the height of the 'subject' of the ECM clause. Thus, for Lasnik's approach to (113a), repeated here,

(113) a. I expected everyone not to be there yet. = scopally ambiguous

it is crucial that *everyone* not raise overtly to Spec, Agr_O. But Lasnik provides an array of binding-theoretic (and other) evidence that *everyone* HAS raised overtly. To give just one of many important paradigms (see Lasnik), we get binding in (121), but not in (122) and (123) (Lasnik and Saito 1992).

(121) The DA proved [two men to have been at the scene of the crime] during each other's trials.

(122) *?The DA proved [that two men were at the scene of the crime] during each other's trials.

(123) *The DA proved [there to have been two men at the scene of the crime] during each other's trials.

---

47. Boeckx (2001) points out that some speakers '. . . have a marked preference for overt raising' in the *make out* construction. Thus:

   (i)   Mary made Bill out to be a fool
   (ii)   %Mary made out Bill to be a fool

So, the scopal ambiguity of (113a) indicates that the lower 'subject' has *not* raised overtly, while the licit binding in (119) indicates that the very same subject *has* raised overtly, a phenomenon that Lasnik has addressed in a number of papers (see particularly Lasnik 1999). Lasnik (1999) suggests that this apparent conflict is not a contradiction, but rather that overt raising to Agr_O of ECM verbs is optional. Thus 'all of these phenomena simply indicate that raising is possible, available when necessary but not necessarily obligatory' (Lasnik 1999:149). Critically, Lasnik argues that there are no cases where the evidence indicates that the ECM subject both has raised and has not raised. Under our alternative approaches traced above (adopting our one-step movement of the lower subject and adopting (118)), we also account for (121)–(123) and (113a) vs. (115c). The ECM subject raising overtly accounts for the various effects that Lasnik discusses, but with the extended scope domain as in (118), we arguably 'get' the scopal effects as well. This leaves the particle-shift cases (see Bošković 2002 for an EPP-free approach).

5 *Exploring architecture*

5.1 Derivational architecture of C_{HL}

In this chapter we explore certain aspects of the derivational model proposed in DASR, the general model being presupposed up to this point. We put in place 'conceptual' and technical details that will allow a more complete examination of a range of important data. We are particularly concerned with our hypothesis (somewhat different from that in DASR; see below) that LF and PF *necessarily* evaluate linguistic entities at *every* point in the derivation. Thus, if X and Y are merged creating C, then C is necessarily input to both LF and PF, which are purely interpretive and interpret as much of C as possible, while C may serve as input to subsequent derivational operations. Explanatory and empirical consequences of this view are considered, with primary focus on certain existential constructions; and more generally, on the nature of 'violations' in the syntax; in particular, we show that 'violation' has a very different status than in GB. In any phasal system, a violation at one point in a derivation does not necessarily 'endure' in later points. Crucially, in our framework, this is different from there being (the GB notion of) 'repair' or 'salvation'. As we will show, the notion of salvation, repair, or 'overcoming an earlier violation' are *not* properties of the step-by-step derivational system that we propose, as we will explain below.

5.1.1 Existentials, Case and the derivation

We begin with a question: Why is *there* present in a simple existential construction such as (1)?

(1)   There will be a man outside.
        (cf. *Will be a man outside.)

We assume, as is standard, that it is the associate (*a*) *man* that checks the agreement features of T, thus accounting for the well-known agreement facts shown in (2).

(2)   a. *There is three men outside.
        b. There are three men outside.

(The precise mechanism of agreement-checking will be considered later.)

How is Case checked? The CT analysis assumes that the (relevant feature of the) associate *a man* covertly checks the Case of T via LF movement to that position, while DBP's (and MI and BEA's) Probe-Goal analysis postulates that Case of *a man* is valued in situ. Under each analysis, *there* is a pure EPP checker. Thus *there* is present in (1) to check a (strong) feature of T (featural EPP) or to satisfy an overt 'phrase structural requirement' (structural EPP).

We obviously cannot adopt such analyses of existentials, since we seek to eliminate any appeal to the EPP. But in fact there is independent evidence against treating *there* as a pure EPP-checker: it does not account for the ill-formedness of (3).[1]

(3)   *It would be likely (for) [there to seem that Fred left]

If *there* checks only the EPP feature, then if *to* HAS only the EPP feature (contra our hypothesis that *to* checks nothing), (3) should be fine. The same incorrect prediction follows from the hypothesis that *there* is a purely structural EPP satisfier.

We thus assume, following Groat (1995), Lasnik (1995), and Martin (1992), that *there* CHECKS CASE, AND ONLY CASE. (This assumption similarly accords with the predictions of a GB-type Case Filter, given that *there* is a phonetically overt NP, hence it requires Case.)

If *there* checks the Case feature of T (and thus *there* is present since if it were not, the presence of the uninterpretable Case feature of T would cause the derivation to crash at LF), then an alternative account of the Case of the associate is required, since once the Case feature of T is checked by *there*, it is presumably deleted and hence unavailable to check the Case of the associate. On independent grounds, Belletti (1988) and Lasnik (1995) argue that the associate checks the partitive Case

---

1. See Hazout (2004), and references therein, for related discussion.

of the copula *be*. Thus, let us assume that in (1), *there* is present not because of the EPP, but in order to locally check the nominative Case of T while the associate checks the partitive Case of *be*. If *there* were a pure EPP-checker and, in addition, Case could be checked on *a man* (in situ) under Probe-Goal matching with φ-complete T, the following types of cases, noted by Lasnik (2001) (pre-dating the Probe-Goal analysis) would be overgenerated.

(4)   *There will not have [$_{VP}$ a man slept]
      (cf. *A man will not have slept.*)

(5)   *There seems [$_{TP}$ to [$_{VP}$ a man like fish]]
      (cf. *A man seems to like fish.*)

Thus, we adopt the Lasnik-Belletti partitive-Case-from-*be* analysis and concomitantly reject Chomsky's hypothesis that Case can be checked in situ under Probe-Goal matching with φ-complete T. We also reject the assumption that *there* is a pure EPP-checker. For us, it checks Case locally.

As concerns this locality, recall that, for us, relations are derivational, hence not definable on derived tree representations. The Spec-Head relation, as is well known, is not a c-command relation, so we can't appeal to it, nor can we ('conveniently') define m-command (alongside c-command), thereby allowing the relation from Head-to-Spec.

But if there is no Head-to-Spec relation, how can *there* check Case of φ-complete T? If *there* is first merged into Spec, T, then *there* itself could probe T under derivational c-command. But, as we'll argue below, we cannot allow Case-checking to apply under mere asymmetric c-command, since T merely asymmetrically c-commands *a man* in

(6)   *T will not have [a man slept]

Thus asymmetric c-command, as sufficient for Case-checking, incorrectly predicts that (6) converges.

To force raising of *a man* (without EPP), we argue that symmetric c-command (sisterhood) is required for Case-checking. In the representation in (6), T c-commands *a man*. If *a man* raises to Spec, T, then *a man* c-commands T, thus they c-command each other, which is sisterhood, the simplest relation.[2] But if symmet-

---

2. See Groat (1995), DASR, and also Fitzpatrick (2002) for extremely insightful discussion of numerous locality conditions including derivational sisterhood.

ric c-command is required for Case-checking and *there* is first merged into Spec, T, then *there* c-commands T, but T fails to c-command *there*. Thus, we need T to c-command *there* in order to effect Case-checking under symmetry. There are at least two ways to achieve this result, and importantly each has been independently motivated in the literature. One approach hypothesizes that expletives raise from a lower position to Spec, TP, as proposed in Moro (1997) (but cf. Bošković 2002).[3] If that's right, symmetric c-command (sisterhood) is attained; i.e. before expletive raising, T c-commands the expletive. After expletive-raising, the expletive c-commands T. Another approach assumes T raising to C (V2), which Epstein (1998) speculates is universal but sometimes 'covert'. This too might yield derivational symmetric c-command between T and *there*.

What about agreement features? Let us assume just for the moment (this will be modified below) that the associate covertly checks the agreement feature of T.

Notice that under this approach, we would need to assume Enlightened Self Interest (ESI) (Lasnik 1995) over Greed. Covert movement of the associate to check agreement is allowed by ESI but prohibited by Greed since agreement features on the DP associate are +interpretable, and hence need not be checked. Interestingly, our analysis overcomes a problem for ESI discussed by Lasnik (1995). Consider (7), patterned after an example from Lasnik:

(7)   *it seems [John to be likely [t will go]]

Precisely because of the EPP, Lasnik points out that in (7), *John* is allowed under ESI to move to check the EPP feature of *to*, and thus the structure is incorrectly predicted to be fine. Lasnik's approach (what he calls a 'technical solution') to this problem is to assume that 'once Case is checked off, no further movement is possible.' But notice that this amounts to invoking two distinct constraints, with Greed disallowing Case-position departures, and ESI allowing non-Greedy EPP-checking. Under our approach this dissolution of the theory of purposeful movement is not required. For us, (7) is out (even assuming ESI), for the simple reason that *to* checks no features (since *to* has no features, there can be no checking relation between *to* and *John*, hence movement of *John* is prohibited). Thus, our analysis

---

3. Under Moro's analysis, there are certain expletives in certain constructions that do not necessarily raise, e.g. *it* co-occurring with *likely*. These would remain problematic for our analysis. See also Bošković (2002) for arguments for a non-movement analysis of *all* expletives.

overcomes a potentially serious problem confronting the theory of movement. (See also Bošković 1997 for an analysis supporting Greed.)

Under the derivational approach assumed here, a new conception of a derivation arises, and crucially there can be no uniquely overt component, no uniquely covert component, no re-cycling within components, nor stipulation of special categories as phases. None of these postulates are possible since for us (as discussed further below) both PF and LF interpret the output of each transformational operation.

We assume that LF necessarily accesses each syntactic object at each point in a derivation; LF does not wait until the 'end of the line' to interpret these objects.[4] Nor is *interpretation* postponed until the phases vP and CP are built (as in DBP). PF is assumed to operate in the same manner. One way to think of this is as an *iterated* Y-model; i.e. after each transformation applies (be it Merge or Remerge), the derived representation is fed into both PF and LF:[5,6]

---

4. Epstein *et al.* (1998) assume that PF and LF need not wait until the end-of-the-line to interpret an expression. However, it is not assumed that (at least) LF must interpret the output of a derivational operation as soon as possible, which we do assume above. In fact, in Chapter 2 of Epstein *et al.*, LF interpretation of reflexives is argued to be optional, hence it can be delayed. In this way, the Epstein *et al.* analysis can account for reconstruction effects of the sort illustrated in (i) (indices used only for exposition)

    (i)   Which picture of himself$_{i,j}$ did Bill$_i$ say that Tom$_j$ liked best?

    At the point in the derivation shown in (ii)

    (ii) Bill$_i$ said that Tom$_j$ likes which picture of himself$_j$?

    the reflexive may or may not be interpreted. If it is interpreted, it may take the local antecedent Tom; however, interpretation of *himself* can be delayed until after the container of the reflexive moves to a higher position, specifically the lower Spec of C, and there *himself* may take *Bill* as antecedent. Thus, rather than having reconstruction downward to associate with the lower antecedent, it is assumed that interpretation may take place 'upward' during the derivation. In the development of the derivational approach being presented here, this delayed interpretation would be precluded. The consequences of this for A′ reconstruction, and specifically the issue of how to handle (i), is left for further research. See Contreras (2003). One approach is to assume that the reflexive in (i) is really a logophor, in the sense of Pollard and Sag (1992), and thus that these cases are essentially non-syntactic, the interpretation of the reflexive being done 'in' the LF representation. We might also assume that such delayed interpretation is possible only with semantically dependent elements like anaphors; thus, we could maintain our strong form of 'immediate' interpretation while still adopting the essence of the Epstein *et al.*, Chapter 2, analysis for cases like (i).
5. See Fernandez-Salgueiro (2003) for arguments that LF interprets each object while PF is delayed.
6. (8) might be misleading since, for example, c-command relations involved in Attract are not 'in' the representation but rather in the derivation; i.e. c-command relations are not read off R#1, which

(8)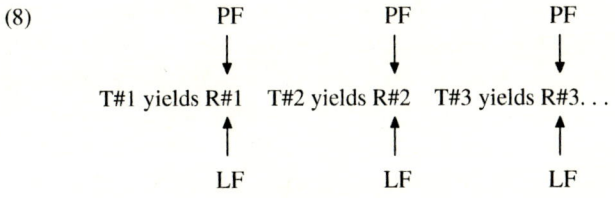

(T = transformational operation, and R = representation)

A number of important consequences of this view merit attention.

For one thing, within this view (which is not fully recognized in DASR), we cannot adopt a GB-type characterization of 'grammatical sentence'. Consider GB-type well-formedness:

(9) a. All and only grammatical sentences have 'well-formed' derivations.
b. A derivation is well formed only if at every point in the derivation no principle is violated.

Importantly, under (9b), if there is any violation of any principle at any level, ungrammaticality is predicted. Informally, within GB, a derivation is not well formed if there appears one or more violations at any point in the derivation. Once a principle is violated, the 'crime' can't be pardoned even if later in the derivation, the criminal features or configurations are erased. For example, if a DS representation violates the θ-Criterion, the *derivation* containing this representation is forever doomed as ill-formed. This works only given privileged points in the derivation, i.e. levels, and principles that apply at them.

Under strong derivationality as in (8), this is not tenable (we are indebted to Sam Gutmann, personal communication, for realizing and raising this entire issue); i.e. if as we propose, LF and PF access each derivational point as in (8), then if we were also to adopt (9), *no well-formed derivations of grammatical sentences would ever be generable.* To see this, consider, for example, the derivation of a simple transitive sentence like *Birds like seed*. In our derivational model, first *like* and *seed* are merged, and the representation *like seed* is evaluated immediately by both PF and LF. The representation *like seed*, however, violates (at least) the

serves as input to T#2. It is important to note in this regard that in an optimal derivational model, it shouldn't be merely non-explanatory to define relations on trees or representations. It should be formally impossible to do so.

θ-Criterion/Full Interpretation. Thus in contrast to GB we cannot assume that a sentence is ungrammatical if any violation occurs in the (best) derivation of it. Indeed, there is such a θ violation in the derivation of every transitive sentence. Similarly, a subject merged into Spec, vP, before higher functional categories are yet merged in still bears an uninterpretable Case-feature which will be detected by LF in the model (8), causing crash at the LF interface within the derivation of every agentive structure.

5.1.2 The Gutmann Problem

Herein lies what we'll call 'The Gutmann Problem'. As just shown, the derivational model in (8) must be formulated so that the θ-Criterion violation in [like seed] does *not* entail that [Birds+[like seed]] is also a θ-Criterion violation.[7] Now here's the problem:

(10) The problem:
      If in order to generate the θ-Criterion-satisfying *Birds like seed* we violate the θ-Criterion after First Cyclic Merge of [like+seed], how can we account for the fact that a string such as *like seed*, BY ITSELF, is in fact ungrammatical?

One could (unsatisfactorily) reply as follows:

(11) An unsatisfactory solution:
      'If we have [like seed] and the derivation continues, adding [birds] later, then the theory predicts it's grammatical. But if we have [like seed] and this is the end of the derivation i.e. an "end-of-the-line" LF representation, then the theory predicts it's ungrammatical.'

The problem with this approach is that in trying to get the derivational model to generate anything, it crucially appeals to the standard Y-model notion 'end-of-the-line LF representation', a concept that must be abandoned under any derivational/phasal approach. The derivational model proposed here, with each generated representation being evaluated by PF and LF, is a satisfactory alternative to the Y-model only if all points in the derivation are treated alike, with no special status afforded to 'the final LF representation', a defining construct of the standard

---

7. For expository purposes, we focus only on the θ-Criterion here, ignoring other violations. One violation is sufficient to illustrate our point.

Y-model.[8] So, what can the derivational model do? It must 'allow' violations (like the θ-Criterion violation in [like seed]) in the course of deriving [birds like seed], but it must disallow violations, in order to predict cases of ungrammaticality such as *like seed. Thus,

(12)   Violations must be pardonable ([birds [*like seed]]) but not pardonable ([*like seed])!

The contradiction cannot be resolved by saying, 'If [like seed] is the final representation, then it's ungrammatical; but if it's not the final representation, then its not necessarily ungrammatical.' This is to implicitly incorporate an end-of-the-line Y-model, antithetical to the derivational approach.

There is a potentially interesting solution to the Gutmann Problem, we believe. In fact, it not so much a solution as a discovery of an unnoted and arguably attractive inherent property of the derivational model, and is, in fact, part of any phase-based model that generates 'nonfatal' crashing by virtue of sending incomplete (i.e. as yet nonconvergent) phasal representations to the interfaces (see Epstein 2003 regarding this aspect of Chomsky's phasal system). Consider again the derivation of *Birds like seed*. First, we merge *like* and *seed* yielding *like seed*. This representation is immediately interpreted by PF and LF. LF rightly says 'This representation violates the θ-Criterion,' and this is (by hypothesis) correct. A native speaker knows that *like seed* is ungrammatical and that the ungrammaticality is lexico-semantic having to do with the meaning of *like*. At the next derivational step, suppose *birds* is merged in, yielding

(13)   [[birds] [like seed]]

This new representation, like every representation generated (see (8)), is immediately interpreted by PF and LF. Still ignoring, for the sake of argument, non-θ properties, LF says, 'This is OK: the θ-Criterion is satisfied.' This seems like exactly the right prediction regarding *birds like seed*.

Thus the representation *like seed* violates the θ-Criterion, but the representation *birds like seed* does not – exactly the right predictions. Thus, we assume:

---

8. On these grounds too we do not want to say that the representation derived by exhausting the Numeration has some special status, different from other representations (see CT, p. 241). On the elimination of numerations see Collins (1997), Frampton and Gutmann (2002), and Epstein and Seely (2002).

(14)   Each syntactic object O generated at each derivational point P is evaluated by PF and LF which, naturally enough, assess the properties of O, i.e. the legitimacy of O.

Thus, there is no contradiction in the fact that [birds like seed] does not contain a θ-violation, even though the derivation that produced it involves an object that does. Under (14), the Gutmann Problem is solved: each output of each transformational rule application is evaluated and its new and unique properties are assessed.

Thus, in solving the Gutmann Problem, we must abandon the GB 'law' stating that 'if there is any violation at any point in the derivation of a sentence S, S is predicted ungrammatical.' But note that this is exactly as is to be expected since we are proposing a radically different computational architecture; thus, our proposal is not so much a solution as a consequence (a welcome one, we believe) of that architecture: each representation is interpreted by PF and LF. Each generated representation (i.e. syntactic object) has PF and LF properties. If α is non-convergent, it does not follow that β containing α (β a new object) will also crash.[9]

This model creates a certain terminological confusion concerning the term 'derivation'. On the one hand, for us,

(15)   Each single rule application is a self-contained 'Y model' derivation: the syntactic object generated is interpreted by PF and by LF.

However, such single-rule-application derivations can be continued, creating bigger derivations which contain derivations. We will use the term 'unit derivation' to refer to a derivation consisting of a single rule application, and will use 'extended derivation' to refer to non-unit derivations (i.e. those involving more than one rule application, hence containing at least two derivations within).

To illustrate, consider

(16)   1st merge: like+seed;   2nd merge: birds+[like seed];
        PF and LF interpret   PF and LF interpret

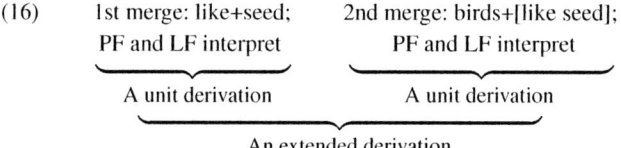

Again restricting attention to just the θ-Criterion, we see here that even though the first unit derivation violates the θ-Criterion, the terminus of the second unit

---

9. For implications of this model regarding so-called non-sentential speech, see Fortin (2004).

derivation (which is equivalent to the terminus of the extended derivation) satisfies the θ-Criterion. Thus, we can 'go from' violation to non-violation. Conversely, we can also 'go from' non-violation to violation. This can be achieved in the case at hand by adding a third unit derivation to the above extended derivation, namely

(17) Third Merge: Fred

as is possible if Merge is unconstrained, as in BEA. Thus, we have

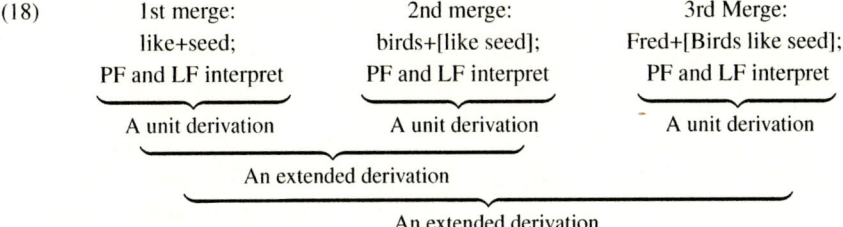

and the θ-Criterion is violated.

Again, in the model proposed here, EACH *newly generated* SYNTACTIC OBJECT UNDERGOES (IS ASSIGNED) A *new* PF AND LF INTERPRETATION, SINCE EACH OBJECT HAS ITS OWN UNIQUE INTERPRETATION AND PROPERTIES.

5.1.3 *On feature checking in the derivational model: Why there can't be a covert component*

In this section we consider, in a preliminary way, consequences of our derivational model for feature checking, addressing in particular certain issues involving feature checking in existentials.

One consequence of our approach is that *covert* movement of an element with phonetic content is simply not possible. To see why, consider again (1), repeated here:

(1) There will be a man outside.

Suppose we have built up to (1). Recall that LF and PF interpret each step as in (8). At the stage represented by (1), suppose, just for the purposes of illustration, we

184   *Derivations in Minimalism*

try to 'covertly' raise *a man*, adjoining it to *there* (as in Chomsky 1986) in order to check the agreement feature of T. The result is (19):

(19)   [there a man] T will be __ outside

The result of this operation, i.e. the object (19), is interpreted by both LF *and* PF, just like all derivational points. So PF necessarily 'sees' that *a man* has moved. What 'covert movement' means is 'movement the output of which is not fed to PF.' But this simply can't happen under our derivational architecture. We can't have e.g. a syntactic object like *is a man outside* interpreted solely by PF and then merge *there* and interpret this solely at LF.

At this point a potential difficulty arises. Following the general idea of interpretability of features, we assume that in (1) T bears uninterpretable Case, contra Chomsky (DBP), and agreement features, all of which must be checked. The Case feature of T is checked by *there*, which for us is a pure Case-checker (following Lasnik 1995 and Groat 1995). The Case feature of *a man* is checked by *be* (adopting the guiding ideas of Belletti 1988 and Lasnik 1992, 1995). What remains are the agreement features of T. How are they checked? It can't be through covert movement of the associate *a man*, since, as we just argued, there can be no covert (i.e. unseen) movement of a category in our model. If we move *a man*, then we necessarily evaluate the newly formed object *[there a man] will be outside*, and not the string (1) – and we assume that the object *[there a man] will be outside* is phonetically illegitimate.[10] A key question, then, is: How do we generate the agreement phenomenon displayed in (1)? We consider below two general approaches to this question. The first involves checking under feature movement (as in CT), while the second involves the in situ feature-checking idea of MI and DBP.

5.1.3.1   Agreement-checking through feature movement   A logical tack to pursue for (1) is the feature movement analysis of CT (although DASR rejects feature movement, as does MI). Suppose, for example, that it is not the whole category *a man* that moves, but just some of its features. Which features? CT assumes that the Case feature of *a man* raises and checks the Case of T, while *there* checks the EPP

---

10. Again, it is simply not possible at derivational point Px, for LF or PF to look back solely at point Px-1. Earlier points in the derivation, of course, play a role in determining the nature of Px, but Px itself (and only Px) is the object under evaluation by LF and PF (at any individual point in the derivation). Px is what it is, and LF and PF have no choice but to evaluate *it*.

feature of T. This won't do for us: under our approach *there* is a Case-checker (and can't be an EPP-checker since we have eliminated the EPP). *There* and *a man* can't BOTH check the Case feature of T (putting aside the issue of 'covert' movement for the moment) since checking involves deletion of the uninterpretable feature(s) in the checking relation. Thus, if *there* checks Case of T, then the Case feature of *a man* is left stranded, and if *a man* checks the Case of T (through raising of the Case feature of *a man*; see directly below for discussion of the possibility of 'covert' feature raising), then *there* is stranded. In essence, then, we are led to adopt the Lasnik/Belletti analysis whereby *be* checks the Case of *a man*.

What about the agreement features of *a man*: could just these features raise to check with T? Assuming that the agreement features themselves (as formal features) have no phonetic content, they could move; i.e. assuming the object

(20)   there T will be a man outside

as input to Move/Attract, just the agreement feature of *a man* could be moved and not be 'seen' by PF. Thus, we could derive (21):

(21)   there [Agr+T] will be a man outside
       (where Agr = the moved agreement features of *a man*)

In fact this object is convergent at both PF and LF (i.e. there are no unchecked features). *There* checks Case of T; *be* checks partitive Case of *a man*; and the raised agreement feature would check agreement of T, provided the features match.[11]

Although this might get the right result in our target example, it raises certain questions. First, it seems clear that we do not want to allow movement of the Case feature, although we just proposed allowing the movement of an agreement feature. To see why, consider, for instance, (22):

(22)   a.   *T will [$_{VP}$ a man go]   (understood as a declarative)
       b.   *T is [a man outside]   (understood as a declarative)

If both the Case and agreement features of *a man* are allowed to raise to T, thereby

---

11. There is a potential problem in that in *this* LF representation, the agreement features of *man* no longer reside in the noun but have moved to T. The question then arises as to how this object can be interpreted as containing the SEMANTICALLY SINGULAR NOUN *man*. We cannot appeal to feature chains, nor copies, given our approach.

licensing feature checking, then (22) is predicted to be well formed: T is satisfied since its uninterpretable Case and agreement features are checked (by the raised Case and agreement features of *a man*), and *a man* is satisfied since its uninterpretable Case feature is checked (again through the Case feature raising to T). Of course, we cannot appeal to the EPP in this case to fill the Spec of T, given our elimination of the EPP.

A feature movement analysis would therefore seem to require the following stipulation:

(23) a. An agreement feature may move by itself.
      b. A Case feature may not move by itself.[12]
          (Where 'by itself' means that the feature can move without bringing the entire category bearing it along for the ride.)

Under the stipulated constraint (23), (22) is correctly out since the Case feature of T is unchecked (since the Case feature of *a man* can't move by itself). And an existential like *there will be a man outside* would be generated (see (21)): *there* checks Case of T, *be* checks partitive Case of *a man*, and the agreement feature of T is checked through raising of the agreement feature of *a man* (such agreement feature movement being allowed by (23a)). Note that the Case vs. Agr distinction in the stipulation (23) might be generalized to the following description:

(24) Interpretable features may move by themselves (i.e. without the whole category), but uninterpretable features cannot.

In a sense, this is the opposite of Greed – it's perhaps a form of 'altruism', as al-

---

12. The Case feature cannot be allowed to move by itself, nor can it move just with agreement features; Case must always move with its host category (see below). Another approach to the same problem might assume that the Case feature *can* move by itself, but such pure feature-raising does not yield the symmetric c-command (derivational sisterhood) necessary for Case-checking, precisely because the raised *feature* itself fails to c-command T. Under this approach to Case, in order to maintain Probe-Goal-checking of agreement in situ, it would have to be assumed that *the category* T asymmetrically c-commanding THE N⁰ CATEGORY *man*, which in turn *contains* Agr features, suffices to delete the matching Agr features on T. These potential unclarities regarding the theory of featural relations in a category-based syntax are not particular to our approach. It has never been clear (to us) that feature 'movement' is a formal operation reducible to a syntactic-category movement, or whether feature movement as proposed is a different, additional, transformational rule type. For a revealing overview and analysis of feature movement in English existentials, see e.g. Jang (1997).

Exploring architecture 187

lowed by ESI. The only features that may move (by themselves) are those that (i) do not themselves need to be checked (i.e. they are interpretable on the host) and (ii) moving will allow the checking of some X whose features are uninterpretable. In other words, X may move by itself only if X contains interpretable features.[13] At this point, it is simply unclear to us how the (somewhat cumbersome) (24) might be derived, and we leave the matter open; but see below for some further discussion.

A potential problem with such a feature movement account concerns 'scattered features'. (CT states that 'isolated features and other scattered parts of words may not be subject to its [i.e. PF's] rules, in which case the derivation is canceled...' [CT, p. 263].) Thus if a proper subset of the features of a syntactic category X move before Spell Out, the result is that X has some of its features in one place and some in another; this, by assumption, renders X uninterpretable by PF, and therefore pure feature movement is never overt. In effect PF can interpret the phonetic features of X only if the total feature set of X is in exactly one place.

It should be noted that Chomsky's 1995 prohibition against overt (PF) feature-scattering seems to induce yet another redundancy with the EPP. Overt feature-scattering is barred so as to exclude 'SS'/PF representations such as the English example:

(25)   *I wonder [$_{CP}$ C^0$_{+WH}$ [$_{IP}$ John saw what$_{+WH}$]]

---

13. Thus, the agreement feature of an N may move by itself since the feature is interpretable. A whole DP/NP like *a man* in (23) and *a man* in *is a man outside* may move since it too is an X that contains an interpretable (agreement) feature (even though it also may contain uninterpretable Case features). However, the Case feature itself can't move since it is an X that consists of only uninterpretables (we must assume further that the Case feature can't move together with just the agreement feature).

This gives the right results for our target cases but empirical/technical issues remain. Note that we still correctly exclude **there seems a man to be outside*: We assume that movement is not gratuitous and since *to* has no features, movement of *a man* would be gratuitous (hence excluded) in this case. But consider next (i):

(i)   *there seems a man left

Here, *there* checks the case of the matrix T. The Case of the lower T, the Case of *a man* and the agreement of the lower T is checked by raising of *a man* to Spec of the lower T. Suppose now that the agreement feature of *man* raises to check agreement of the matrix T, something allowed by what we have said so far. We can exclude (i) perhaps by appeal to locality; hence we could exclude the agreement movement in (i) by appeal to locality (in effect the Tensed S Condition). We might also appeal to the MI notion of 'activeness', discussed in the next subsection.

If the (English) requirement that there be overt *wh*-movement (imposed by C; see Lasnik and Saito 1984, 1992) could be satisfied by mere feature movement, then movement of just the Q or *wh*-feature of *what* to C^0 would satisfy the requirement, and (25) would be overgenerated. Thus, the prohibition against scattered features blocks (25). But notice that (25) is widely assumed to be blocked by the EPP: i.e. EPP feature(s) in C require that there be an overt categorial specifier at PF. Similarly,

(26)   *was arrested a man.

is excluded by EPP in T, but also redundantly by scattered features in the derivation in which the Case feature *overtly* raises to T, thereby checking Case.

There is also a potential implementation problem. How would PF be able to determine that features *have been scattered*? If PF sees just phonological feature bundles, it's not clear how PF could see that lexical features of one head *have been moved* to another head. Two approaches are to assume (i) feature-copies or (ii) PF 'consultation' with the lexicon so as to compare PF-feature distribution. Either would seem to be technically sufficient for PF to detect that the process of scattering has been applied.

But if this scattered feature idea is right, then there is an interesting consequence for our derivational model: feature movement is impossible. Since for us PF 'looks in' at all points in a derivation, then as soon as features move, the result will be fed to PF, and PF will find feature scattering and hence illegitimacy.[14]

Of course for us, as just noted, a derivational violation at one point does not necessarily yield an enduring or persistent crash; i.e., the derivation can continue, creating new syntactic objects with their own formal properties. If indeed such feature scattering yields PF illegitimacy, one can imagine the violation being corrected by moving the relevant features back into *a man*, thereby reconstituting this original lexical feature bundle, after scattering achieves checking. However, a number of potential problems confront such a scatter-check-reconstitute account. First, as has been noted, the structural change effected by feature raising has never been entirely clear. Second, reconstituting feature movement would be similarly unclear. Third, clearly, reconstitution movement is movement to a non-c-commanding ('downward') position, violating cyclicity and the derivational theory of relations.

---

14. So there would be no 'covert' movement of any type of an element that has phonetic content.

Moreover, the movement does not seem to result in feature *checking* in the formal sense; hence, it potentially threatens the Minimalist Theory of featurally purposeful operations. Notice, to avoid all such problems, one can try to establish a relation from T to *a man* without movement of features or movement of *any kind*. This is precisely the approach reflected in Chomsky's Probe-Goal analysis, discussed next.

5.1.3.2 Agreement checking in situ: a Probe-Goal analysis of agreement, but not Case   To avoid the problems of feature-scattering approaches, a second approach that we might take to the issue of agreement checking (in existentials) appeals to the MI, DBP, BEA analyses, wherein certain kinds of checking can take place in situ, without movement.

If there is no 'covert' category movement nor feature movement, then we still face the question: how is agreement checking carried out in (1), repeated here?

(1)   There will be a man outside.

Developing the analysis outlined in Section 5.1.1, one could adapt certain aspects of Chomsky's Probe-Goal analysis, according to which the Agr features of T in (1) are valued (or may be) under Probe-Goal Matching with *man*. (We maintain that Case on T is checked by *there*, accounting for the presence of the expletive without appeal to the EPP.) Let's start with a quick review of crucial MI mechanisms:

(27)   a.   Active:
             Any element with uninterpretable features is *active*. (This is a generalization of MI, pp. 37–39; see also DBP.)
         b.   Dual Activation Requirement:
             Only active elements may participate in syntactic operations (specifically Agree and Move, and perhaps also Merge). (MI, p. 39)

Recall, arguably it is the case that the *dual* activation condition is needed because of the EPP. That is, if one hypothesizes pure EPP-checking by *to*, then single activation wrongly permits movements such as the following for pure EPP-checking.

(28)   *[John to seem t is sad] upset Mary.

Thus, X and Y can participate in some operation only if both X and Y are active;

thus, both X and Y must contain uninterpretable features. Any element with only *interpretable* features is syntactically inert.

(29) Probe:
An active element may be a *probe* P. A probe seeks something to get rid of the probe's uninterpretable features; this is what MI calls 'suicidal greed'. The probe seeks out the local matching features that will destroy it, i.e. delete those features.[15] A probe seeks a goal G.

(30) Match:
Match is a relation between elements X and Y (specifically between a probe and a goal). We'll say that a probe *matches* a goal if for every relevant feature of the probe, there is an identical feature on the goal – the probe's features are a subset of the goal's. (The features are identical but not necessarily the feature value).

Furthermore, the probe must *locally* c-command the goal. Thus, a probe P Matches a goal G if and only if:

> The features of P are a subset of the features of G,
> *and* P (derivationally) c-commands G,
> *and* G is the *first* Matching set that P 'finds'. (= local c-command/'search')

At first glance, this might look like a structural relation between nodes in a phrase marker, a relation that is defined on a representation. But, crucially for us, the relation is established derivationally. That is, Chomsky's Command Condition (Probe must c-command Goal) is by hypothesis derivationally explicable by the *general* theory of relations in DASR and assumed here.[16,17]

Thus, in

(31) T will be a man outside

---

15. Note that this is similar to the Frampton and Gutmann (1999) hypothesis that certain features are 'instructions' to the syntax to apply certain operations.
16. Notice that there is a potential redundancy between *first* in '*first* Matching goal' and Chomsky's Phase Impenetrability Condition (PIC). Ideally, given PIC, the *first* Matching goal is the only visible matching goal; hence, *first* need not be stipulated.
17. For explicit discussion reducing aspects of the conditions on Probe-Goal searching to derivational c-command, see Epstein (2001).

the φ-features of T Match with the φ-features of *man* under local c-command.

(32)   Agree:
Agree is a syntactic operation which deletes (or values) uninterpretable features. Agree is constrained by Match. Thus, a probe P can Agree with a goal G only if P Matches G. If P Matches G (and G is local to P), uninterpretable features of P and/or G delete via Agree, or are valued by this operation. (See Epstein and Seely 2002 for discussion of the motivation for and implementation of the mechanisms of valuation.)

Let's review a target example to see how it works. Consider (33) (cf. (1)):

(33)   there T will be a man outside

T has a full set of φ-features, which (on T) are uninterpretable. T is active (since it has uninterpretable features). Since active, T can be a probe. Assume it is a probe. As a probe, T seeks out a G (to Match with in order to Agree with). T 'looks down' and finds in its local (derivational) c-command domain the goal *man*, specifically the φ-features of *man* (which are interpretable). There is a Match between T and *man* (for every feature of T – person, gender, and number – there is an identical feature on *man*; and recall that features, not feature values, must be identical). Since there is Match and since both T and *man* are active (each bearing uninterpretable features), Agree can apply. Agree deletes (or values) the φ-features of T and the Case feature of *man* (since these features are uninterpretable). Thus, the Agr features of T are 'checked' by *man* in situ, and no category or feature movement, covert or overt, is employed. Taken this far, we have directly adopted the agreement checking analysis of MI.[18]

However, our analysis radically differs from MI with respect to Case- and EPP-checking, the feature content of *there*, the content of raising *to*, basic derivational architecture, and the driving force of movement.

Consider Case-checking first. In MI, Case-'checking' is dependent on agreement 'checking'. Contra our proposal here, in MI T does not have a Case feature. Rather, the Case feature of a DP is deleted only if there is some element that can 'check' (by virtue of having a full set of φ-features) the φ-features of that DP; thus, if DP Agrees with T, then the case feature of DP deletes, as an 'ancillary' process.

---

18. Recall that the MI analysis does not incorporate the Belletti-Lasnik partitive Case hypothesis.

Crucially, under such ancillary mechanisms, *there is deletion without feature identity*; i.e., the Agreement features of T value the Case feature of *man*.

The MI analysis of (33) with respect to Case runs in this way: T Matches with the φ-features of *man*, and Agree takes place, deleting the uninterpretable φ-features of T under identity (featural identity, not value identity) with the φ-features of *man*. What also happens here, as a dependent and 'ancillary' operation, is that the Case feature of *man* deletes; the Case feature deletes as a 'reflex' of the φ-complete Agree operation. Again, in MI, T has no Case feature. Rather, it's the φ-set of T that ultimately (but indirectly) causes the Case feature of *man* to delete (and it is the Case feature of *man* that renders it active, hence eligible for Agree-application given the dual activation requirement in (27b)).[19] Another way of looking at this is that a full set of φ- features on tensed (φ-complete) T deletes Case of the DP associate. Crucially, note that under the Belletti (1988) and Lasnik (1992, 1995) analyses of existentials, which involves partitive Case-checking of the associate by *be*, there is an account of the Definiteness Effect. The basic idea is that partitive Case '...selects an indefinite meaning for the NP that carries it' (Belletti 1988:5). If the associate left in situ overtly must bear partitive as opposed to any other Case, (Belletti and particularly Lasnik 1992, 1995 provide compelling arguments for this), then the definiteness effect in existentials follows; and more generally, the definiteness effect for unaccusatives follows. Crucially, our analysis adopts this partitive Case analysis and thus can maintain the Belletti/Lasnik account of the definiteness effect. The MI analysis, on the other hand, whereby the Case of the in situ associate is checked ultimately by T seems to provide no natural account of the definiteness effect.

Note further that, as just discussed, agreement and Case-'checking' may both be done in situ for MI. As long as probe and goal are active and as long as they are in the Match relation, then Agree takes place. Note specifically that both Case (of *man*) and agreement (of T) are deleted *without any movement* in (33) in MI. This is different from CT, where movement is driven by feature checking. Specifically, it's assumed in CT that features can check (delete) only in the spec-head (or head-adjoined-to-head) relation, and this drives movement (leaving out familiar details).

---

19. There is a potential problem with the MI analysis: If T values the Case feature of *man* in situ as indicated above, then *man* is effectively 'deactivated' and hence inaccessible for further operations, including movement to Spec, T (to satisfy, under the MI approach, the EPP feature). Given the general purposefulness of operations, then, movement to Spec, T would be (incorrectly in this case) disallowed.

Note in addition that the operation of Agree can take place only if the goal, *man*, is active (i.e. contains an uninterpretable feature). In (33), *man* is active, as it bears the uninterpretable Case feature. This in turn allows T to 'check' its uninterpretable agreement features, under φ-feature identity with *man*, and this in turns allows the Case feature of *man* to be 'checked'. Interestingly, Case in MI is a mechanism that activates a DP for agreement checking. Because DP has Case, it is active. If it's active, φ-features on T can 'check' the DP's uninterpretable Case, and the DP's φ-features can check the uninterpretable φ-features of the 'checker' (=T). So there is a clear but unexplained dependency of Case on agreement. Once a DP's Case is checked, then in the normal instance that DP has no more uninterpretable features and hence is inactive, thus syntactically inert (not available for operations like Move or Agree).

So a crucial question for the Probe-Goal analyses is: what drives movement in (34) below?

(34)   A man will be [__ outside]

The answer within Probe-Goal analyses is 'the EPP', in many cases. But this raises important issues regarding the entire theory of movement, feature checking and interpretability. If the Case feature of *a man* and the agreement features of T are valued in situ (under Probe-Goal), then, in fact, movement of *a man* is impossible, since the dual activation pre-condition for movement is rendered inapplicable due to in situ Probe-Goal valuation. That is, it is not the case that T and *a man* are both active after in situ Probe-Goal agreement. And recall, we have suggested above (following Bošković 2002) that the dual activation condition is itself motivated to block pure EPP-checking, as in (35).

(35)   *[John to seem __ is sad] upset Mary.

So how can the movement in (34) be generated, given that *a man* is deactivated in situ, under Probe-Goal? Within Chomsky's framework a number of possibilities have arisen. First, one could say that movement is a 'reflex' of agreement (and in (33) the reflex is blocked by Merge-over-Move, a constraint we discussed in detail, and sought to eliminate, in Chapter 2). A second, related approach assumes that in situ valuation and movement are simultaneous, but as argued in Chapter 4 and Epstein and Seely (2002), simultaneity is in a sense incompatible with a step-by-step transformation-based derivational approach, so we cannot adopt it here. Another approach assumes that T has, in addition to φ-features, an EPP feature of some kind. But this in and of itself does not overcome the ban on moving *a man*. That is, regardless of whether T has or lacks an EPP feature, *a man*'s Case is valued in situ and movement is blocked by the dual activation condition. Of course, one other approach to this problem is to say: 'movement for the EPP is (mysteriously) different. Dual activation can be violated and EPP can never be checked in situ, but imposes a (construction-specific) structural requirement demanding an (overt?) specifier of certain special categories, one of which is T.'

We have presented in earlier chapters what we believe to be good reasons for eliminating the EPP. We therefore cannot drive movement in (34) by appealing to the EPP. The elimination of the EPP has another consequence as well: we cannot adopt the MI analysis of Case-checking since then we would have no driving force for movement. Consider (36):

(36)   *Will be a man outside.

Here, both the Case of man and agreement of T can be checked in situ; thus the probe T Matches and Agrees with the goal *man* thereby deleting Agr of T and Case of *man* (just as in *there is a man outside* in MI). But then if there is no EPP, we predict that (36) is fine. Thus, all else equal, we must not assume that Case-checking 'freely occurs' with agreement-checking (as in MI), but rather that Case and agreement are differently checked (as in CT). We can achieve the required (by hypothesis) dissociation of Case and agreement in the following way:

(37)   Agreement-Case Dissociation:
      a. Agreement is checked under the Probe-Goal analysis as in (27), (29), (30), (32).
      b. Case is checked under spec-head. (Or, without appeal to m-command, Case is checked under derivational sisterhood: x c-commands y and y c-commands x, as discussed above.)

Notice that our approach, like others, unattractively multiplies the types of checking configurations and stipulates that for certain features only one of the many checking configurations suffices. We return to this momentarily.

As a reminder of the previous components of our analysis:

(38) a. We assume the general features of the derivational model of DASR.
      b. There is no EPP, hence no EPP feature checking. Nor is there a 'structural' EPP.
      c. *There* is a pure Case-checker.
      d. Copular *be* assigns partitive Case.
      e. We assume that there is no gratuitous movement.

This gets the right result for the cases currently under consideration, the most relevant of which we repeat here for ease of reference:

(39) a. *Will be a man outside.   (as a declarative)
      b. There will be a man outside.
      c. The man will be outside.
      d. *There seems [a man to be outside]
      e. *There [$_{VP}$ a man left]   (See Lasnik 1995)

In (39a) the agreement feature of T is checked by *man* (under Probe-Goal), and the Case of *man* is checked optionally by *be* (partitive Case).[20] However, the Case feature of T remains and the derivation crashes. (39b) works in the same way except that in this instance the Case feature of T is checked by *there* (which raises to Spec, T under Moro 1997). In (39c) all is well, since here *the man* must raise to check the Case feature of T. (39d) is out since the movement of *man* is gratuitous, by virtue of the fact that *to* has no features to check (see Chapters 2, 3). Finally, (39e) is rejected since although the Case of T is checked by *there*, and the agreement of T is checked (under Probe-Goal) by *man*, the Case feature of *man* is unchecked (*leave* is not a partitive Case-checker, nor does it have any other relevant Case). So notice that for us, the driving force for movement into Spec, (finite and null Case-checking) T is Case-checking, as is roughly the case in GB. (But following Groat 1995 and DASR, we assume neither government, nor head-to-spec, nor m-command to implement the relation, if indeed expletives raise and/or T moves to C, either operation creating derivational sisterhood between T and the associate.)

One important question to raise now is this: why is there a difference between agreement- and Case-checking (i.e. why (37))? Limiting ourselves to independently

---

20. For us, partitive Case, which is semantically linked, must be checkable in situ.

motivated lexical features and their interpretation at the interfaces, the difference might well concern the fact that in the agreement-checking relation one element is interpretable while the other is uninterpretable; with Case, on the other hand, both elements are uninterpretable. Thus, in agreement checking between T and DP we have (40a), but with Case-checking we have (40b):[21]

(40)   T   DP
      a.   [− phi-interpretable] ← [+ phi-interpretable]
      b.   [− interpretable] ↔ [− interpretable]
            Case   Case

Suppose that feature checking of X, X an uninterpretable feature, can take place only if X locally derivationally c-commands Y, and X and Y Match. The idea is that to be 'satisfied' an uninterpretable feature must look down and see a Matching feature (where 'look down' means local derivational c-command). If this is true of *all* uninterpretable features, then we can in effect get the distinction in (37), exploiting (40). Recall that we are basically trying to explain why Case requires movement (the establishment of spec-head (37b)), whereas agreement can be checked in situ. The 'facts', but not the theory, comport with GB: i.e. (the) Case (Filter) but not agreement drives movement. Consider (41):

(41)   T [$_{vP}$ a man left]

T contains the uninterpretable agreement feature. This feature does locally derivationally c-command a matching feature (the +interpretable agreement feature of *a man*). But notice that for us (contra DBP) *both* T and *a man* contain an uninterpretable *Case* feature. So here, it is not enough for T to locally c-command *a man*; it is also true that the uninterpretable Case feature of *a man* must act as a probe and, for its own satisfaction, the uninterpretable probing Case feature of *a man* must locally c-command the goal T. In its merge site (Spec, vP) *a man* does not c-command T. However, notice that were it to move to Spec, T, then the uninterpretable Case feature of *a man* could successfully probe – under local derivational c-command – the identical matching feature in T.[22]

---

21. See Bošković (2002) for adoption and further exploration of this proposal.
22. Perhaps problematically, this seems to require that a maximal projection, not just a lexical item, can be a probe. However, interestingly, Uriagereka (1999) argues that by the LCA, a branching (maximal)

Thus, by virtue of DP raising to Spec, T in (41), we derive sisterhood, i.e. mutual derivational c-command. That is, T c-commanded *a man* before *a man* moved, and after *a man* moves, *a man* c-commands T. Thus there is mutual derivational c-command; i.e. the two are sisters, as are all spec-heads derived by such movement. But it is not entirely clear in DASR why there are two syntactic relations: derivational asymmetric c-command, and derivational sisterhood (= derivational symmetric c-command). Under the current set of ideas the answer is this: there is in fact only one relation, derivational c-command. Derivational sisterhood falls out automatically from the nature of feature checking, and specifically the idea that ALL *uninterpretables must c-command an element that they Match with*. We then simply appeal to the independently motivated (and perhaps irreducible) fact that Case is uninterpretable on *both* elements of the Case-checking relation, while only one element is uninterpretable with the agreement-checking relation. Ideally, we do not need to stipulate that Case takes place under derivational sisterhood while, by contrast, agreement takes place under derivational asymmetric c-command. Rather, it is exactly the same relation in both types of checking. The difference reduces to the nature of the individual elements, the atomic units, in the checking relation: a probe must be in a relation to (i.e. derivationally c-command) a matching goal. The asymmetry between Case necessitating Move/Attract, while Agr does not require movement, would to some degree follow from the independently motivated featural difference between uninterpretability of Case vs. Agr, as in (40).[23]

5.2 Some final notes on the derivational model; eliminating feature strength and 'obligatory' transformational rule application

Given what was said in Section 1, a potentially important aspect of the derivational model can now be made clear. Consider the object [was arrested a man]. In every syntactic model exhibiting Y-model architecture, it is required that *a man* must move to subject position before the split-off to Spell Out/PF, so as to ensure that

---

specifier position must be converted 'on line' to a lexical item. This however requires much further research.

23. Another approach to existentials which we do not pursue here hypothesizes that, contra Moro (1997), the associate is first merged in Spec, V (= *be*), not as the subject of a small clause complement of *be*. See Cresti and Tortora (1999), whom we thank for discussion of this analysis, and see also Epstein and Seely (1999) for further discussion.

was arrested a man is correctly predicted to be 'ungrammatical'. In standard theory, Passive was stipulated to be an obligatory transformation. As was recognized (Chomsky and Lasnik 1977), this is descriptive. The question 'why is it obligatory?' is answerable only by 'because *was arrested a man* is ungrammatical and I have no principled way to rule it out.'

In more contemporary analyses (e.g. Chomsky 1993, CT), a similarly descriptive account is provided. Certain features are stipulated to be strong, so if unchecked before the level of PF there is crashing at that level, while other features are weak. Again, this is non-explanatory, as is noted in e.g. CT (p. 233).[24]

A third approach is formulated in Frampton and Gutmann (1998): uninterpretable features are instructions to Attract, 'telling' Attract to apply whenever it should, in order to get the correct predictions. This too is somewhat descriptive and to the extent that [−interpretable] features are instructions for Attract to apply, and Attract is required to apply when instructed to by a [−interpretable] feature, the account seems to embrace strength and obligatory transformational application.

This of course is a very serious fundamental problem: Why does the 'meaning representation' not constitute the sound representation? Why are there transformations? Why must we pronounce it *A man was arrested*? That is, why can't we pronounce it *was arrested a man*?

The derivational framework does not need to incorporate any of the non-explanatory apparatus invoked to explain the fundamental facts: not strength, nor obligatory transformations, nor features as (obligatory) instructions to Attract. Consider again *was arrested a man*. In the derivational model, this object is interpreted by PF and LF. There appears an unchecked nominative Case feature on *a man*, and another on T. Thus, this object crashes, and this correct result is obtained without 'forcing' movement. Rather, if *a man* remains in situ, there is crashing and this is obtained with no new ad hoc descriptive mechanisms forcing *a man* to move. Rather the derivational model, married to independently motivated hypotheses concerning the interface interpretability of features, might suffice in this regard.

24. "...formulation of strength in terms of PF convergence is a restatement of the basic property, not a true explanation. In fact, there seems to be no way to improve upon the bare statement of the properties of strength" (CT, p. 323).

References

Alexiadou, A. and E. Anagnostopoulou. 1998. 'Parameterizing AGR: word order, V-movement and EPP-checking', *Natural Language and Linguistic Theory* 16:491–539.

Allen, Margaret. 1978. 'Morphological investigations', PhD diss., University of Connecticut, Storrs.

Baker, Mark. 1988. *Incorporation: A theory of grammatical function changing*, Chicago: University of Chicago Press.

Baltin, Mark. 1995. 'Floating quantifiers, PRO, and predication', *Linguistic Inquiry* 26:199–248.

Belletti, Adriana. 1988. 'The case of unaccusatives', *Linguistic Inquiry* 19:1–35.

Belletti, Adriana and Luigi Rizzi. 1988. 'Psych-Verbs and (Theta)-Theory', *Natural Language and Linguistic Theory* 6:291–352.

Berwick, Robert and Samuel D. Epstein. 1995. 'On the convergence of "minimalist" syntax and categorial grammar', in A. Nijholt, G. Scollo, and R. Steetkamp (eds.), *Algebraic Methods in Language Processing 1995: Proceedings of the Twente Workshop on Language Technology 10, jointly held with the First Algebraic Methodology and Software Technology (AMAST) Workshop on Language Processing*, Universiteit Twente, Enschede, The Netherlands.

Bobaljik, Jonathan. 2001. 'Floating quantifiers: Handle with care', to appear in the second *State of the Article*, Berlin: Mouton.

Boeckx, Cedric. 1999. 'Conflicting c-command requirements', *Studia Linguistica* 53:227–250.

— 2000. 'Minimal obviation constraints', ms., University of Connecticut, Storrs.

— 2001a. 'Scope reconstruction and A-movement', *Natural Language and Linguistic Theory* 19:503–548.

— 2001b. 'Mechanisms of chain formation', PhD diss., University of Connecticut, Storrs.

Borer, Hagit. 1986. 'I-subjects', *Linguistic Inquiry* 17: 375–416.

Bošković, Željko. 1994. '*Wager*-class verbs and existential constructions: A case for greed, lowering, and partitive case assignment', ms., University of Connecticut, Storrs.

    1995. 'Principles of economy in nonfinite complementation', PhD diss., University of Connecticut, Storrs.

    1997. *The syntax of nonfinite complementation: An economy approach*, Cambridge, MA: MIT Press.

    2001. 'Floating quantifiers and theta-role assigment', *Proceedings of NELS 31*, Amherst, Mass.: GLSA Publication, pp. 59–78.

    2002. 'A-movement and the EPP', *Syntax* 5:167–218.

Bošković, Željko and Howard Lasnik. 2003. 'On the distribution of null complementizers', *Linguistic Inquiry* 34:527–546.

Bošković, Željko and Daiko Takahashi. 1998. 'Scrambling and last resort', *Linguistic Inquiry* 29:347–366.

Brody, Michael. 1993. 'Theta theory and arguments', *Linguistic Inquiry* 24:1–23.

    1995. *Lexico-logical form: A radically minimalist theory*, Cambridge, MA: MIT Press.

    2001. 'One more time', *Syntax* 4:126–138.

Castillo, Juan Carlos, John Drury and Kleanthes K. Grohmann. 1999. 'Merge over move and the extended projection principle', in Sachiko Aoshima, John Drury and Tuomo Neuvonen (eds.), *University of Maryland Working Papers in Linguistics* 8:63–103. University of Maryland, College Park: Department of Linguistics.

Chomsky, Noam. 1957. *Syntactic Structures*, The Hague: Mouton.

    1965. *Aspects of the theory of syntax*, Cambridge, MA: MIT Press.

    1970. 'Remarks on nominalizations', in R. Jacobs and Peter S. Rosenbaum (eds.), *English transformational grammar*, Waltham, MA: Ginn, pp. 184–221.

    1975. *Reflections on language*, New York: Pantheon Books.

    1980. *Rules and Representations*, New York: Columbia University Press and Oxford: Blackwell.

    1981. *Lectures on government and binding*, Dordrecht: Foris.

    1986. *Knowledge of language: Its nature, origin, and use*, New York: Praeger.

    1991. 'Some notes on economy of derivation and representation', in Robert Freidin (ed.), *Principles and parameters in comparative grammar*, Current Studies in Linguistics Series, no. 20, Cambridge, MA: MIT Press, pp. 417–54.

1993. *Language and thought*, Wakefield, RI: Moyer Bell.
1995. *The minimalist program*, Cambridge, MA: MIT Press.
1999. 'Derivation by Phase', *MIT Occasional Papers in Linguistics*, no. 18, Cambridge, MA: MIT Working Papers in Linguistics, Department of Linguistics and Philosophy.
2000. 'Minimalist inquiries: the framework', in Roger Martin, David Michaels and Juan Uriagereka (eds.), *Step by step: Essays in honor of Howard Lasnik*, Cambridge, MA: MIT Press, pp. 89–155.
2001a. 'Derivation by phase', in Michael Kenstowicz (ed.), *Ken Hale: A life in language*, Cambridge, MA: MIT Press, pp. 1–52.
2001b. 'Beyond explanatory adequacy', ms., MIT. A revised version to appear in Adriana Belletti (ed.) *Structures and beyond: current issues in the theory of language*, Oxford: Oxford University Press.

Chomsky, Noam and Howard Lasnik. 1977. 'Filters and control', *Linguistic Inquiry* 8:425–504.
1993. 'Principles and parameters theory', in Joachim Jacobs, Arnim von Stechow, Wolfgang Sternefeld, Theo Vennemann (eds.), *Syntax: An international handbook of contemporary research*, Berlin: De Gruyter, pp. 506–569.

Collins, Chris. 1994. 'Economy of derivation and the generalized proper binding condition', *Linguistic Inquiry* 25:45–61.
1997. *Local economy*, Cambridge, MA: MIT Press.
1999. 'Multiple verb movement in Hoan', *Linguistic Inquiry* 33:1–29.
2002. 'Eliminating labels', in Samuel D. Epstein and T. Daniel Seely (eds.), *Derivation and explanation in the minimalist program*, Oxford: Blackwell, pp. 42–64.

Contreras, Heles. 2003. '*Wh*-movement without intermediate traces', ms., University of Washington.

Cresti, Diana and Christina Tortora. 1999. 'Aspects of locative doubling and resultative predication', *Proceedings of the 25th Annual Meeting of the Berkeley Linguistics Society*.

den Dikken, Marcel. 1995. 'Binding, expletives, and levels', *Linguistic Inquiry* 26:347–354.

Edelman, Shimon and Morten H. Christiansen. 2003. 'How seriously should we take minimalist syntax?', *Trends in cognitive sciences* 7.2:60–61.

Einstein, Albert. 1954. *Ideas and Opinions*, New York: Bonanza Books.

Emonds, Joseph. 1986. [1985?] *A unified theory of syntactic categories*, Dordrecht: Foris.
Enç, Mürvet. 1987. 'Anchoring conditions for tense', *Linguistic Inquiry* 18:633–657.
　1991. 'The semantics of specificity', *Linguistic Inquiry* 22:1–26.
Epstein, Joshua M. 1999. 'Agent-Based Computational Models and Generative Social Science', *Complexity* 4:41–60.
Epstein, Joshua M. and Robert L. Axtell 1996. *Growing artificial societies*, Cambridge, MA: MIT Press.
Epstein, Samuel D. 1990. 'Differentiation and reduction in syntactic theory', *Natural Language and Linguistic Theory* 8:313–323.
　1994. 'The derivation of c-command', paper presented at Harvard University Forum for Linguistic Theory, Harvard University.
　1998. 'Overt scope marking and covert V2', *Linguistic Inquiry* 29:181–227.
　1999. 'UN-principled syntax: the derivation of syntactic relations', in Samuel D. Epstein and Norbert Hornstein (eds.), *Working minimalism*, Cambridge, MA: MIT Press, pp. 317–345.
　2001. 'Deriving the Proper Binding Condition', Paper presented at TiLT, University of Utrecht.
　2003. 'Intermodal deduction and I-functional explanation', to appear in *Syntax*.
Epstein, Samuel D. and Norbert Hornstein (eds.). 1999. *Working minimalism*, Cambridge, MA: MIT Press.
Epstein, Samuel D. and T. Daniel Seely. 1999. 'SPEC-ifying the GF "subject": Eliminating A-chains and the EPP within a derivational model', ms., University of Michigan and Eastern Michigan University.
　2002. 'Rule applications as cycles in a level-free syntax', in Samuel D. Epstein and T. Daniel Seely (eds.), *Derivation and explanation in the minimalist program*, Oxford: Blackwell.
Epstein, Samuel D., Erich Groat, Ruriko Kawashima, and Hisatsugu Kitahara. 1998. *A derivational approach to syntactic relations*, Oxford: Oxford University Press.
Epstein Samuel D., Acrisio Pires and T. Daniel Seely. 2004. 'EPP in T?', ms., University of Michigan and Eastern Michigan University.
Epstein, Samuel D., Höskuldur Thráinsson and C. Jan-Wouter Zwart. 1996. 'Introduction', in Werner Abraham, Samuel D. Epstein, Höskuldur Thráinsson and

C. Jan-Wouter Zwart (eds.), *Minimal ideas*, Amsterdam/Philadelphia: Benjamins, pp. 1–66.

Ferguson, K. Scott. 1994. 'Deriving the invisibility of PP nodes for command from Agr^0 and P^0 Case-checking', *Harvard Working Papers in Linguistics* 4, edited by Samuel D. Epstein, Höskuldur Thráinsson and Susumu Kuno. Associate editor Steve Peter.

Ferguson, K. Scott and Erich Groat. 1993. 'Shortest move', ms., Harvard University.

Fernandez-Salgueiro, Gerardo. 2003. 'Level-free Syntax, Linearization and Phonetic Realization of Chain Links', ms., University of Michigan.

Fitzpatrick, Justin M. 2002. 'On miminalist approaches to the locality of movement', *Linguistic Inquiry* 33:443–463.

Fortin, Catherine. 2004. 'On the Syntax of Nonsententials', ms., University of Michigan.

Frampton, John and Sam Gutmann. 1999. 'Cyclic computation, a computational efficient minimalist syntax', *Syntax* 2:1–27.

2002. 'Crash-proof syntax', in Samuel D. Epstein and T. Daniel Seely (eds.), *Derivation and explanation in the minimalist program*, Oxford: Blackwell.

Freidin, Robert. 1992. *Foundations of generative syntax*, Cambridge, MA: MIT Press.

Freidin, Robert. 1994. 'Conceptual shifts in the science of grammar: 1951–1992', in Carlos P. Otero (ed.), *Noam Chomsky: Critical assessments*, vol. 1, London: Routledge, pp. 653–690.

1997. 'Binding theory on minimalist assumptions', in Hans Bennis, Pierre Pica and Johan Rooryck (eds.), *Atomism and binding*, Dordrecht: Foris.

Freidin, Robert and Jean-Roger Vergnaud. 2001. 'Exquisite connections: some remarks on the evolution of linguistic theory', *Lingua* 111.9:639–666.

Fukui, Naoki and Margaret Speas. 1986. 'Specifiers and projections', *MIT Working Papers in Linguistics* 8:128–172.

Gajewski, Jon. 2000. 'Noncyclic operations and the LCA in a derivational theory', *Linguistic Inquiry* 31:722–731.

Groat, Erich. 1995. 'English expletives: A minimalist approach', *Linguistic Inquiry* 26:354–365.

Grohmann, Kleanthes K., John Drury and Juan Carlos Castillo. 2000. 'No more EPP', in Roger Billery and Brook Danielle Lillehaugen (eds.), *Proceedings of the 19th West Coast Conference on Formal Linguistics*, Somerville, MA: Cascadilla Press, pp. 153–166.

Grohmann, Kleanthes and Cedric Boeckx. 2004. 'Reflections on Phases', Talk presented at the University of Michigan, August 26, 2004.

Hazout, Ilan. 2004. 'The syntax of existential constructions', *Linguistic Inquiry* 35:393–430.

Higginbotham, James. 1983. 'Logical form, binding, and nominals', *Linguistic Inquiry* 14:395–420.

1985. 'On semantics', *Linguistic Inquiry* 16:547–593.

Holmberg, Anders. 2000. 'Am I unscientific? A reply to Lappin, Levine, and Johnson', *Natural language and linguistic theory* 18.4:837–842.

Hornstein, Norbert. 1995. *Logical form: From GB to minimalism*, Oxford: Blackwell.

1998. 'Movement and chains', *Syntax* 1:99–127.

2001. *Move! A minimalist theory of construal*, Oxford: Blackwell.

Huang, C.-T. James. 1993. 'Reconstruction and the structure of VP: Some theoretical consequences', *Linguistic Inquiry* 24:103–138.

Jacobson, Pauline. 1992. 'Raising without movement', in Richard Larson *et al.* (eds.), *Control and grammatical theory*, Dordrecht: Kluwer, pp. 149–194.

Jaeggli, Osvaldo. 1982. *Topics in Romance syntax*, Dordrecht: Foris.

Jang, Young-Jun. 1997. 'Minimal feature movement', *Journal of linguistics* 33:2.

Jelinek, Eloise. 1984. 'Empty categories, case, and configurationality', *Natural Language and Linguistic Theory* 2:39–76.

Johnson, Kyle. 1991. 'Object positions', *Natural Language and Linguistic Theory* 9:577–636.

Kayne, Richard S. 1984. *Connectedness and binary branching*, Dordrecht: Foris.

1994. *The Antisymmetry of syntax*, Cambridge, MA: MIT Press.

Kitahara, Hisatsugu. 1995. 'Target alpha: Deducing strict cyclicity from derivational economy', *Linguistic Inquiry* 26:47–77.

1997. *Elementary operations and optimal derivations*, Cambridge, MA: MIT Press.

2003. 'Some notes on Minimalist theorizing', *Current issues in English linguistics*, volume 2:1–24.

Koizumi, Masatoshi. 1995. 'Phrase structure in minimalist syntax', PhD diss., MIT.

Lappin, Shalom, Robert D. Levine, and David E. Johnson. 2000a. 'The structure of unscientific revolutions', *Natural language and linguistic theory* 18.3:665–671.

2000b. 'The revolution confused: a response to our critics', *Natural language and linguistic theory* 18.4:873–890.

Lasnik, Howard. 1992. 'Case and expletives', *Linguistic Inquiry* 23:381–405.

1995. 'Verbal morphology: *Syntactic structures* meets the *Minimalist program*', in Paula Kempchinsky and Héctor Campos (eds.), *Evolution and revolution in linguistic theory: essays in honor of Carlos Otero*, Washington, D.C.: Georgetown University Press, pp. 251–275.

1998. 'Exceptional case marking: Perspectives old and new', in Željko Bošković, Steven Franks, and William Snyder (eds.), *Formal Approaches to Slavic Linguistics: The Connecticut Meeting 1997*, Michigan Slavic Publications, pp. 187–211.

1999. 'Chains of arguments', in Samuel D. Epstein and Norbert Hornstein (eds.), *Working minimalism*, Cambridge, MA: MIT Press, pp. 189–216.

2001. 'A note on the EPP', *Linguistic Inquiry* 32:356–362.

2002. 'On the Extended Projection Principle', ms., University of Maryland, College Park.

2003. *Minimalist investigations in linguistic theory*, London: Routledge.

Lasnik, Howard, and Mamoru Saito. 1984. 'On the nature of proper government', *Linguistic Inquiry* 15:235–289.

1991. 'On the subject of infinitives', in Lise Dobrin, Lynn Nichols, and R. Rodriguez (eds.) *Papers from the 27th regional meeting of the Chicago Linguistic Society*, pp. 324–343.

1992. *Move alpha: Conditions on its application and output*, Cambridge, MA: MIT Press.

Lasnik, Howard and Juan Uriagereka. 1988. *A course in GB syntax: Lectures on binding and empty categories*, Cambridge, MA: MIT Press.

Lebeaux, David. 1988. 'Language acquisition and the form of grammar', PhD diss., University of Massachusetts, Amherst.

1991. 'Relative clauses, licensing, and the nature of the derivation', in Susan Rothstein (ed.) *Syntax and semantics: Perspectives on phrase structure: Heads and licensing*. Academic Press.

1995. 'Where does the binding theory apply?', *University of Maryland Working Papers in Linguistics* 3:63-88.

Lobeck, Anne. 1990. 'Functional heads as proper governors', *Proceedings of the 20th Northeastern Linguistics Society Conference*, GLSA, University of Massachusetts, Amherst.

Manzini, M. Rita and Anna Roussou. 2000. 'A minimalist theory of A-movement and control', *Lingua* 110:409–447.

Martin, Roger. 1992. 'On the distribution and case features of PRO', ms., University of Connecticut, Storrs.

1996. 'Minimalist theory of PRO and control', PhD diss., University of Connecticut, Storrs.

1999. 'Case, the extended projection principle, and minimalism', in Samuel D. Epstein and Norbert Hornstein (eds.), *Working minimalism*, Cambridge, MA: MIT Press, pp. 1–26.

McCloskey, James. 1986. 'Inflection and conjunction in Modern Irish', *Natural Language and Linguistic Theory* 4:245–281.

1991. '*There, it* and agreement', *Linguistic Inquiry* 22:563–567.

1996. 'On the Scope of Verb Movement in Irish,' *Natural Language and Linguistic Theory* 14:47–104.

1997. 'Subjecthood and subject positions,' in Liliane Haegeman (ed.), *Elements of Grammar*, Dordrecht: Kluwer Academic Publishers, pp. 197–235.

McCloskey, James and Ken Hale. 1984. 'On the syntax of person-number inflection in Modern Irish', *Natural Language and Linguistic Theory* 1:487–533.

McGilvray, James. 1999. *Chomsky: language, mind and politics*, Malden, Mass.: Polity Press.

Moro, Andrea. 1997. *The raising of predicates: Predicative noun phrases and the theory of clause structure*, Cambridge: Cambridge University Press.

Muysken, Pieter. 1982. 'Parameterizing the notion "head"', *Journal of Linguistic Research* 2:57–75.

Myers, Scott. 1984. 'Zero-derivation and inflection', *MIT Working Papers in Linguistics* 7:53–69.

Nuñes, Jairo. 1999. 'Linearization of chains and phonetic realization of chain links', in Samuel D. Epstein and Norbert Hornstein (eds.), *Working minimalism*, Cambridge, MA: MIT Press, pp. 217–250.

2001. 'Sideward movement', *Linguistic Inquiry* 32:303–344.

2004. *Linearization of chains and sideward movement*, Cambridge, MA: MIT Press.

Ormazabal, Javier. 1995. 'The syntax of complementation: On the connection between syntactic structure and selection', PhD diss., University of Connecticut, Storrs.

Pesetsky, David. 1991. 'Zero syntax, vol. 2: Infinitives', ms., MIT.

Phillips, Colin and Howard Lasnik. 2003. 'Linguistics and empirical evidence: reply to Edelman and Christiansen', *Trends in cognitive sciences* 7.2:61–62.

Piattelli-Palmarini, Massimo. 2000. 'The metric of open-mindedness', *Natural language and linguistic theory* 18.4:859–862.

Pires, Acrisio. 2001. 'The syntax of gerunds and infinitives: Subjects, case and control', PhD. diss., University of Maryland, College Park.

Pollard, Carl and Ivan Sag. 1992. 'Anaphors in English and the Scope of Binding', *Linguistic Inquiry* 23.2:261–303.

Poole, Geoffrey. 1996. 'Transformations Across Components', PhD diss., Harvard University.

Reuland, Eric. 2000. 'Revolution, discovery and an elementary principle of logic', *Natural language and linguistic theory* 18.4:843–848.

Rizzi, Luigi. 1986. 'Null objects in Italian and the theory of pro', *Linguistic Inquiry* 17.3.

1990. *Relativized minimality*, Cambridge, MA: MIT Press.

Roberts, Ian. 2000. 'Caricaturing dissent', *Natural language and linguistic theory* 18.4:849–857.

Rooryck, Johan. 1997. 'On the interaction between raising and focus in sentential complementation', *Studia Linguistica* 50:1–49.

Rosenbaum, Peter S. 1967. *The grammar of English predicate complement constructions*, Cambridge, MA: MIT Press.

Rothstein, Susan. 1983. 'The syntactic forms of predication', PhD diss., MIT.

Ruwet, Nicholas. 1982. 'Les Phrases Copulatives', in *Recherches Linguistiques* (University of Paris–Vincennes) 143–191.

Sag, Ivan. 1978. 'Floated quantifiers, adverbs, and extraction sites', *Linguistic Inquiry* 9:146–150.

Saito, Mamoru and Keiko Murasugi. 1990. 'N' deletion in Japanese', *UConn Working Papers in Linguistics* 3:87–107.

Seely, T. Daniel. 1992. ' "Together," operators, and plurality', ms., Eastern Michigan University.

2000. 'On projection free syntax', ms., Eastern Michigan University.

Smith, Neil. 1999. *Chomsky: Ideas and ideals*, Cambridge: Cambridge University Press.
Speas, Margaret. 1986. 'Adjunction and projection in syntax', PhD diss., MIT.
Sportiche, Dominique. 1988. 'A theory of floating quantifiers and its corollaries for constituent structure', *Linguistic Inquiry* 19:425–449.
Stowell, Tim. 1981. 'Origins of phrase structure', PhD diss., MIT.
   1982. 'The tense of infinitives', *Linguistic Inquiry* 13:561–570.
   1991. 'Small clause restructuring', in Robert Freidin (ed.), *Principles and parameters in comparative grammar*, Cambridge, Mass.: MIT Press, pp. 182–218.
Takahashi, Daiko. 1994. 'Minimality of movement', PhD diss., University of Connecticut, Storrs.
Torrego, Esther. 2002. 'Arguments for a Derivational approach to Syntactic Relations based on Clitics', in Samuel D. Epstein and T. Daniel Seely (eds.), *Derivation and explanation in the minimalist program*, Oxford: Blackwell.
Uriagereka, Juan. 1998. *Rhyme and reason*. (Appendix authored by Jairo Nuñes and E. Thompson), Cambridge, MA: MIT Press.
   1999. 'Multiple spell-out', in Samuel D. Epstein and Norbert Hornstein (eds.), *Working minimalism*, Cambridge, MA: MIT Press, pp. 251–282.
   2000. 'On the emptiness of "design" polemics', *Natural language and linguistic theory* 18.4:863–871.
Whitehead, Alfred North. 1938. *Modes of Thought*, New York: The Free Press.
Williams, Edwin. 1980. 'Predication', *Linguistic Inquiry* 11:203–238.
   1982. 'The NP cycle', *Linguistic Inquiry* 13:277–295.
   1989. 'The anaphoric nature of theta roles', *Linguistic Inquiry* 20:425–456.
   1994. *Thematic Structure in Syntax*. Cambridge, MA: MIT Press.

Index

A-bar
  chains 5
  movement 127
  reconstruction 178
A-bound 131, 145
ACC *see also* Case 70, 72, 73, 74, 75, 76, 77, 78, 79, 80, 81, 82, 83, 86, 87, 88, 91, 94, 96, 97, 98, 100, 101, 102, 111
A-chain *see also* chain 5, 14, 15, 17, 18, 19, 20, 21, 23, 24, 25, 27, 28, 29, 31, 32, 33, 35, 36, 37, 39, 41, 42, 43, 44, 45, 46, 47, 49, 51, 113, 116, 121, 156
  elimination of 4, 14, 15, 17, 18, 19, 20, 21, 22, 23, 24, 25, 27, 28, 29, 31, 32, 34, 36, 37, 39, 41, 42, 43, 44, 45, 46–47, 113, 121, 156
Agr *see also* Agreement 184, 185, 186, 189, 191, 192, 193, 194, 197
Agreement 15, 30, 33, 50, 51, 86, 175, 177, 184, 185, 186, 187, 189, 191, 192, 193, 194, 195, 196, 197, 199
  agreement checking 175, 189, 191, 193
Agreement-Case Dissociation 194
Alexiadou, A. 51
Allen, Margaret 106
A-movement *see also* movement 16, 20, 32, 42, 43, 44, 46, 113, 114, 116, 117, 119, 130, 131, 132, 133, 134, 135, 139, 143, 147, 150, 156, 157, 164, 166, 177
  'long distance' 49
  partial A-movement 56
Anagnostopoulou, E. 51
anaphor 178
  anaphoric relations 131
A-reconstruction 137, 144, 148, 150, 167
associate 175, 176, 177, 178, 184, 192, 195, 197
asymmetric c-command 27, 176, 197
A-traces *see also* traces 43, 47, 144, 151
Attract 22, 33, 34, 41, 48, 117, 121, 122, 135, 142, 178, 185, 197, 198
Axtell, Robert 7

Baker, Mark 65, 83
Baltin, Mark 161
Bare Output Condition (BOC) 65, 66
Bare Phrase Structure (BPS) 27
Beddor, Pam 1
BELIEVE (verb class) 11, 49, 72, 73, 75, 78, 99, 116
Belletti, Adriana 136, 139, 175, 176, 184, 185, 191, 192
Berwick, Robert 30
binding 115, 118, 119, 130, 131, 132,

136, 139, 143, 144, 146, 147, 149, 151, 153, 165, 168, 172, 173
Binding Theory
  Condition A 114, 118, 132, 133, 134, 135, 136, 137, 139, 143, 144, 148, 149
  Condition C 119, 124, 131, 135, 138, 139, 144, 145, 149, 150, 151
Bobaljik, Jonathan 12, 161, 163, 164
Boeckx, Cedric 114, 116, 125, 131, 132, 136, 137, 139, 140, 147, 148, 149, 150, 167, 172
Borer, Hagit 116
Bošković, Željko 9, 11, 12, 30, 43, 49, 51, 52, 53, 57, 65, 70, 71, 72, 73, 74, 75, 76, 77, 80, 82, 83, 86, 87, 88, 98, 99, 101, 103, 104, 105, 106, 107, 109, 112, 113, 114, 116, 117, 118, 119, 120, 121, 122, 123, 124, 125, 126, 127, 128, 130, 133, 137, 146, 150, 151, 152, 153, 154, 155, 156, 159, 160, 161, 164
BPS *see* Bare Phrase Structure
Brody, Michael 8, 25, 29, 36, 45, 70
Burzio, Luigi 73
Burzio's Generalization 73, 77

Case 21, 30, 33, 34, 37, 38, 40, 41, 42, 43, 50, 51, 52, 56, 57, 58, 59, 60, 67, 68, 69, 70, 71, 72, 73, 74, 75, 76, 77, 78, 79, 81, 82, 83, 84, 85, 86, 87, 88, 89, 90, 91, 93, 94, 96, 97, 98, 99, 100, 101, 102, 103, 104, 105, 106, 109, 111, 113, 114, 115, 116, 117, 139, 140, 141, 142, 146, 148, 149, 159, 164, 165, 166, 167, 168, 170, 174, 175, 176, 177, 180, 184, 185, 186, 187, 188, 189, 191, 192, 193, 194, 195, 196, 197, 198, 199
  Case checking 57, 86, 89, 97, 104, 176, 177, 191, 194, 195, 196, 197
  Case Filter 34, 56, 57, 59, 67, 83, 94, 102, 109, 175
Castillo, Juan Carlos 53, 68, 114, 116, 131, 145
c-command 5, 19, 27, 28, 29, 30, 115, 119, 131, 132, 133, 134, 135, 136, 137, 138, 139, 141, 142, 143, 144, 145, 146, 147, 148, 149, 153, 154, 176, 177, 178, 186, 188, 190, 191, 194, 196, 197, 199
  asymmetric 27, 176, 197
chain 14, 15, 16, 17, 18, 19, 20, 21, 22, 23, 24, 25, 26, 27, 28, 29, 30, 31, 32, 33, 34, 35, 36, 37, 38, 39, 40, 41, 42, 43, 44, 45, 46, 47, 49, 50, 51, 113, 116, 117, 120, 121, 123, 124, 126, 129, 133, 150, 151, 156, 167, 175
Chain Condition 36, 38
chain formation *see also* chain, Form Chain 34, 35, 36
head chains 5
function chains 44
C_{HL} 15, 16, 19, 20, 21, 22, 28, 30, 39, 40, 49, 56, 65, 174
checking
  Case 57, 86, 89, 97, 104, 176, 177, 191, 194, 195, 196, 197
  domain 40
  relation 33, 37, 39

Index   211

Chomsky, Noam 4, 5, 6, 8, 9, 12, 13, 14, 16, 17, 19, 20, 21, 23, 24, 25, 26, 27, 28, 29, 30, 31, 32, 33, 34, 35, 36, 37, 38, 39, 40, 41, 43, 44, 45, 46, 47, 48, 49, 50, 51, 52, 53, 54, 56, 57, 58, 60, 66, 85, 90, 97, 99, 100, 103, 105, 106, 114, 117, 120, 123, 127, 129, 131, 135, 142, 143, 146, 147, 150, 155, 166, 167, 168, 169, 175, 176, 178, 181, 183, 184, 187, 189, 190, 192, 193, 196, 198
Christiansen, Morten 9
clause, small 76, 89, 90, 95, 96, 98, 197
Collins, Chris 18, 24, 59, 61, 83, 87, 126, 181
Condition A 114, 118, 132, 133, 134, 135, 136, 137, 139, 142, 144, 148, 149
Condition C 119, 124, 131, 135, 138, 139, 144, 145, 149, 150, 151
configurational requirement 50
conjecture (verb class) 70, 71, 72, 73, 74, 75, 76, 77, 78, 79, 80, 81, 82, 83, 84, 85, 86, 87, 88, 91, 94, 96, 97, 101, 102, 104, 107, 108, 109, 110, 111, 113
Contreras, Heles 178
control *to* 48
converge 176, 181, 182, 185, 198
copy theory 14, 16, 17, 18, 21, 35
counter-cyclicity 123, 126
covert movement 177, 184, 185, 188
Cresti, Diana 22, 197
c-selection 92, 113

Deletion 15, 34, 37, 38, 39, 40, 41, 42, 48
den Dikken, Marcel 86
derivation 16, 20, 22, 24, 25, 27, 28, 29, 30, 31, 32, 34, 35, 36, 38, 39, 40, 41, 42, 43, 44, 45, 46
derivational model 174, 179, 180, 181, 183, 188, 195, 197, 198
derivation-internal deletion 38
extended 182, 183
unit 182, 183
Dirac, Paul 1
Drury, John 53, 68, 114, 116, 131, 145
D-structure 6, 168, 169
dual activation approach 99, 189
Dual Activation Requirement 189

ECM *see* Exceptional Case Marking
ECM ACC *see also* case 91, 166
Edelman, Shimon 9
Einstein, Albert 3, 7
elimination of A-chains 4, 14, 15, 17, 18, 19. 20, 21, 22, 23, 24, 25, 27, 28, 29, 31, 32, 34, 36, 37, 39, 41, 42, 43, 44, 45, 46–47, 113, 121, 156
Emonds, Joseph 55
empirical
  adequacy 29
  coverage 1
  overlap 9
Enç, Mürvet 79
Enlightened Self Interest (ESI) 57, 67, 177, 186
enriched representational objects 8
Epstein, Josh 1, 7

Epstein, Samuel D. 1, 4, 5, 7, 8, 9, 11, 12, 13, 17, 20, 22, 25, 26, 27, 38, 30, 31, 33, 34, 41, 43, 45, 46, 51, 52, 59, 61, 62, 84, 105, 116, 118, 122, 124, 128, 129, 132, 135, 141, 143, 158, 168, 174, 176, 177, 178, 179, 181, 184, 190, 191, 193, 195, 197
Exceptional Case Marking (ECM) 43, 49, 52, 57, 69, 70, 77, 79, 81, 82, 91, 115, 159, 161, 165, 166, 167, 173
experiencer 134, 135, 136, 137, 138, 139, 140, 141, 142, 143, 144, 145, 146, 147, 148, 149, 154
expletives 71, 82, 84, 86, 95, 97, 101
  expletive raising 177
  there-insertion 56
extended derivation 182, 183
Extended Projection Principle (EPP) 8, 9, 10, 11, 12, 15, 35, 43, 48, 49, 50, 51, 52, 53, 54, 55, 56, 57, 58, 59, 60, 63, 64, 67, 68, 69, 70, 71, 72, 76, 77, 78, 79, 88, 89, 90, 91, 94, 96, 97, 98, 99, 100, 101, 102, 103, 105, 106, 107, 108, 109, 110, 111, 113, 114, 115, 116, 117, 118, 119, 120, 124, 126, 127, 128, 129, 130, 131, 132, 133, 134, 135, 136, 139, 143, 144, 146, 150, 155, 156, 157, 158, 164, 165, 166, 167, 169, 170, 171, 172, 173, 175, 176, 177, 184, 185, 186, 187, 188, 189, 191, 192, 193, 194, 195
Extension Condition 123, 125, 126

feature 15, 16, 31, 32, 33, 34, 36, 37, 39, 40, 41, 50
  checking 48, 50, 57, 59, 68, 71, 99, 104
  feature-driven 117, 122, 125, 126, 128, 129
  formal 33, 39, 40
  Theta 190, 191, 192, 193
Feature-Relativized Minimality 49
Ferguson, K. Scott 49, 135, 139
Fernandez-Salgueiro, Gerardo 178
Fitzpatrick, Justin 176
Form Chain *see also* chain 36, 40, 43, 120, 122, 123, 124, 126, 129, 133, 176
Fortin, Catherine 182
Fox, Danny 131
Frampton, John 61, 62, 181, 190, 198
Freidin, Robert 3, 21, 26, 131
Fukui, Naoki 11, 51, 116
Full Interpretation (FI) 34, 66, 90, 96, 180
function chains 44

Gajewski, Jon 4
GB *see* Government and Binding Theory
Generative Social Science 7
Government and Binding Theory 6, 33, 44, 46, 55, 57, 67, 69, 175, 179, 180, 182, 195, 196
Grammatical Function 31
grammatical relations 6
Greed 57, 65, 67, 116, 177, 178, 186
Groat, Erich 11, 13, 17, 20, 31, 41, 43, 49, 132, 168, 174, 175, 176, 179,

184, 190, 195, 197
Grohmann, Kleanthes 53, 68, 114, 116, 125, 131, 145, 146
Gutmann, Sam 13, 61, 62, 179, 180, 181, 182, 190, 198
Gutmann Problem 180, 182

Hale, Ken 54
Hazout, Ilan 175
head chains 5
head-movement 8
Higginbotham, James 30, 131
Holmberg, Anders 9
Hornstein, Norbert 4, 15, 19, 37, 114, 167
Huang, C.-T. James 136

I-bar invisibility 22
IFC (Instantaneous Form Chain) 124, 133
Impure Merge 67
Inclusiveness 14, 16, 32
indexing 16
infinitival 48, 49, 52, 53, 54, 55, 57, 58, 61, 63, 68, 70, 71, 72, 75, 76, 77, 79, 83, 98, 101, 102, 103, 106, 108, 109, 110, 111, 112, 114, 116
   complements 48, 49, 52, 55, 71, 72, 76, 79, 83, 98, 102, 106
   control *to* 48
   non-control *to* 99, 100, 112
   raising *to* 48, 53, 56, 68, 69
INFL 41
information structure 51
inherent Case *see also* Case 81, 101, 103, 104

interface levels 15
Internal Subject Hypothesis 53
interpretable 15, 16, 20, 21, 22, 27, 33, 34, 36, 37, 40, 43
iterative rule application 6

Jacobson, Pauline 53
Jaeggli, Osvaldo 163
Jang, Young-Jun 186
Jelinek, Eloise 65
Johnson, David 9
Johnson, Kyle 69, 136, 166

Kawashima, Ruriko 13, 17, 20, 31, 41, 43, 132, 168, 174, 176, 179, 184, 190, 195, 197
Kayne, Richard 6, 27, 28
Kitahara, Hisatsugu 5, 9, 13, 17, 20, 31, 41, 43, 123, 131, 132, 139, 140, 147, 148, 168, 174, 176, 179, 184, 190, 195, 197
Koizumi, Masatoshi 69

label 14, 15, 17, 18, 23, 24, 25, 33
Lappin, Shalom 9
Larsonian shell structures 30
Lasnik, Howard 6, 9, 11, 13, 23, 25, 26, 28, 34, 47, 49, 51, 57, 69, 71, 73, 77, 84, 88, 102, 104, 106, 107, 108, 109, 113, 114, 115, 116, 117, 118, 120, 131, 132, 136, 137, 143, 144, 146, 147, 150, 164, 165, 166, 167, 168, 169, 170, 171, 172, 173, 175, 176, 177, 184, 185, 188, 191, 192, 195, 198
Last Resort 19, 33

late insertion 154, 155
LCA *see* Linear Correspondence Axiom
Lebeaux, David 132, 139, 145, 148, 150, 151, 152, 153, 154
level-free model 6
Levine, Robert 9
lexical items 14, 15, 16, 32, 33
l(=lexical)-selection 73
LF *see* Logical Form
Linear Correspondence Axiom (LCA) 6, 27, 28, 196
Lobeck, Anne 158
locality 117, 118, 121, 122, 124, 125, 128, 129, 130, 133, 134, 135, 136, 142, 155, 156, 164, 176
  locality constraint 51, 118, 122, 125, 155, 156
Logical Form (LF) 6, 8, 12, 13, 20, 21, 22, 26, 27, 29, 31, 33, 34, 36, 37, 38, 39, 40, 41, 42, 45, 46, 56, 57, 59, 62, 65, 66, 67, 90, 174, 175, 178, 179, 180, 181, 182, 183, 184, 185, 198

Manzini, Rita 53, 114
Martin, Roger 9, 11, 51, 53, 72, 73, 76, 78, 97, 104, 105, 106, 107, 109, 110, 116, 159, 175
Match 189, 190, 191, 192, 194, 196, 197
McCloskey, James 9, 53, 54, 55, 86
McGilvray, James 9, 27
Merge 5, 17, 18, 20, 22, 25, 27, 28, 29, 30, 31, 32, 34, 37, 40, 41, 46, 54, 55, 59, 60, 61, 63, 64, 65, 66, 67, 68, 90, 91, 93, 114, 116, 122, 124, 129, 140, 174, 176, 177, 178, 179, 180, 181, 182, 183, 184, 189, 193, 196, 197
  Impure Merge 67
  Merge over Move 58, 59, 60, 61, 63, 64, 65, 67, 68
  Pure Merge 66, 67
  Re-Merge 25
Minimalism *see* Minimalist
Minimalist 5, 6, 7, 8, 9, 14, 16, 18, 20, 22, 24, 25, 26, 27, 28, 30, 32, 34, 36, 38, 40, 42, 44, 45, 46, 48, 50, 56, 57, 58, 59, 60, 61, 62, 63, 64, 65, 67, 68, 69, 122, 126, 128, 129, 166, 168, 170, 175, 184, 187, 188, 189, 190, 191, 192, 193, 194
  framework 6
  method 3
Minimize Chain Links Principle (MCLP) 117, 120, 129, 130
model
  derivational model 174, 179, 180, 181, 183, 188, 195, 197, 198
  interface levels 15
  level-free model 6
  Y-model 6, 178, 180, 181, 197
Mood 55
Moro, Andrea 80, 85, 88, 89, 90, 91, 92, 93, 94, 95, 96, 98, 100, 111, 115, 177, 195, 197
motherhood 23, 24, 25, 26
Move (Attract) 5, 15, 17, 18, 19, 20, 27, 28, 29, 30, 31, 32, 33, 34, 35, 36, 39, 40, 41, 42, 43, 44, 45, 46, 48, 50, 51, 57, 58, 59, 60, 61, 63, 64,

65, 66, 67, 68, 69, 115, 117, 118, 120, 121, 122, 123, 124, 125, 126, 128, 129, 167, 176
  covert 177, 184, 185, 188
  Move-α 6, 33, 44, 122
  Move-F 33
Movement *see* Move
  head-movement 8
Multiple Spell Out 5
Murasugi, Keiko 158
Muysken, Pieter 21, 26
Myers, Scott 105
Myers' Generalization 105, 110

Negative Polarity Item 137
NOM *see also* Case 97
non-control *to* 99, 100, 112
null complementizers 51, 107, 108
numeration 16, 37, 40, 60
Nuñes, Jairo 16, 28

Ormazabal, Javier 11, 104, 106, 107, 108, 109
Ouali, Hamid 51

PAH *see* Pronominal Argument Hypothesis
partial A-movement 56
passive 25, 60, 71, 72, 76, 79, 80
  short Passive 63
Pesetsky, David 11, 80, 81, 82, 104, 105, 107, 109, 131
  Pesetsky's Generalization 81
PF *see* Phonological Form
phase 60, 61, 62, 63, 64, 67, 68
Phase Impenetrability Condition (PIC) 127, 128, 129, 190
φ-complete T 176
phi feature 88, 99, 103, 190, 191, 192, 193, 194
Phillips, Colin 9
Phonological Form (PF) 6, 12, 13, 20, 28, 34, 45, 56, 62, 66, 112, 174, 178, 179, 180, 181, 182, 183, 184, 185, 187, 188, 197, 198
Piattelli-Palmarini, Massimo 9
PIC *see* Phase Impenetrability Condition
pied piping 138
Pires, Acrisio 11, 52, 79, 84, 105, 130
Pollard, Carl 178
Poole, Geoffrey 36
pragmatic considerations 131
principle, unclarity of 4
pro 153, 154
PRO 70, 75, 97, 159
Probe 175, 176, 186, 189, 190, 193, 194, 195, 200
Probe-Goal 175, 176, 186, 189, 190, 193, 194, 195
projection
  single-bar 21, 27
Pronominal Argument Hypothesis (PAH) 65
proposition 61, 62, 63, 70, 75, 76, 77, 78, 79, 81, 82, 84, 85, 86, 87, 91, 101, 104
propredicate placeholder 90, 91, 93
Pure Merge 66, 67

Q-float 115, 118, 119, 126, 130, 155, 156, 158, 160, 162, 163

raising
  infinitival 52, 53
  predicate 54, 55
  to 48, 53, 56, 68, 69
Reconstruction 115, 168
redundancy 51, 52, 53, 90, 94, 96, 98, 99, 101, 109
redundant 48, 51, 52, 53, 69, 105
Re-Merge 25
repair 174
representational 8, 17, 22, 25, 27, 28, 29, 30, 31, 32, 36, 37, 43, 44, 45, 46
representational objects, enriched 8
Reuland, Eric 9
R-expression 16, 145, 149
Rizzi, Luigi 25, 36, 49, 136, 139
Roberts, Ian 9
Rooryck, Johan 83
Rosenbaum, Peter S. 85
Rothstein, Susan 51, 52
Roussou, Anna 53, 114
rule
  iterative rule application 6
Ruwet, Nicholas 92

Sag, Ivan 161, 178
Saito, Mamoru 34, 69, 131, 158, 166, 170, 172
Seely, T. Daniel 1, 4, 7, 8, 9, 11, 12, 13, 18, 24, 26, 28, 45, 52, 61, 84, 105, 116, 122, 124, 158, 162, 181, 191, 193, 197
short Passive 63
single-bar projections 21, 27
sister 17, 18, 21, 22, 23, 25, 26, 28, 30, 31, 32, 34, 42
small clause 76, 89, 90, 95, 96, 98, 197
Smith, Neil 9
Speas, Margaret 11, 21, 51, 116
Spell Out 187, 197
Sportiche, Dominique 12, 115, 119, 156, 157, 161, 162, 163, 164
s-selection 70, 72, 73, 92
S-structure 56, 57, 67, 168, 170, 171, 187
Stowell, Tim 11, 48, 55
Structural Description 30, 31
subject
  Internal Subject Hypothesis 53
successive cyclic A-movement *see also* A-movement, movement 5, 8, 31, 32, 34, 41, 42, 43, 48, 49, 52, 56, 57, 58, 60, 68, 113, 114, 116, 117, 119, 130, 132, 133, 134, 135, 139, 150, 156, 164, 166
Suicidal Attract 67
Suicidal Greed 57
Superiority 138
syntactic filters 7
syntactic object (SO) 14, 15, 16, 17, 18, 19, 20, 24, 29, 31, 36, 39, 40, 41, 42, 46, 61, 62, 86
syntactic operation 114
syntactically accessible 15, 16

Takahashi, Daiko 31, 65, 117, 120
Tense 48, 55, 61, 136, 171, 172
that-clause 85, 86, 90, 91, 93, 94, 95, 101
theme-rheme 51
there-insertion 56

Theta
  assignment 33
  Criterion 66, 67, 96, 155, 168, 179, 180, 181, 182, 183
  features 190, 191, 192, 193
  marking 65, 80, 81
  position 35, 42, 43, 117, 160
Thom, René 1
Thompson, E. 28
Torrego, Esther 12, 48, 55, 139, 140, 141, 142, 143, 146, 147, 148
Tortora, Christina 197
trace 8, 16, 17, 19, 20, 32, 34, 35, 37, 38, 39, 40, 41, 42, 43, 44, 45, 46, 47, 48, 56
trace theory 8

unclarity of a principle 4

unit derivation 182, 183
Universal Grammar (UG) 4, 12, 13, 15, 43, 49, 51, 53, 55
Uriagereka, Juan 6, 9, 27, 28, 196

Vergnaud, Jean-Roger 3

Whitehead, Alfred North 7
wh-movement *see also* movement 117, 127, 133, 138, 152
Williams, Edwin 12, 51, 52, 161, 162, 163

X-bar invisibility 21, 23, 25, 26, 27, 28, 30, 31

Y-model 6, 26, 178, 180, 181, 197

Printed in the United States
50724LVS00002B/94